What people are saying about …

# FROM GENESIS TO JUNIA

"*From Genesis to Junia* is one of the most compelling, encouraging, and comprehensive books I've read regarding what the Bible really says about women in leadership. And Preston's thorough biblical scholarship is well balanced by his approachable humility, which makes this material read like genuinely inviting dialogue as opposed to an agenda-driven diatribe. I'll be buying this book by the case to give to friends as well as to intentionally leave behind on planes, in restaurants, and in pastor's offices I'm invited to visit while on the road!"

**Lisa Harper**, bestselling author, Bible teacher, and host of the *Back Porch Theology* podcast

"Few recent Christian books on gender roles in home and ministry have done the tough, needed work on all the key biblical texts and themes to come to their conclusions. Preston Sprinkle has done his homework in this area, and whether one agrees with every view he articulates, his careful and detailed handling of Scripture is exemplary. Gracious in tone and measured in his exegesis. A model for us all."

**Craig L. Blomberg**, PhD, distinguished professor emeritus of New Testament at Denver Seminary, author of *Jesus the Purifier* and *The Historical Reliability of the New Testament*

"Preston Sprinkle learned his faith in contexts where women were not invited into roles of leadership. Most would feel comfortable staying within the boundaries of those familiar spaces. But, as is characteristic of Preston, his love for Scripture, the church, and the individual believer has driven him further. Inviting 'egalitarians' and 'complementarians' to the table, Sprinkle engages a difficult topic with grace and a high view of Scripture. As his training predicts, his primary contributions are on the New Testament side of things. But what is best about this book is Preston's unique ability to keep everyone at the table until the conversation is finished. What does he decide? I guess you will need to join the conversation to find out!"

**Sandra L. Richter**, Robert H. Gundry Chair of Biblical Studies, Westmont College

"*From Genesis to Junia* represents the culmination of Preston Sprinkle's years-long search to understand what the Bible says about women in leadership. Having engaged in wide-ranging public and private dialogue, his book offers both rigorous scholarship and pastoral wisdom. I highly recommend this book—it will enrich and deepen your understanding, wherever you stand on this important debate."

**Gerry Breshears**, PhD, professor of theology, Western Seminary, Portland

"*From Genesis to Junia* is a unique and refreshing take on women in leadership. Preston Sprinkle invites us to join him on his own journey as he examines the issue without presupposing either a complementarian or egalitarian position. The result is a fascinating exploration of the biblical witness as he skillfully guides us through the interpretive issues and provides a careful and measured rationale for his own conclusions. He makes an important contribution by demonstrating a hermeneutical approach that recognizes the complexity of the evidence while personally modeling a humility that includes a willingness to be wrong. Although he lands on one position, the book is less an apologetic and more an invitation to constructive dialogue. Thoroughly researched, highly engaging, and very accessible, this is a much-needed work that provides a most valuable example to the church of how to study this difficult and heated topic."

**Michelle Lee-Barnewall**, affiliate professor of New Testament at Talbot School of Theology, award-winning author of *Neither Complementarian nor Egalitarian*

"Evenhanded, deeply researched, and refreshingly honest, *From Genesis to Junia* takes readers on a compelling journey through one of the church's most urgent debates. Preston Sprinkle's typical willingness to engage both sides with rigor and charity makes this work both thought-provoking and disarmingly humane. Whether or not readers share all his conclusions, they'll find themselves drawn afresh to the humble Christ and grateful for the conversation."

**Sandra Glahn**, PhD, seminary professor and author of *Nobody's Mother: Artemis of the Ephesians in Antiquity and the New Testament*

"I appreciate how Preston includes us in his academic journey. The book is easy to read, well researched, and doesn't fall into academic details (except when necessary). While I don't always agree with his conclusions, I do appreciate him, and he did change my mind on some of the issues."

**William Mounce**, PhD, author of *The Pastoral Epistles*, in the *Word Biblical Commentary*

"*From Genesis to Junia* represents Sprinkle's exhaustive analysis of the biblical text and thorough exploration of current theories, culminating in a compelling case for his conclusion. With his characteristic conversational tone, Sprinkle invites readers to join his *Honest Search for What the Bible Really Says About Women in Leadership*. Sprinkle provides scholars, students, and pastors an accessible and charitable pathway to conversation around this important topic."

**Lynn H. Cohick**, PhD, distinguished professor of New Testament, Houston Christian University

"Through solid exegesis and self-examination, Sprinkle comes to a fair and reasoned conclusion. Even if the reader disagrees, they'll learn much from the journey."

**Rev. Dr. Michael F. Bird**, deputy principal, director of research, and lecturer in New Testament, Ridley College, Melbourne

# FROM GENESIS TO JUNIA

# FROM GENESIS TO JUNIA

## AN HONEST SEARCH FOR WHAT THE BIBLE REALLY SAYS ABOUT **WOMEN IN LEADERSHIP**

PRESTON SPRINKLE

*NEW YORK TIMES* BESTSELLING AUTHOR

DAVID C COOK

A MINISTRY OF COOK MEDIA GLOBAL

FROM GENESIS TO JUNIA
Published by David C Cook
4050 Lee Vance Drive
Colorado Springs, CO 80918 U.S.A.

A Ministry of Cook Media Global

Integrity Music Limited, a Division of David C Cook
Brighton, East Sussex BN1 2RE, England



Library of Congress Control Number 2025947651
ISBN 978-0-8307-8580-3
eISBN 978-0-8307-8581-0



The Team: Michael Covington, Stephanie Bennett, Greg Coles,
Judy Gillispie, Karissa Silvers, Susan Murdock
Cover Design: Leah Von Fange

Printed in the United States of America
First Edition 2026

2 3 4 5 6 7 8 9 10 11

031226

# CONTENTS


May 2022: My Journey into the Women in Leadership Debate 11

Chapter 1: Adam, Eve, and Genesis 1–3 19
Chapter 2: Women in the Old Testament 39
Chapter 3: Women in the Ministry of Jesus 65
Chapter 4: Leaders and Leadership in the Early Church 93
Chapter 5: Women in the Ministry of Paul (Rom. 16) 119
Chapter 6: Female Prophets in the New Testament 151
Chapter 7: Marriage, Headship, and Submission (Eph. 5:21–33) 171
Chapter 8: Man Is the Head of Woman (1 Cor. 11:3–12) 193
Chapter 9: Women Be Silent in All the Churches (1 Cor. 14:34–35) 219
Chapter 10: Women, Teaching, and Authority (1 Tim. 2–3) 239

Landing the Plane 287
Acknowledgments 297

# MAY 2022: MY JOURNEY INTO THE WOMEN IN LEADERSHIP DEBATE

I'm writing this introduction in real time. It's May 2022, and I'm about to embark on a theological journey to figure out what I think the Bible says about women in church leadership.

I'm a bit nervous about this journey, since I don't know my destination. I honestly don't know where I'll end up. Authors typically write their book's introduction last, after they've written the rest of the book and sorted out their conclusions. That's how I wrote most of my previous books.

But this one is different. I'm not starting with a settled conclusion and then writing the book to convince you of it. Rather, I'm inviting you to peek over my shoulder as I journey through Scripture to figure out what I believe it says about this contentious issue.

Most Christians I know have strong opinions on the matter, and I used to be one of them. I grew up in a staunchly complementarian context where only men could be pastors and leaders. I believed this was the only valid biblical position—any view that allowed women to teach and preach was a direct violation of God's Word. Over the years, though, I've seen some problems with this view. Some arguments seem solid. Others seem forced and unconvincing. I'm not sure it's wrong; I'm just not sure it's right.

The same goes for the egalitarian view. I've come across some compelling arguments for women in leadership. But I've seen some terrible arguments too. I'm not sure it's wrong; I'm just not sure it's right.

So, for the last several years, I've remained undecided about what I think the Bible says about women in leadership.

Why stay undecided for so long? Well, I'm a bit obsessive when it comes to researching a topic, especially a hotly disputed one. I want the depth of my study to determine the strength of my conclusion. I never want to give thin answers to thick questions. And there are a lot of thick questions surrounding this issue that I haven't had time to thoroughly research. Until now.

This fall (2022), I'm taking a sabbatical and setting aside my other ministry responsibilities to focus on the question of women in leadership. I doubt I'll be able to finish my book in six months, but at least I'll have a running start. After the sabbatical is over, I'll keep researching the topic until I feel like I can land on a view with some level of confidence.

I can't promise you that I'll be an unbiased researcher—nobody is totally free from bias! What I can say is that I don't have external pressures—a job, a church, relationships—nudging me toward one view over another. If I were teaching at the Southern Baptist Theological Seminary (which is staunchly complementarian) or at Fuller Seminary (which is firmly egalitarian), I'd have a lot of financial and practical reasons to arrive at a certain conclusion. If I were a pastor at a complementarian church, I'd need to agree with its view (unless I was looking for a job change). If my wife were a senior pastor, my motivation might be tainted. If all my friends were on one side of the debate, my perspective might be clouded.

But I don't work for a church or a seminary, my wife would rather stroll barefoot through a room filled with broken glass than be a pastor, and I have friends on all sides of this debate. And since my friends are real friends, I won't lose them if I end up on the "wrong side" of this question.

No matter what I conclude in this book, I expect to keep all my jobs and ministry roles, make the same amount of money, and keep speaking at both egalitarian and complementarian churches. I won't lose my ordination status (because I'm not ordained), and I won't be kicked out of my denomination (because I'm not part of a denomination). My wonderful publisher doesn't need me to uphold a particular position; they publish books that examine all sides of the issue.

Even personally—and I guess you'll have to take my word for it—I really don't have major leanings in either direction. As I said before, I see strong and weak arguments for each view. But all my thoughts and questions so far are half-baked and under-researched—hence this book. Maybe I'll become more convinced of arguments I've found unconvincing, and maybe I'll see problems with arguments I previously thought were strong. I might even be embarrassed by ignorant things I've said in this introduction!

Although I don't know exactly how this book will unfold, here are some key topics and passages I plan on studying. I'll need to spend time in Genesis 1–3 and the relationship between the first humans. Adam's alleged "headship" over Eve forms the bedrock for the complementarian view that I grew up with, and I'm eager to see if the text actually supports this. I'm also curious what the rest of the Old Testament says about women's leadership, especially how it portrays female prophets like Huldah and Deborah. But since my main focus is *church* leadership, I'll probably devote more time to the New Testament.

Even here, I'll have to be selective. I know I want to look at how women participated in the ministries of Jesus and Paul. I'll also spend a good deal of time in three important passages: 1 Corinthians 11:2–16; 1 Corinthians 14:34–35; and 1 Timothy 2:8–15. I'm pretty sure I'll study the so-called household code in Ephesians 5:22–33, since *church* roles and *household* roles were sometimes related in the first century. And I want to understand the nature of New Testament prophecy, since women were clearly prophesying in the early church. Is prophecy akin to preaching or teaching? Is it an authoritative activity? These are significant questions I'll try to address.

In a study like this, it's important that we don't understand things like "leadership" and "church" from a modern perspective. I don't want to simply drape the New Testament in the robes of modern Western church structures and call it the same thing. Whatever Paul was saying to Timothy in the first century, it probably didn't involve deciding whether a woman could step under bright stage lights next Sunday and deliver a polished sermon to an audience of five thousand. My aim in this study is to step back into the dusty streets and crowded homes of the first believers and explore the question of women in church leadership according to *their* understanding of church and leadership, not ours. What today's churches choose to do with that portrait lies beyond the scope of my study.

What do I mean by *leader* and *leadership*? I'm hesitant to start with an overly precise definition and then project this definition onto the text of Scripture. I'd rather have the Bible itself shape our understanding of leadership as we journey through our study. But since I'll be using the term *leader* from the get-go, here's a general definition of what I mean at this early stage of our journey. A leader is a person who (1) holds a recognized title or position of authority (such as "king" or "elder"), (2) guides and directs a group of people toward a specific goal or mission, or (3) speaks or acts in a way that expects others to follow their direction.

I offer these descriptions only as flexible frameworks, not fixed barriers. Again, our understanding of leadership should arise from the text, not be forced upon it. I'll be sure to revisit and fine-tune this definition once we get to the portions of the New Testament that deal with leadership in the church. In any case, I'll try to be clear where and why I think someone is considered a leader, based on this general definition.

A few quick words before we dive in. First, I'll be wading through lots of academic literature on this topic, but I plan to write in a conversational tone. I want this book to represent the scholarly debates responsibly, but I also want it to be readable for people who don't have a seminary degree. If you're a scholar, you might find my tone too colloquial. If you're a non-scholar, you might be annoyed by the copious footnotes. Either way, I hope this book can help bridge the gap between the academy and the church.

Second, I know the terms *egalitarian* and *complementarian* are highly disputed. Some have ditched these terms for others like *mutualist* (instead of *egalitarian*) and *patriarchal* (instead of *complementarian*). But while *egalitarian* and *complementarian* may be frayed, the other labels have their own loose threads.[1] Whichever term we use, I believe the most respectful approach is to call a view what its proponents call it. In other words, I don't think it's helpful when egalitarians label the other view *patriarchal* if its proponents don't use that label. Likewise, it's misleading to slap *feminist* on the opposing view if they don't use it themselves—that term carries connotations that many egalitarians reject.

Since most complementarians seem to prefer this term, it's the one I'm going to use. While *mutualist* is gaining traction, I think *egalitarian* is still the more recognizable term, so I'll use it throughout the book. But I want to be clear about what I mean by each word. In this book, *egalitarian* refers to the view that women can serve in all areas of church leadership, and *complementarian* refers to the view that certain positions of church leadership are reserved for men. Both terms can carry lots of other implications and assumptions, but when I use them here, I mean nothing more than what I've just said.

There are, of course, variations within both groups. For instance, "soft complementarians" believe that women can teach and preach in churches as long as they're under the authority of male elders. Some egalitarians believe that men and women are equal in every way, while

---

1 I don't mind *mutualist* (instead of *egalitarian*), but complementarians believe that men and women exist in a mutual relationship with different roles. I really don't like *patriarchal*, since there are so many definitions of this term. Plus, some who use *patriarchy* to mean male domination often fail to appreciate the sociological and economic complexity of the ancient patriarchal world. *Hierarchical* is problematic, since Christian leadership itself is not hierarchical. If only men are to be leaders, this does not mean they exist in some hierarchical relationship over those they lead. The term *egalitarian* can be problematic, since it can have secular connotations or imply that there are no male-female differences. And *complementarian* can suggest that non-complementarians don't believe that men and women complement each other. We can continue to dissect each term and show why it's good, bad, or ugly. But I'm simply going to use the familiar terms *egalitarian* and *complementarian* as I define them in this introduction.

others are happy to celebrate the differences between men and women. I'll tease out these variations where they're relevant.

Lastly, my study will be strictly exegetical in nature. It will focus on what the Bible says about women in church leadership *in its own context.* I'm not going to offer modern-day applications, nor will I address the modern problems that sometimes develop in complementarian or egalitarian churches. These issues are worth addressing! But it would take a whole other book to do so, and I'm not sure I'm the right person to do that. My goal here is to provide an honest evaluation of the biblical arguments—I'll leave the application questions to other scholars, and to readers like you.

I just ordered a truckload of books, which should be here in a couple of days. I'll spend the next few months reading as deeply and widely as I can. And then, once I've taken copious notes, maybe I'll start to think about putting pen to paper.

See you in a few months (or a few years)!

Chapter 1

# ADAM, EVE, AND GENESIS 1–3

I know you just turned the page, but I've actually been shored up in my study for several months. I've combed through several books on women in leadership, just to get my head around the debate. And then I decided to delve deep into the most logical starting place: the creation of the first human pair and the implications they bring to our debate.

Studying Genesis 1–3 has felt like watching a theological Ping-Pong match: Egalitarians and complementarians rally back and forth with arguments, counterarguments, and counter-counterarguments. But there's one thing both sides agree on: Genesis 1–3 is pivotal for the debate. Some say it's the most crucial passage of all. "As Genesis 1–3 go," writes Ray Ortlund, "so goes the whole Biblical debate."[1]

I think Ortlund overstates his case, but I agree that Genesis 1–3 plays a key role in our topic. Paul refers to Adam and Eve's relationship

---

1 Raymond C. Ortlund, "Male-Female Equality and Male Headship: Genesis 1–3," *Recovering Biblical Manhood and Womanhood: A Response to Evangelical Feminism*, ed. John Piper and Wayne Grudem (Crossway, 1991), 95.

in two important passages about women in the church (1 Cor. 11:8–9; 1 Tim. 2:13–14). And this creation story is fundamental for Christian theology as a whole.[2] There are many shiny theological objects we could chase in this passage, so we'll have to stay focused on the question most relevant for our study: Does Genesis 1–3 depict Adam as a leader who exercises authority over Eve as part of God's original creational design for male-female relations in the home and the church?

Our answer depends in part on how Paul interprets the passage, but we'll address that later in the book. For now, I want to look at Genesis 1–3 on its own terms. What does it say about authority, leadership, and male-female relations? Much of this debate boils down to five key questions.

## 1. Do Adam and Eve Exercise Mutual Rule in Genesis 1?

Complementarians like to camp out in Genesis 2–3 to highlight Adam's authority over Eve, but egalitarians are quick to point out that Genesis 2–3 should be read in light of Genesis 1.[3] There, "male and female" are "the image of God"; both are commissioned to "fill the earth and subdue [*kabash*] it" and "rule" (*radah*) over the animal kingdom (1:26–28). There's no hint of man ruling, leading, or exercising authority over woman.[4] Both male and female are subduing and ruling.

---

2 I don't think it matters to our interpretation whether Genesis 1–3 is a nonhistorical myth or literal history (or a blend of both). I believe the passage is historical, though it may contain some mythical elements. But even if it were wholly mythical, it's still designed to establish theological truth. The New Testament writers and Jesus certainly understood this passage to be theologically significant.

3 Some see Genesis 1 as a different creation account than Genesis 2–3. I don't think this reading is correct, but even if it were, the final form of Genesis 1–3 suggests that we should read the passage as a cohesive whole.

4 See Gail Taylor, "Women in Creation and Redemption," *Journal of Christian Brothers Research Fellowship* 26 (1974): 17.

The authority structure is one where God rules over creation and commissions both man and woman to mediate his rule over the animals. "There is nothing in the first creation narrative," writes Mary Conway, "to indicate that the subordination of women, whether in regard to their nature or function, was part of Yahweh's original intention for humanity."[5]

Complementarians agree that Genesis 1 establishes ontological equality between man and woman and that both are called to mediate God's rule. But they argue that the chapter doesn't detail *how* man and woman will collaborate to subdue and rule the earth. It's in Genesis 2 where their individual roles are spelled out, and man's authority over woman exists within this framework of ontological equality.[6]

I can see the validity of both perspectives. The only explicit authority language used in Genesis 1–2 is ascribed to both male and female, as they "rule" over creation (1:26). And Genesis 1 precedes Genesis 2, so it naturally influences the interpretation of the latter. Genesis 1, however, doesn't delve into specific male and female roles, which Genesis 2 addresses more directly (though *roles* might not be the best term). It's possible that Genesis 2 depicts a scenario where man holds authority over woman, while both are ontologically equal and called to rule over creation (Gen. 1).

I think it's best to table a firm response to this first question until we've worked through the others.

---

5 Mary L. Conway, "Gender in Creation and Fall: Genesis 1–3," in *Discovering Biblical Equality: Biblical, Theological, Cultural, and Practical Perspectives*, 3rd ed., ed. Ronald W. Pierce and Cynthia Long Westfall (IVP Academic, 2021), 39.

6 As Grudem notes, "Equal value and equal honor and equal personhood and equal importance do not require that people have the *same roles* or the *same authority*." Wayne Grudem, *Evangelical Feminism & Biblical Truth: An Analysis of More Than 100 Disputed Questions* (Crossway, 2012), 104 (italics in original).

## 2. Why Was Adam Created First?

Some argue that Adam occupies a leadership role in the created order because he was created first.[7] Genesis was written in a culture that held to a principle of primogeniture, which passed leadership to the firstborn son. Therefore, Tom Schreiner says, "the Hebrew reader would be disposed to read the second creation in terms of *primogeniture*," where the "firstborn male has authority over the younger brothers after the father dies."[8] Since God created Adam first, he had authority over Eve, who came after him.

I used to think this argument was compelling, but I now see several flaws with reading Genesis 2 through the lens of primogeniture. Eve is Adam's wife, not his sibling and definitely not his younger brother. Also, the primogeniture principle states that the firstborn male becomes the patriarch *after the father dies*. I guess we could say God functions like Adam's father in this story, but according to the Newsboys, God's not dead. Most significantly, God often subverts the primogeniture principle throughout Scripture, especially in Genesis. God gives priority to Isaac, not the firstborn Ishmael; to Jacob, not Esau; to Joseph, not his older brothers; to Ephraim, not Manasseh; to Perez, not Zerah. This pattern is repeated at key points elsewhere in the Old Testament story: God chooses Moses over Aaron and David over his seven older brothers. "In

---

7 It's not just conservative complementarian scholars who argue for Adam's authority over Eve in Genesis 2. Plenty of progressive scholars find Genesis 2 to be a male chauvinistic presentation of man's superiority over woman. See e.g., David J. A. Clines, "What Does Eve Do to Help? And Other Irredeemably Androcentric Orientations in Genesis 1–3," in *What Does Eve Do to Help? And Other Readerly Questions to the Old Testament*, ed. David J. A. Clines, *Journal for the Study of the Old Testament Supplement Series* 94 (JSOT Press, 1990), 25–48.

8 Thomas R. Schreiner, "Women in Ministry: Another Complementarian Perspective," in *Two Views on Women in Ministry*, rev. ed., ed. James R. Beck (Zondervan, 2005), 291 (italics in original). See also Craig Blomberg, "A Complementarian Perspective," in *Two Views on Women in Ministry*, rev. ed., ed. James R. Beck (Zondervan, 2005), 128. On the definition of *primogeniture* and its occurrence in Genesis, see Udogu Chukwuebuka, "Primogeniture, a Cultural Tool for the Interpretation of Genesis Narratives," *International Journal of Social Sciences and Scientific Studies* 1, no. 1 (2021), https://ijssass.com/index.php/ijssass/article/view/7/2.

spite of the Near Eastern custom of giving preference to firstborn sons, at critical junctures God *almost always subverts* this custom," writes Philip Payne.[9] Even if early readers would have read Genesis 2 through the lens of primogeniture—and it's not clear they would have—it's unlikely that God was establishing a universal principle of primogeniture, since he was so fond of overturning it.

To me, the strongest argument for man's primogeniture status comes not in Genesis 2 but in the letters of Paul, who seems to ascribe some kind of priority or authority to man since he was created first (1 Cor. 11:8–9; 1 Tim. 2:13–14). The passages in 1 Corinthians and 1 Timothy will be significant for our study, and both are fraught with interpretive difficulties. It would be naive to simply cite these Pauline texts to prove Adam's primogeniture status. One would first need to hack through the interpretive jungle surrounding these two passages, which we'll do in later chapters.

For now, I'm mainly concerned with the author's intention in Genesis 1–3.[10] And I don't think Genesis alone demands that Adam's first-created status establishes male authority over woman. Later, we'll see if Paul begs to differ.

## 3. Does Eve Being Adam's "Helper" Imply That Adam Is in Charge?

Eve was created to be "a helper fit for" Adam (Gen. 2:18, 20 ESV). Some take this to mean that Adam held authority over Eve, whose created role was to support him. "The word 'helper' ... suggests the woman's

---

9 Philip Payne, *The Bible vs. Biblical Womanhood: How God's Word Consistently Affirms Gender Equality* (Zondervan, 2023), 7 (italics in original).

10 I take the author to be Moses, whose work was revised by inspired editors, but I'll keep using "author" so as to not distract those who disagree with Mosaic authorship. The author's identity doesn't ultimately matter for our purposes.

supportive role," writes Ray Ortlund.[11] "The man was not created to help the woman, but the reverse."[12] Ortlund then raises the question, "Was Eve Adam's equal?" To which he responds: "Yes and no. She was his spiritual equal ... but she was not his equal in that she was his 'helper.' A man," says Ortlund, "by virtue of his manhood, is called to lead for God. A woman, just by virtue of her womanhood, is called to help for God."[13]

Ortlund and other complementarian scholars stress that Eve's (and every woman's) status as "helper" does not imply ontological subordination.[14] All people are created in God's image and possess equal value, worth, and dignity. But relationships in which people have different roles, where one leads and another helps, can exist among people of equal worth.

I think this logic is reasonable. Just because your boss holds authority over you doesn't mean you're not both equal in worth and value as images of God. All humans are ontologically equal, even if some are called to lead, while others are to follow. The question is, Does the term "helper" imply that woman was created to follow man's leadership?

I don't think it does. The Hebrew word for "helper," *ezer*, rarely refers to the role of a subordinate. *Ezer* occurs nineteen other times in Scripture, and it most often refers to a stronger ally or a deliverer.[15] In

---

11 Ortlund, "Male-Female Equality," 104.

12 Ortlund, "Male-Female Equality," 101–2.

13 Ortlund, "Male-Female Equality," 102. See also Schreiner, "Women in Ministry," 292–94.

14 E.g., Ortlund, "Male-Female Equality," 102–3; Grudem, *Evangelical Feminism*, 104, 117–21.

15 Philip Payne goes so far to say that *all* nineteen "occurrences of *ezer* refer to a savior or deliverer" (*Bible vs. Biblical Womanhood*, 3). Craig Blomberg, however, disagrees: *Ezer* refers "to someone in a subordinate role" in three other passages: Isaiah 30:5, Ezekiel 12:14, and Daniel 11:34 ("Complementarian Perspective," 129–30). I don't agree with Blomberg's take on Isaiah 30:5. Here, *ezer* describes Egypt, and God rebuked Israel for seeking an alliance with Egypt, a "people who can't *help*" and "are of no benefit, they are no *help*" (30:5 CSB). Egypt was not Israel's subordinate; it was clearly a more powerful nation than Israel at this time. Blomberg might be right about Ezekiel 12:14, where King Zedekiah's military troops (or possibly foreign allies) are described as his "helpers" (ESV). These "helpers" were subordinate to the king, though they were stronger than the king, which is why he wanted them at his side. As far as Daniel 11:34 goes, I don't think it's clear whether the ones who "help" were subordinate to the ones they were helping.

at least fifteen of the nineteen occurrences, it refers to God "helping" Israel.[16] Clearly, God is not subservient to Israel, nor was he playing a mere supportive role under Israel's leadership.[17] The Septuagint (the Greek translation of the Old Testament) supports the notion that *ezer* does not imply a subservient role when it translates *ezer* as *boethos*. In almost every one of its other forty-five occurrences in the Septuagint, *boethos* refers to help coming "from a stronger one, in no way needing help."[18]

Complementarian scholars are obviously aware of these other uses of *ezer*, but they still argue that Eve's status as "helper" implies that she is subordinate to Adam. For instance, Ray Ortlund recognizes that *ezer* is often used of God helping Israel, but he says, "It is entirely possible for God to subordinate Himself, in a certain sense, to human beings. He does so whenever He undertakes to help us. He does not 'un-God' Himself in helping us; but He does stoop to our needs, according to His gracious and sovereign will."[19] Ortlund illustrates his point by saying that he subordinates himself to his children whenever he helps them with their homework.[20] Wayne Grudem agrees: "The person

---

16 Exodus 18:4; Deuteronomy 33:7, 26, 29; Psalm 20:2; 33:20; 70:5; 115:9, 10, 11; 121:1, 2; 124:8; 146:5; Hosea 13:9; cf. Payne, *Bible vs. Biblical Womanhood*, 3–4; Linda Bellville, "An Egalitarian Perspective," in *Two Views on Women in Ministry*, rev. ed., ed. James R. Beck (Zondervan, 2005), 27–28.

17 David Clines acknowledges that superiors can help inferiors but then makes the odd claim that "in the act of helping they are being 'inferior.'" He goes on to say, "Their help may be necessary or crucial, but they are *assisting* some task that is already someone else's responsibility" ("What Does Eve Do to Help?," 6, italics in original).

18 Victor Hamilton, *The Book of Genesis: Chapters 1–17*, New International Commentary on the Old Testament (Eerdmans, 1990), 176, citing J. M. Higgins, "Anastasius Sinaita and the Superiority of the Woman," *Journal of Biblical Literature* 97, no. 2 (1978): 253–56. Hamilton notes three exceptions: 1 Chronicles 12:18, Ezekiel 12:14, and Nahum 3:9. See note 15 on Ezekiel 12:14. I don't know why Hamilton lists 1 Chronicles 12:18, since it clearly refers to God who "helped you" (CEB). Nahum 3:9 mocks Nineveh for having "helpers" (allies) like Put and Libya who fail to deliver.

19 Ortlund, "Male-Female Equality," 10.

20 Ortlund, "Male-Female Equality," 104.

doing the helping puts himself in a subordinate role to the person who has primary responsibility for carrying out the activity."[21]

I'm not quite convinced of Ortlund's and Grudem's logic here. The question is not whether a person in authority could ever stoop to meet the needs of someone under their authority. The question is whether the word *ezer* implies being under the authority of someone else. Ortlund's examples still portray God, the *ezer*, in a position of authority, not in a position of submitting to someone else's authority. Likewise, a father doesn't relinquish his authority when he helps his kids with math.

So I don't think *ezer* in Genesis 2 implies that Eve was subordinate to Adam, or that "women" were created to "help men by supporting the[ir] leadership," as Schreiner says.[22] The task Eve is created to "help" with in Genesis 2 is the creation mandate of Genesis 1:26–28: populating, cultivating, and ruling over the earth.[23] And Genesis 1 makes no distinction between male and female in their ruling roles. For instance, they're both given the same command to procreate (Gen. 1:28), which obviously requires both partners. Part of Eve's "help" toward Adam, then, is her role in procreation. I'll let the reader decide whether they want to say that women play a supporting or subservient role to men in bearing, delivering, and rearing children.

---

21 Grudem, *Evangelical Feminism*, 37; cf. Blomberg: "What makes an *ezer* a 'helper' in each context is that he or she comes to the aid of someone else who bears the primary responsibility for the activity in question" ("Complementarian Perspective," 130).

22 Schreiner, "Women in Ministry," 293.

23 Clines argues that Eve's only "help" is her role in procreation (see his article "What Does Eve Do to Help?"). It does seem that her role in procreation is a point of emphasis throughout Genesis 1–3. But I disagree with Clines that Eve's only help is procreation. The commands to "subdue" the earth and "rule" over the animals are given to both male and female (Gen. 1:28), and Eve also "helps" Adam by creating community and thus solving the problem of his aloneness.

Moreover, in Genesis 2:18 and 2:20, *ezer* is combined with *kenegdo* ("suitable" NIV; "just right" NLT), which implies a mutual partnership, not a relationship where one exercises authority over another. *Kenegdo* occurs only here in 2:18 and 2:20, and it combines two Hebrew words, *ke*, which means "as, like, similar," and *neged*, which means "opposite," "in front of," or "against." The combination of both words (*ke* + *neged* = *kenegdo*) captures Eve's similarity to Adam and her difference from Adam.[24] She's "like" Adam, since she's human, and she's "different from" Adam, since she's a female. Together, *ezer kenegdo* refers to Eve's essential role as a fellow human whose sex difference is necessary for the human pair to procreate and fill the earth. This phrase by itself doesn't suggest a relationship between a person in authority (Adam) and his subordinate (Eve).[25]

As the narrative unfolds, Adam and Eve are treated as mutual partners in the task of ruling over creation. Both sin against God.[26] Both realize they are naked (3:7). Both hide from God (3:8). Both are ashamed of their actions. Both shift the blame (3:12–13). When God confronts them, he addresses them both. We do see themes of authority in Genesis 1–2, but it's an authority where God rules over humans and humans mediate God's rule over creation.[27] If we are going to identify Adam's leadership and authority over Eve, I think we need to find it elsewhere, not from the phrase *ezer kenegdo*.

---

24 See my book *Does the Bible Support Same-Sex Marriage? 21 Conversations from a Historically Christian View* (David C Cook, 2023), 39.

25 See Phyllis Trible, *God and the Rhetoric of Sexuality* (Fortress Press, 1978), 90.

26 "The NT, intriguingly, blames Adam exactly twice (Rom. 5:12–14; 1 Cor. 15:22) and Eve exactly twice (2 Cor. 11:3; 1 Tim. 2:14) in its discussions of the original sin" (Blomberg, "Complementarian Perspective," 131).

27 Carol Meyers, *Rediscovering Eve: Ancient Israelite Women in Context* (Oxford University Press, 2013), 74.

## 4. Does Adam's Naming of Eve Demonstrate His Authority over Her?

Another argument for Adam's authority over Eve comes from Genesis 2:23, where he calls her "woman":

> Then the man said,
>
> "This at last is bone of my bones
> and flesh of my flesh;
> she shall be called [*qarah*] Woman [*ishah*],
> because she was taken out of Man [*ish*]." (ESV)

In the ancient world, giving someone a name often implied that the name-giver was exercising authority over the one named.[28] For instance, Nebuchadnezzar's chief eunuch changed the names of Daniel, Hananiah, Mishael, and Azariah to Belteshazzar, Shadrach, Meshach, and Abednego (Dan. 1:7). Pharaoh Necho did the same when he changed the name of Eliakim to Jehoiakim (2 Kings 23:34).[29] Even in Genesis 1, God exercised his sovereignty over creation when he "called [*qarah*]" the light "day," the darkness "night," and so on (v. 5). The same is true of Adam when he named the animals: "And whatever the man *called* [*qarah*] each living creature, that was its name" (2:19). Some scholars therefore argue that Adam also exercised authority

28 See Gerhard von Rad, *Genesis: A Commentary*, trans. Dorothea Barton (Fortress Press, 1961), 80–83; K. D. Sakenfeld, "The Bible and Women: Bane or Blessing?," *Theology Today* 32 (1975): 225.

29 For other instances where the act of naming suggests authority, see Genesis 41:45; Numbers 32:41–42; Joshua 19:47; 2 Samuel 5:6–9; 2 Kings 24:17.

when he declared that his new fellow human "shall be *called* [*qarah*] Woman" (2:23 ESV).[30]

But there are several challenges to this argument. First, while naming often conveys authority, there are some notable exceptions.[31] The clearest is Genesis 16:13, where Hagar names God: "So she *called* [*qarah*] the *name* of the LORD who spoke to her, 'You are a God of seeing'" (ESV). Hagar was not exercising authority over God. Later in Genesis 26:17–21, Isaac named certain wells as he *relinquished* control over them. Naming here is the opposite of exercising authority. Other instances of naming show an awareness of God's presence[32] or commemorate an act of God[33] without the person giving the name appearing to exercise authority over the thing being named.

Second, the word *woman* is not a proper name but a common noun. It designates Eve's sex, not her personal name.[34] Adam doesn't name the woman "Eve" until Genesis 3:20, but this naming occurs in the context of the fall rather than God's original design. If Adam naming his wife "Eve" in 3:20 demonstrates his authority, it very well could be a kind of authority poisoned by the fall.[35]

---

30 Gordon J. Wenham, *Genesis 1–15*, Word Biblical Commentary 1 (Word, 1987), 70; Ortlund, "Male-Female Equality," 103.

31 See e.g., George W. Ramsey, "Is Name-Giving an Act of Domination in Genesis 2:23 and Elsewhere?," *Catholic Biblical Quarterly* 50, no. 1 (1988): 33–34.

32 When Jacob names Bethel (Gen. 28:19; 35:7, 15), Peniel (Gen. 32:31), and an altar (Gen. 33:20), the point doesn't seem to be that Jacob has authority over these places. George Ramsey is probably correct that Jacob "exhibits awareness of God's activity and presence" and that "there is no basis in the text for concluding that this act of naming by Jacob establishes for him a measure of control over the respective places named" ("Name-Giving," 34).

33 For example, the naming of Simeon (Gen. 29:33), Dan (Gen. 30:6), Gilgal (Josh. 5:9), and Ichabod (1 Sam. 4:21); see Ramsey, "Name-Giving," 33.

34 Phyllis Trible, "Depatriarchalizing in Biblical Interpretation," *Journal of the American Academy of Religion* 41 (1973): 38; see also Richard Davidson, *Flame of Yahweh: Sexuality in the Old Testament* (Baker, 2007), 18.

35 Trible notes that the naming formula in 3:20 is very close to 2:19, which suggests that "the man reduces the woman to the status of an animal by calling her a name" (*God and the Rhetoric*, 133).

Third, Genesis 2:23 is followed by a curious statement in 2:24 that might challenge male authority: "That is why a man leaves his father and mother and is united to his wife, and they become one flesh." In Israel's culture, it was the woman who would leave her family and join the home of her husband's father and mother. But Genesis 2:24 spins it around. The man leaves his home and joins his wife's home. Sandy Richter believes "this is an intentional reversal on the part of the biblical author."[36] The point, she says, is something like this: "Young man, although you have all the benefits and comforts in this system, from this day onward you shall live your life as though you too have left."[37]

I wouldn't go as far as some egalitarians do when they argue that the wife in 2:24 "seems to be a free agent, in command of her own life."[38] But I do think 2:24 would have been startling to the original audience. If the goal of 2:23 is to highlight the man's authority over his wife, 2:24 is a very strange way to follow it.

Some scholars have suggested that it's not so much the *act* of naming that conveys authority but the authority *already possessed* by the name-giver.[39] We see this dynamic throughout the Old Testament when parents name their kids.[40] So, whenever God names someone or something, it's an authoritative act because he's God, not because the act of naming ascribes him this authority. The same could be true of conquerors changing the names of the conquered.[41] It's their status as the conqueror that

---

36 Sandra L. Richter, *The Epic of Eden: A Christian Entry into the Old Testament* (IVP Academic, 2008), 38; cf. Davidson, *Flame*, 44.

37 Richter, *Epic*, 38.

38 Gilbert Bilezikian, *Beyond Sex Roles: What the Bible Says About a Woman's Place in Church and Family* (Baker Academic, 2006), 34; rightly critiqued by Grudem, *Evangelical Feminism*, 126.

39 Hamilton, *Genesis*, 177.

40 We'll discuss this in chapter 2.

41 See Daniel 1:7, for example.

invests them with the authority to rename the conquered. This might make sense of most cases, but not all of them. The name-giver doesn't always possess authority over the thing or person being named, as in the case of Hagar.

In any case, if it's the *status* of the name-giver and not simply the *act of naming* that signals authority, where does this leave us with the man and woman? Some might quickly say: The man *is* the woman's authority and *therefore* his act of naming displays his authority. But this, of course, begs the question. We're evaluating the man's authority, not assuming it.

In sum, many acts of naming in the Bible signal the authority of the name-giver, but some do not. There's little clear evidence that the man in Genesis 2:23 was exercising authority when he named the woman. At the very least, we should be cautious about simply citing the naming of the woman in 2:23 as clear proof that the man was the woman's authority.

## 5. Does "He Will Rule over You" Mean Men *Should* Rule over Women?

"Perhaps no single verse of the Hebrew Bible is more troubling for issues of gender relations and women's roles than Genesis 3:16," writes Carol Meyers.[42] This is where God tells the woman: "Your desire [*teshuqa*] will be for your husband, yet he will rule [*mashal*] over you" (3:16 CSB).

Is Adam's "rule" (*mashal*) over Eve part of God's created intention, or is it a negative consequence of sin's curse? The verb *mashal* by itself doesn't give us enough information to answer that question. The

42 Meyers, *Rediscovering*, 81.

term can refer to a positive or negative kind of rule.[43] We need context to determine whether *mashal* is positive or negative.

Wayne Grudem rightly points out that the same two verbs from Genesis 3:16, "desire" and "rule," also occur together just a few verses later (4:7). The Hebrew construction of 3:16b is nearly identical to 4:7b:

> *Your desire* [*teshuqa*] will be for your husband, yet *he will rule* [*mashal*] over you. (3:16b CSB)
>
> *Its desire* [*teshuqa*] is for you, but *you must rule* [*mashal*] over it. (4:7b CSB)

I can't help but think that the author is intentionally drawing a parallel here. In 4:7, sin's "desire" for Cain is surely negative, which suggests that whatever is meant by the woman's "desire" for her husband is probably also negative.[44] Since Cain's "rule" over sin refers to his defeat or domination over it, the same sense could be implied in Genesis 3:16.[45] Thus, the man's "rule" over the woman is not a good sort of rule; it's one of domination and therefore part of the curse, not God's original design.[46]

---

43 Positive rule: Genesis 45:26; Psalm 66:7; 89:9. Negative rule: Judges 14:4; 15:11.

44 For various interpretations, see Susan Foh, "What Is the Woman's Desire?," *Westminster Theological Journal* 37 (1975): 376–83. *Teshuqa* occurs only one other time in the Old Testament, Song of Songs 7:10, where it's used positively. Given the Edenic imagery throughout the Song, it's likely that Song of Songs 7:10 represents the reversal of the negative "desire" in Genesis 3:16 (Davidson, *Flame*, 552–53).

45 Hamilton, *Genesis 1–17*, 202.

46 One could say that Cain's "ruling" over sin would be a good thing and therefore Genesis 4:7 views such "rule" positively. This may be true, but "rule" would still convey domination. For Cain to defeat and dominate sin would be a good thing. But Adam defeating and dominating his wife would be a bad thing—not some kind of gentle godly leadership.

The larger context supports this reading. Genesis 3 is like a divine trial investigation, where God pronounces judgment on the snake (vv. 14–15), the woman (v. 16), and the man (vv. 17–19).[47] The husband's "rule" is announced alongside cursed ground, pains in childbirth, and snakes licking up dust, as part of God's judgment. I think it's more likely, then, that man's "rule" over his wife is one of domination, not godly leadership. It's tempting to wander down the rabbit hole of divine agency to figure out whether God is causing, allowing, or simply foreseeing that husbands will rule over their wives in a negative manner. But I'll leave this for the theologians to figure out. For our purposes, we only need to note that Genesis 3:16 probably isn't commanding husbands to exercise godly leadership over their wives.

It's not just egalitarians who hold this view—lots of complementarians say the same thing. Wayne Grudem, for instance, boldly declares: "We should never try to promote Genesis 3:16 as something good!" He emphasizes that this passage "should never be used as a direct argument for male headship in marriage."[48] According to this complementarian view, Adam's "rule" over Eve in 3:16 is a distortion of the godly leadership prescribed for husbands over their wives in Genesis 1–2. Obviously, egalitarians don't see any spousal leadership prescribed in the first two chapters of Genesis. But either way, both groups agree that Genesis 3:16 isn't a good way to defend a complementarian view.

---

47 Davidson, *Flame*, 67–70; Hamilton, *Genesis*, 230–31.
48 Grudem, *Evangelical Feminism*, 40.

## Other Interpretive Issues

In addition to the five major questions we've looked at, several other features in the text deserve to be mentioned at least briefly.

First, some scholars point out that God gave his command to Adam and not Eve in Genesis 2:16–17, suggesting male leadership. According to Tom Schreiner, God's command to Adam signals "Adam's responsibility for leadership and teaching in the relationship."[49] After all, God didn't speak the command directly to woman. She recalled it in her conversation with the serpent in Genesis 3, which means she must have learned it from Adam.

Was Adam, therefore, Eve's teacher? The text doesn't clearly say this. God might have given his command to the man simply because he was the only one around at that point (the woman was created later). Plus, whatever God's reason is for commanding Adam first in Genesis 2:16–17, God commands *both* male and female in his original mandate in Genesis 1:26–28. And after both have sinned, God addressed them individually (3:16–19) and held the woman accountable for her own sin. The man did not speak on behalf of the woman, nor was he the only one held responsible, even though the command was given directly to him. So I don't think we can draw too much out of God commanding Adam in Genesis 2—the only human alive at that point.

Second, what about the serpent approaching the woman and not the man in order to deceive her? Does this tell us anything about male authority and female submission? Some older interpreters say the serpent approached Eve because she was "inferior to Adam in knowledge, and strength and presence of mind."[50] But this argument could run both

---

49 Schreiner, "Women in Ministry," 291.

50 Matthew Henry, cited in Taylor, "Women in Creation and Redemption," 19n29.

ways. On the one hand, Satan might have targeted Eve because she was the intellectually weaker of the two, and he knew the man wouldn't fall for his tricks. On the other hand, it took the craftiest, most deceitful being in the universe to deceive the woman. All it took for the man to sin was for his wife to offer him some fruit. If the woman was so gullible, what does this say about the man?

Some recent interpreters suggest that the serpent approached the woman "to get her to take responsibility for leading the family into sin, and inverting the order that God had established at Creation."[51] But this seems to add more to the text than what's clearly stated. If anything, Eve's sin had to do with her lack of leadership, not with her exercising too much of it: She failed to "subdue" the snake as both woman and man were commissioned to do back in Genesis 1:26–28.[52] In the end, the passage simply tells us that the snake approached Eve and deceived her, but it doesn't tell us why. Perhaps we shouldn't read too much psycho-anthropology into why the narrative plays out the way it does.

Finally, some suggest that Eve's creation from Adam's "side" (*tsela*) implies that Adam has some kind of priority over Eve.[53] Indeed, Paul makes a point about the woman being created from man in 1 Corinthians 11:8, which we'll deal with later. As far as Genesis 2 goes, the word for Adam's "side," *tsela*, does not mean "rib," as is often assumed. *Tsela* is used more than forty other times in the Hebrew Bible, and it never refers to a person's "rib."[54] Most often, it refers to the side of a sacred

---

51 Grudem, *Evangelical Feminism*, 36.

52 See Carmen Joy Imes, "Eve's Legacy Is Both Sin and Redemption," *Christianity Today*, May/June 2023.

53 For example, Bruce Ware, "Male and Female Complementarity in the Image of God," in *Biblical Foundations for Manhood and Womanhood*, ed. Wayne Grudem (Crossway, 2002), 82–84.

54 See John Walton, *The Lost World of Adam and Eve: Genesis 2–3 and the Human Origins Debate* (IVP Academic, 2015), 77–81.

piece of architecture, like the tabernacle or temple.[55] Eve's creation from the side of Adam, rather than his head or his feet, would seem to stress mutuality, not subordination. In the words of twelfth-century Bishop Peter Lombard, "Eve was not taken from the feet of Adam to be his slave, nor from his head to be his ruler, but from his side to be his beloved partner."[56]

In other words, it's very unlikely that the manner of the woman's creation suggests male authority. If anything, the word *tsela* argues against it. It's true that the woman was derived from the man, but derivation doesn't necessarily imply submission. Adam was derived from the ground, but this doesn't mean he should submit to the ground.[57]

## Summary and (Lack of a) Conclusion

I resonate with what Francis Watson says about male headship in Genesis 2–3: "Certain interpretive statements are 'possible,' although not explicitly demanded by the text."[58] I might even offer a slightly stronger conclusion: Genesis 1–3 alone does not teach male headship over women, or husbands' authority over their wives, as some universal principle etched into creation. Some male-headship arguments have more merit than others, but none of them is without problems. The two times authority language is employed, it refers to the mutual rule of male and

---

55 An interesting use of *tsela* comes in 1 Kings 6:34, where it describes two halves of a double door. The doors are the same, except their hinges are on opposite sides. "The imagery is remarkably apt for Eve and Adam," notes Carol Meyers. "They are virtually the same, and their combination produces humanity; but a male or female 'side' without the other could never produce the whole" (Meyers, *Rediscovering*, 75).

56 See Davidson, *Flame*, 17.

57 Davidson, *Flame*, 16.

58 Francis Watson, "Strategies of Recovery and Resistance: Hermeneutical Reflections on Genesis 1–3 and Its Pauline Reception," *Journal for the Study of the New Testament* 14, no. 45 (1992): 92.

female over creation (1:26–28) and a negative kind of rule that husbands wield over their wives in a world cursed by sin (3:16).

Still, we need to suspend judgment until we consider Paul's two allusions to Genesis 2 (1 Cor. 11:8–9; 1 Tim. 2:13–14). My initial glance at these Pauline passages seems to support a complementarian reading of Genesis. But initial glances won't suffice for such an important topic. We'll need to roll up our sleeves and spend considerable time working through these texts. Before we get there, I want to keep exploring what the rest of the Old Testament says about women and leadership in ancient Israel.

Chapter 2

# WOMEN IN THE OLD TESTAMENT

I originally toyed with skipping the rest of the Old Testament, since the debate about women in church leadership is primarily concerned with the New Testament. After all, the Old Testament doesn't talk about church, at least not in its post-Pentecost Spirit-filled form. I'm cautious about mapping Old Testament leadership roles too neatly onto the New Testament church. Just because Jael knows how to wield a tent peg doesn't mean we should hand her a pulpit.

But what happens in Israel doesn't always stay in Israel. The two Testaments are woven together. When Paul wrote that "all Scripture is God-breathed and is useful" for godliness (2 Tim. 3:16), he was referring to what we now call the Old Testament. This was the early church's authoritative "Bible," which is why New Testament writers quoted it over three hundred times. I can't imagine that early Christians would have ignored their Bible (the Old Testament) as they considered whether women should serve as leaders in their churches.

In this chapter, I'll first explore the social context of ancient Israel and the complex roles men and women played in this culture. This part won't directly address our question about women's leadership, but it will help attune us to the Old Testament world and the surprising agency women possessed in a male-dominated society. I'll then sample a few stories where women played significant roles in Israel's redemption story. This part will move us a bit closer to our question at hand. The third section, where I consider female prophets, will be the most relevant to today's debate about church leadership. I'll conclude by wrestling with Israel's all-male priesthood and see how this contributes to the debate.

## The Social World of the Old Testament

People often assume that the Old Testament is emphatically androcentric. It's written by men and primarily addressed to men,[1] and the story is often carried on the backs of men. Named men outnumber women by a factor of about twelve to one, and most of the significant leaders are men.[2] From the patriarchs (Abraham, Isaac, and Jacob) to Moses and Joshua to virtually every judge, king, and prophet—the story of God's covenant with Israel is a drama of God and men. Women aren't absent. They just appear to be insignificant.

1 Men are most often the intended audience, even when we consider the many places where masculine terms are intended to include both men and women. See Carol Meyers, *Rediscovering Eve: Ancient Israelite Women in Context* (Oxford University Press, 2013), 19; cf. 70–71.

2 Meyers, *Rediscovering*, 3.

Plus, fathers held legal authority over their households, including their wives.[3] When the patriarch died, his authority was passed on to the firstborn son, who took over the household.[4] From our modern perspective, this whole system might sound oppressive to women. And maybe some aspects of it were. But we must understand the Old Testament world on its own terms, not through our twenty-first-century Western lens.

Ancient Israel was an agrarian society, and the household was fundamental for the economic life of everyone in the nation. Nobody simply went off to work to make money for themselves, as many of us do today. In ancient Israel, an individual's survival depended on their connection to a household, and everyone in the home played a vital role. The fact that the father had legal authority over his household did not mean that women were inferior to men or that they lacked all agency. Women were just as vital to the survival of the household as men, and they often wielded power in ways that aren't appreciated unless we understand the social context they were living in.

For instance, women were in charge of making bread.

## Bread, Power, and the Ancient Household

Modern readers might find it odd, if not insulting, to talk about women and bread making in an effort to highlight the power of women. But

---

3 See Numbers 30:1–16. This is why we often see the phrase "house of the father," or *bet 'ab* (e.g., Gen. 41:51; 46:31; Ex. 12:3; Num. 18:1). Strikingly, a few passages refer to the "house of the mother" (Gen. 24:28; Ruth 1:8; Song 3:4; cf. 2 Kings 8:1; Prov. 9:1; 14:1; 31:21, 27). Carol Meyers says, "These instances of 'woman's household' suggest that when texts have a female focus, the prominence of women in the myriad household tasks ... meant the identification of the household with the senior female" (*Rediscovering*, 113).

4 For an excellent and accessible overview of the household in ancient Israel, see Sandra L. Richter, *The Epic of Eden: A Christian Entry into the Old Testament* (IVP Academic, 2008), 21–46.

that's the problem. We moderns view ancient life through the lens of our own world, where making bread conjures up images of a passive woman donning a flour-dusted apron and waiting idly for her husband to come home. But in ancient Israel, bread-makers wielded power unlike any we see in our postindustrial age.[5]

In Old Testament times, about 90 percent of people were rural farmers, living in a household that included the nuclear family, grandparents, unmarried kids, married sons with their wives and kids, other relatives, and possibly servants. Survival demanded that everyone work, and roles were often distributed by gender.[6] Although what we call "women's work" may be devalued today, ancient people "valorize[d] women's contributions to household life," which were not "less important than what men [did]."[7] Indeed, women stood at the heart of the household's endurance and vitality.

Bread making was particularly vital for the household and for the existence of society as a whole. In ancient times, more than 70 percent of a person's calories came from grain. But grain had to be ground into flour, which then had to be made into dough and baked to be edible. Grinding grain was an especially arduous task; it took two to three hours for a person to grind enough flour to feed six people. The bread-making process was not only physically demanding but also required "specialized knowledge and technological skills: how fine to grind the flour, how to knead the dough, how to heat the oven, and even how to make the

---

5 See the incisive discussion in Meyers, *Rediscovering*, 121–46.

6 Carol L. Meyers, "The Importance of Bread: Archaeology, the Bible, and Women's Power in Ancient Israel," in *The Biblical World of Gender: The Daily Lives of Ancient Women and Men*, ed. Celina Durgin and Dru Johnson (Cascade Books, 2022), 6.

7 Meyers, *Rediscovering*, 126.

oven!"[8] As we see throughout Scripture, it was women who ruled over this process and therefore wielded "considerable household power" in the ancient world.[9]

In addition to bread, women were also in charge of bearing and raising kids, managing the household, and participating in other aspects of agrarian life. Procreation and child-rearing in particular were not optional; they were socially and economically essential. A home without children stood on the brink of extinction, which is why barrenness was such a life-threatening tragedy. "Give me children, or I shall die!" cried Rachel in Genesis (30:1 ESV).[10] Today's Western world has almost completely inverted this, turning child-rearing into an unnecessary option at best and a financial burden at worst. But in ancient Israel, having kids was a matter of survival. And women (mothers and midwives) were responsible for carrying, delivering, naming, rearing, and educating children.[11]

---

8 Meyers, "Importance," 9.

9 Meyers, "Importance," 9. Women are associated with grinding stones used to turn grain into flour (Judg. 9:53–54; 2 Sam. 11:21; cf. Isa. 47:1–2; Matt. 24:41) and were in charge of baking bread (Lev. 26:26; 1 Sam. 28:24; cf. 1 Sam. 8:13; 2 Kings 4:8). Some women, such as Abigail, wielded power over the distribution of valuable food to others in need (1 Sam. 25:18–19; cf. Prov. 31:14–15, 20). The Shunammite woman also made autonomous decisions over who she could feed and several other matters related to the management of the household (2 Kings 4:8–37; 8:1–6; see Meyers, "Importance of Bread," 10).

10 The seriousness of childlessness is illustrated in the six stories of barrenness in the Hebrew Bible: Sarah (Gen. 16:1–6; 18:1–15; 21:1–7), Rebecca (Gen. 25:19–25), Rachel (Gen. 30:1–8, 22–24), the wife of Manoah (Judg. 13:1–24), Hannah (1 Sam. 1:1–28), and the Shunammite woman (2 Kings 4:8–17).

11 On mothers educating their children, see C. V. Camp, "The Wise Women of 2 Samuel: A Role Model for Women in Early Israel?," *Catholic Biblical Quarterly* 43 (1981): 14–29; Meyers, *Rediscovering*, 136–39. As for naming, it's striking that mothers name their children more frequently than fathers in the Old Testament. See Edward J. Bridge, "A Mother's Influence: Mothers Naming Children in the Hebrew Bible," *Vetus Testamentum* 64, no. 3 (2014): 389–400; Daniel I. Block, "Marriage and Family in Ancient Israel," in *Marriage and Family in the Biblical World*, ed. Ken M. Campbell (InterVarsity, 2003), 33–102 (esp. 67). In the case of Jacob, his free wives name all his sons except for one, which means women gave names to almost all the tribes of Israel (Gen. 29:31–30:24; 35:18; cf. Bridge, "Mother's Influence," 395).

Making bread and making babies. Such "woman's work" is often ridiculed in society today. Ironically, this critique supposes that activities historically performed by men are the standard by which to measure meaningful work—an assumption that is itself misogynistic and male-centered—and it's a good example of why we shouldn't read our modern notions of equality and power into an ancient Near Eastern text. Rather, we need to look at the Old Testament's portrayal of women within their own cultural situation. And in the Old Testament, men's status as the legal heads of the household didn't erase the agency of women.

Another example of female agency comes in that steamy collection of love poems called the Song of Songs.

## Mutual Love in the Song of Songs

Since as early as the mid-nineteenth century, scholars have read the Song as a "melodramatic manifesto for the emancipation of women."[12] The Song certainly exhibits a love relationship between man and woman that is profoundly mutual. There is no hierarchy, where man takes a passive woman as the object of his desire.[13] If any books of the Bible promote male domination, the Song of Songs is not one of them.

The Song begins and ends with the woman speaking (1:2–4; 8:14). And throughout, the woman speaks more (eighty-nine verses) than the man (forty-nine verses).[14] There is no dominant partner; both

12 M. H. Pope, *Song of Songs*, Anchor Bible Commentary (Yale University Press, 1995), 205.

13 Tremper Longman III, *Song of Songs*, New International Commentary on the Old Testament (Eerdmans, 2001), 66.

14 See Richard M. Davidson, "Theology of Sexuality in the Song of Songs: Return to Eden," *Andrews University Seminary Studies* 27 (1989): 8.

pursue each other. Sometimes the man is the initiator (2:10–14), while at other times the woman is (7:11–13). In some places, the woman's passionate advances are more aggressive than the man's (4:16; 7:11–12; 8:2). Throughout the Song, the woman enjoys a certain emotional and sexual power over the man (4:9; 6:5; 7:5). Both lovers indulge in rich and lively descriptions of the beauty of each other's bodies, including erotic depictions of each other's sexual anatomy.[15] It's quite telling that the Song colors its poetry with images of Eden, suggesting that the lovers showcase the kind of male-female relations that God intended before the fall.[16]

## Heroic Women in the Old Testament

From bread making to love making, the Old Testament portrays what Carol Meyers calls the "complexity of gender dynamics." Meyers, herself a nonreligious feminist, goes so far as to say that "patriarchy" is an inaccurate description of ancient Israel.[17] "Israelite women were not dominated in all aspects of Israelite society but rather were autonomous actors in multiple aspects of household and community life."[18]

It's within this framework of "complex gender dynamics" that I want to look at five Old Testament stories where women emulate covenant faithfulness, perform heroic feats, embody wisdom and virtue, or play an essential role in God's unfolding plan of redemption. Strikingly, the male authors often lavish these women with a glowing report *in contrast* to unfaithful, foolish, or fearful men.

---

15 See e.g., Song 4:1–7; 5:10–16.

16 See Davidson, "Theology of Sexuality."

17 Carol Meyers, "Was Ancient Israel a Patriarchal Society?," *Journal of Biblical Literature* 133, no. 1 (2014): 8–27.

18 Meyers, "Ancient Israel," 27.

## Mothers and Midwives in Exodus 1–5

When we think of human heroes in the book of Exodus, we often think of Moses. But Moses is actually a bit of a complicated character. After murdering an Egyptian, he ran away "afraid" (2:14) and married a foreign woman (2:21), and his interaction with God in the burning bush showed more doubt than trust. "Please, Lord, send someone else," he complained, which caused God's anger to burn against him (4:13–14 CSB).

God did ultimately use Moses to redeem his people, and along the way, Moses displayed many admirable qualities (e.g., 2:17–19). But there would have been no Moses—and no redemption, no Red Sea crossing, and no Israel—were it not for several women who turned the Egyptian empire on its head through their heroic acts of political resistance in the early chapters of Exodus.[19]

Midwives prevented the mass murder of the enslaved Hebrews by opposing the king's edict to kill off every male being born (1:15–20). Pharaoh surely didn't think some lowly female midwives were a threat to the empire, which turned out to be one of the greatest miscalculations of the late Bronze Age. Pharaoh then took matters in his own hands and commanded his people to kill every newborn Israelite son (1:22). But a woman named Jochebed defied the king's command by hiding her baby, Moses, and sending him down the Nile River in a basket with his sister Miriam looking on (2:1–4). Miriam witnessed another woman, Pharaoh's daughter, rescue her brother, so she approached the princess and offered to find a Hebrew to nurse the child. Pharaoh's daughter

---

19 See the excellent treatment by Terence Fretheim, *Exodus*, Interpretation (John Knox Press, 1991), 23–41, 80–81.

complied, and in an ironic twist, Moses was given back to his mother (2:7–9).

Midwives, a mother, a sister—all female slaves—and even Pharaoh's own daughter pave the way for God's redemption. The agency of women dominates the first two chapters of Exodus. All the male characters are passive, fearful, or profoundly evil.

As the narrative unfolds, women continue to play critical roles. Israelite women were the ones God said would "plunder the Egyptians" (3:22). And later on, God was about to kill Moses because he had failed to circumcise his son, but his wife, Zipporah, stepped in to rescue Moses's life in a graphic way. She sliced the foreskin from Gershom's penis, tossed it at Moses's feet, rebuked Moses for his negligence, and thus saved Moses's life and the whole project of redemption (4:24–26).

God dismantled political and spiritual oppression in Exodus 1–5, and it was women who "nurture[d] the revolution."[20] As Carmen Joy Imes explains, "Women do not usually take center stage on the pages of Scripture. But in this liberation story ... the narrative presents a dramatic face-off between the man in power and the women who defeat him."[21]

## Rahab: Canaanite, Prostitute, Heroine

Rahab was the first Canaanite to confess faith in Yahweh, and she became a model of courage and faithfulness (Josh. 2:1–24; 6:22–27). Her heroic act of hiding the spies became the catalyst for Joshua's victory over Jericho and, ultimately, the Israelites' entry into the Promised Land.

---

20 Phyllis Trible, "Depatriarchalizing in Biblical Interpretation," *Journal of the American Academy of Religion* 41 (1973): 34.

21 Carmen Joy Imes, "Freedom Fighters of the Exodus," in *The Biblical World of Gender: The Daily Lives of Ancient Men and Women*, ed. Celina Durgin and Dru Johnson (Wipf and Stock, 2022), 44.

From a literary perspective, Rahab and Achan are contrasting characters. Rahab, a Canaanite prostitute, was an outsider who became an insider through her faithfulness. Achan, an Israelite from the tribe of Judah, was an insider who became an outsider.[22] Rahab hid the Israelite spies on her roof, protecting them from the king of Jericho (2:4–7). Achan, in contrast, took and hid forbidden items from Jericho, violating the ban imposed by Joshua (7:1, 20–21).[23] Rahab was a poor Canaanite woman whose actions saved her family. Achan was a wealthy man from the tribe of Judah whose sin destroyed his family.[24]

The juxtaposition of these two characters highlights themes of obedience, faith, and the consequences of people's actions.[25] Achan stands as an unrighteous foil for the righteous Rahab, who ended up marrying into Achan's tribe (Judah) and ultimately became part of the genealogical line of the Messiah (Matt. 1:5).

## Ruth: Outsider, Widow, Agent of Redemption

The books of Judges and Ruth play off each other to form a dialogue of despair and redemption. In Judges, male leaders plunge society into chaos, which leads to the "Canaanization of Israel."[26] Enter Ruth: a poor foreign widow on the brink of death. The book situates her story "during the time of the judges" (Ruth 1:1 CSB), insisting that we read the story of Ruth against the backdrop of the male-led horror show of Judges.

---

22 E. John Hamlin, *Inheriting the Land: A Commentary on the Book of Joshua*, International Theological Commentary (Eerdmans, 1983), 19.

23 David M. Howard Jr., *Joshua*, The New American Commentary 5 (Broadman & Holman, 1998), 97.

24 Howard, *Joshua*, 97.

25 David G. Firth, *Including the Stranger: Foreigners in the Former Prophets*, New Studies in Biblical Theology (IVP Academic, 2019), 24.

26 Daniel Block, *Judges, Ruth*, New American Commentary (Broadman & Holman, 1999), 58.

Instead of staying with her own people, which offered a better chance of survival, Ruth chose to join the people of Israel and worship their God (1:16). Despite being a widow in a foreign land—a death sentence in the ancient Near East—Ruth gained a widespread reputation as a "noble" woman (3:11),[27] showing covenant faithfulness ("kindness," *hesed*, 3:10) to Boaz, her kinsman-redeemer. The book closes with the astonishing revelation that Ruth supplied a vital link in the genealogy of God's redemption (4:18–22). Like Rachel and Leah, two women "who together built the house of Israel" (4:11 CSB), Ruth helped build the messianic line through her daring choice to sojourn in a foreign land. Without Ruth, there would be no David. Without David, there would be no Jesus.

## Abigail: Sage, Saint, Prophet

The Bible's portrait of Abigail is so glowing that it borders on mythical. She's not only a pivotal character in the books of 1 and 2 Samuel, but she also plays a key role in the broader biblical narrative.

David had already been privately anointed king, but he found himself on the run from Saul, who still occupied the throne. David and his men were hungry. They noticed a nearby man, Nabal, who was "very rich" (1 Sam. 25:2 ESV), so they asked for food, but Nabal mocked David and shooed them away (vv. 10–11). Thirsty for revenge, David gathered his four hundred armed men and marched toward Nabal to annihilate him and his household (v. 13). Nabal's servants found out and rushed to

27 The phrase *eshet hayil* ("noble woman") occurs only two other times in Scripture: Proverbs 12:4 and 31:10 (Block, *Judges, Ruth*, 694).

seek counsel from Abigail, Nabal's wife, who took charge of the situation and saved the day (vv. 14–35).

Abigail is among the most noble characters in all of Scripture. She's remarkably intelligent, humble, hospitable, loyal to her husband (despite his stupidity), yet "capable of independent action."[28] Even though David was acting recklessly, she honored him as king. Her male servants looked to her for leadership and obeyed her (vv. 14–17). She commanded her family's resources and gave generously to those in need (vv. 18–19). She not only epitomizes the noble wife of Proverbs 31; she's a model follower of Yahweh worthy of any man or woman's emulation.

Abigail's lengthy speech to David drips with wisdom, kindness, and humility and plays a central role in the story (vv. 23–31). It even has a prophetic flair to it, as she declared God's promise to David in advance: "The LORD is certain to make a *lasting dynasty* [*bayit ne'ĕmān*] for my lord because he fights the LORD's battles" (v. 28 CSB).[29] The phrase "lasting dynasty" (literally, "a secure house") is the same phrase God would later use when he established his everlasting covenant with David (2 Sam. 7:16).[30] Abigail went on to express certainty in David's future: "When the LORD does for my lord all the good he promised you and appoints you ruler over Israel, there will not be remorse or a troubled conscience for my lord because of needless bloodshed or my lord's revenge" (1 Sam. 25:30–31 CSB).

Her revelation of God's plan for David squelched his passion for "needless bloodshed" (v. 31) like some kind of Jedi mind trick and saved

---

28 Phyllis Bird, "Images of Women in the Old Testament," in *Religion and Sexism: Images of Woman in the Jewish and Christian Traditions*, ed. Rosemary R. Ruether (Simon and Schuster, 1974), 65.

29 Elna K. Solvang, "Abigail," in *The New Interpreter's Dictionary of the Bible*, ed. Katharine Doob Sakenfeld, vol. 1 (Abingdon, 2006), 10.

30 H. A. Hoffner Jr., *1 & 2 Samuel*, vol. 1 (Lexham Press, 2015), 832.

her household from disaster. David "obeyed [her] voice" (v. 35 ESV) and blessed Abigail, and then she returned home to find her head of the house "holding a feast fit for a king" (v. 36 CSB). Ten days later, Nabal died, so David sent his servants to bring Abigail back as his wife. After taking the form of "a slave to wash the feet of" David's servants (v. 41 CSB)—a mark of true leadership, from a Christian perspective—she became his wife.

Abigail's selflessness, kindness, humility, and wisdom are clearly contrasted with Nabal's selfishness, harshness, arrogance, and foolishness. Legally, Nabal was the "master" of the household (vv. 14, 17). But practically and morally, Abigail was the obvious leader,[31] even compared to David. Not only did she avert him from needless bloodshed—a sin that would cripple him later (2 Sam. 11:14–21; 16:7–8)—but she also exhibited the virtues fit for a king. The biblical author doesn't critique her for exercising leadership in this story. Just the opposite—she is celebrated for it.

## Esther: Exiled Jew, Cunning Queen

Esther's story begins with King Ahasuerus showing off "the glorious wealth of his kingdom and the magnificent splendor of his greatness for a total of 180 days" (Est. 1:4 CSB). This excessive display of pomp and pride lands him in the narcissistic hall of fame.[32] It's in this context that he summoned Queen Vashti "to show off her beauty to the people and the officials, because she was very beautiful" (v. 11 CSB). The king's

31 "In the Hebrew Bible, it is unusual to find the wife depicted as being superior to her husband; thus this story serves as a striking example of feminine superiority." Kenneth D. Mulzac, "The Role of Abigail in 1 Samuel 25," *Andrews University Seminary Studies* 41, no. 1 (2003): 45.

32 "The operative word in the first chapter of Esther is *excess*." C. M. Bechtel, *Esther*, Interpretation (Westminster John Knox Press, 2002), 21.

objectification of Vashti is the pinnacle of his ego: His queen was just another piece of wealth to flaunt.

Vashti refused to be paraded like a trophy before a hall of drunken men, which struck panic in the hearts of insecure men. "For the queen's action will become public knowledge to all the women and cause them to despise their husbands," warned Memucan, one of the king's "wise" officials (v. 17 CSB; cf. vv. 13–14). Even the "noble women of Persia" (v. 18 CSB) would be inspired to "despise their husbands" (v. 17 CSB)—that is, refuse to be tossed around by pompous men. Memucan therefore told the king to issue a decree throughout the entire Persian Empire that "women will honor their husbands, from the greatest to the least" and that "every man should be master of his own house" (vv. 20, 22 CSB). The whole story is told with delicious humor that plays on the insecurities of the male ego.[33]

In many ways, Vashti's courage against misogyny-run-amuck prefigures the heroic feats of Esther, the woman who would replace her. Even though Esther was more compliant than Vashti, she too disobeyed the king's decree by appearing before him without being summoned (4:11; 5:1–2). Then, through a crafty display of manipulation (5:4; 7:1), she overpowered the king without him even realizing it and convinced him to execute Haman and save the Jewish people.

The book contains creative and ironic themes related to male authority and female submission. The episode in chapter 1 brims with comedic critiques of abusive male authority. Vashti's defiance against her insecure and arrogant husband is portrayed positively and leads to the rise of

---

33 C. A. Moore, *Esther: Introduction, Translation, and Notes*, Anchor Bible Commentary 7B (Yale University Press, 2008), 14.

Queen Esther, who saved her people. Without Vashti's insubordination, the Jews would have been annihilated and God's promises would have come to an end. The king's doubling down on male authority and female submission (1:17–18, 20, 22) was a pagan response to the righteous act of Vashti. Esther worked within the domestic decree by honoring her husband while overpowering him, albeit submissively.

Esther's story does not address every question related to male-female relations in the home. But it does offer a scathing critique of husbands who wield a Genesis 3:16-like rule over their wives. Only pagan men rule as masters of their houses, demanding that their wives obey their every beck and call.

## Summary of Heroic Women

The Old Testament appears to be male-centric, but there are important exceptions. Israel's story unfolds with a steady celebration of the power and faithfulness of women who play essential roles at key junctures in God's redemption of his people. This doesn't necessarily mean all these women were leaders. Not every faithful person is a leader, and God can use non-leaders to carry out his plan of redemption. But these stories at least suggest that biblical women can embody the wisdom and virtues expected of leaders, sometimes in contrast to male leaders who simply hold a title.

Many other women could be mentioned: Hagar, Hannah, Jael, the Shunammite woman, and the wise woman of Tekoa all emerge as pivotal figures in God's redemptive story, embodying faithfulness that often outshines the men surrounding them. What I find fascinating is that the male writers of Scripture chose to highlight the significance of these women, often describing their faithful behavior in contrast to the unfaithfulness of men. As a Christian, I can chalk it up to divine inspiration—God wielding Genesis 1:27 like a broadsword against misogynistic tendencies. Or, from a more naturalistic perspective, perhaps not every ancient Israelite man celebrated male domination over women. Either way, the Old Testament thus far doesn't appear to reinforce some kind of absolute principle of creation, where men are always the leaders and women are designed to help them in their tasks.

## Female Leaders in the Old Testament?

We still need to answer the question, Were there any women who occupied formal leadership positions over men in Israel? All the kings were male—except for the wicked Athaliah, who illegitimately took the throne through a violent coup (2 Kings 11:1). Two foreign queens are portrayed positively in Scripture.[34] But this tells us little about God's intention for his people. The queen mothers of Israel and Judah (i.e., the mothers of the male kings) seemed to wield some level of authority, but they're almost always mentioned in passing, and it's tough to determine what kind of role they played.[35] And, of course, all the priests in Israel were men, an issue I'll explore at the end of this chapter.

If there were any women who played a formal leadership role in Israel, it had to have been female prophets. The Old Testament mentions four female prophets by name: Miriam (Ex. 15:20–21; Num. 12:1–15; Mic. 6:4), Deborah (Judg. 4:4–5), Huldah (2 Kings 22:14–20; 2 Chron. 34:22–28), and Noadiah (Neh. 6:14). It also refers to an unnamed prophetess (Isa. 8:3), women who prophesy (Ezek. 13:17–23), and "daughters"

34 Sheba (1 Kings 10:1–13) and the queen of Chaldea (Dan. 5:10–12).
35 E.g., 1 Kings 2:17–19; 15:2, 10, 13; 2 Kings 24:8, 15; Jer. 13:18; 29:2.

who "shall prophesy" in the future (Joel 2:28 ESV). Daniel Block says, "We should probably add Hannah, whose utterance in 1 Samuel 2:2–10 bears the marks of a prophetic oracle."[36] And while Abigail is never called a prophet, we've just seen that she too offered an oracle-like message to David.

Not everyone agrees, however, that female prophets were leaders over men in Israel. So let's delve into this issue by looking more closely at two in particular: Deborah and Huldah.

Deborah was the first prophet to come on the scene since Moses, and she's the first *named* prophet in what scholars call "Deuteronomic history" (Joshua–2 Kings). Judges 4 describes her this way:

> Deborah, a woman prophet, the wife of Lappidoth [or "fiery woman"], was judging Israel at that time. She held court under the Palm of Deborah between Ramah and Bethel in the hill country of Ephraim, and the Israelites went up to her to have their disputes decided. (vv. 4–5, my translation)

The author highlights Deborah's gender by calling her "a *woman* prophet [*ishah ne'vi*]," the "*wife* of Lappidoth," and later says she is "a *mother* in Israel" (5:7). Some argue that the phrase "wife of Lappidoth" could be translated "fiery woman" or "woman of torches," but Sandy Richter counters that "wife of Lappidoth" is surely the better translation, since it would have been quite normal for a woman to be identified by

36 Block, "Marriage and Family," 68n160.

her husband's name.[37] The location where she judged (between Ramah and Bethel) is similar to Samuel's jurisdiction (1 Sam. 7:15–17), and this parallel seems intentional.[38] Indeed, Deborah and Samuel were the only two judges who were also prophets.[39]

In the book of Judges, Deborah is the only judge cast "in an unequivocally positive light," and "each judge who succeeded her represents a decline in quality and character."[40] She occupied a public position of judicial, spiritual, and military leadership.[41] People sought her out for legal decisions, she mediated God's word to Barak, and she embodied the virtues of courage, wisdom, and utter dependence on God throughout the narrative.

Wayne Grudem, however, argues that Deborah was not a leader over men in Israel. Rather, "she affirmed the rightness of male leadership" when she "encouraged Barak" to summon the people to battle.[42] Grudem goes on to suggest that "Deborah refused to lead the people in military battle, but insisted that a man do this (Judges 4:6–7, 14)."[43] As for her judging activity, Grudem sees this as "not a picture of public leadership" but a "private settling of disputes through both arbitration and judicial decisions."[44]

---

37 I thank Sandy Richter for pointing this out to me.

38 Hugh Williamson, "Prophetesses in the Hebrew Bible," in *Prophecy and Prophets in Ancient Israel: Proceedings of the Oxford Old Testament Seminar*, ed. J. Day (Continuum, 2010), 69.

39 Interestingly, Huldah is the last-named prophet in the same section of Scripture (Joshua–2 Kings), which makes two female prophets, Deborah and Huldah, the bookends of Israel's preexilic history (Williamson, "Prophetesses," 70).

40 Block, *Judges, Ruth*, 194–95.

41 Block questions Deborah's judicial function. He argues that when the sons of Israel come to her for judgment (4:5), "they are not asking her to solve their legal disputes but to give them the divine answer to their cries" (Block, *Judges, Ruth*, 197).

42 Wayne Grudem, *Evangelical Feminism & Biblical Truth: An Analysis of More Than 100 Disputed Questions* (Crossway, 2012), 132.

43 Grudem, *Evangelical Feminism*, 133.

44 Grudem, *Evangelical Feminism*, 133.

I don't find Grudem's interpretation persuasive, for three reasons. First, Deborah didn't "encourage" Barak to gather the people; she "summoned" (*qa'ra*) him to travel to her (v. 6 CSB)—subordinates don't summon superiors. She then prophetically relayed God's word to him and commanded him to deploy the troops while articulating a precise battle plan (vv. 6–7). Deborah behaved more like a four-star general organizing an army than someone avoiding battle to preserve male leadership. In every way, Deborah acted as Barak's superior.

Second, the verb "to judge" (*shaphat*) cannot be limited to "private settling of disputes" as Grudem thinks.[45] *Shaphat* means "to govern, administer, exercise leadership,"[46] and every time it's used in Judges, it describes a broader sense of rulership.[47] Even though Deborah settled legal disputes (vv. 4–5), this doesn't seem to be *all* she did as a judge. She clearly wielded mad leadership and military skills throughout Judges 4 and was celebrated as the primary catalyst for the battle: "Villagers in Israel would not fight; they held back until I, Deborah, arose, until I arose, a mother in Israel" (5:7).

Third, the text gives no indication that Deborah was judging only privately and not publicly. When Deborah was "judging Israel," the "Israelites went up to her" (4:4–5 CSB); this was a public affair. She strategically set herself up "between Ramah and Bethel in the hill country" (v. 5), which was centrally located, making her "accessible to the entire

---

45 Grudem, *Evangelical Feminism*, 133

46 See Block, *Judges, Ruth*, 23.

47 The verb *shaphat* describes four major judges—Othniel (Judg. 3:10), Deborah (4:4), Jephthah (12:7), and Samson (15:20; 16:3)—and five minor judges—Tola (10:1–2), Jair (10:3), Ibzan (12:8–9), Elon (12:11), and Abdon (12:13–14). In 1 Samuel 8:5, it depicts a king's rule over his people, and it's also used as a "general designation for the leaders of Israel in 2:16–19, from which we may infer that the leaders described in the book may be so designated" (Block, *Judges, Ruth*, 22). Block goes on to note: "Since the judges functioned as princes, rulers, and chieftains over specific territories and clans, the term *shophetim* is best understood generally to mean 'tribal rulers, leaders, governors' rather than 'judges'" (*Judges, Ruth*, 23).

nation," as Daniel Block points out.[48] The text also says she sat under a tree, which may seem like a mundane detail. But Deborah is clearly being described as "the Israelite counterpart to Sisera," the Canaanite military leader who also "sat" in a nearby region.[49] Plus, it was common for rulers to exercise leadership while sitting under trees (1 Sam. 14:2; 22:6).

The text seems rather clear: Deborah played a key leadership role in Judges 4–5. While her leadership seems to be an anomaly—she's the only female judge and one of a few female prophets—there's nothing in the text that criticizes her for exercising leadership. Rather, her leadership is worthy of praise and imitation. I don't think this means Deborah has to be some kind of proto-pastor, and we should be cautious about using her as an example of female leaders in the church. The text simply celebrates her as an eminent leader over men in ancient Israel.

Huldah is another female prophet who came on the scene at a climactic moment in Israel's history, right at the turning point of Josiah's reforms in Judah (2 Kings 22:14–20). The high priest at the time, Hilkiah, discovered the book of the law in the temple, so he gave it to the royal scribe, Shaphan, who read it (v. 8). Shaphan then went to King Josiah and read it again in the king's presence (v. 10). King Josiah understood the meaning of the text to some extent, but he still felt the need to ask a prophet about its full implications. "Go and inquire of the LORD for me," Josiah said, "and for the people and for all Judah about what is written in this book that has been found" (v. 13). He sent Hilkiah and Shaphan to find the prophet Huldah, and he added three more men to the delegation: Ahikam, an influential court official (Jer. 26:24); Akbor,

---

48 Block, *Judges, Ruth*, 195.

49 Block, *Judges, Ruth*, 193. See Judges 4:2.

one of Josiah's key officials (2 Kings 22:12); and Asaiah, who's simply called "the king's servant" (22:12 CSB).[50]

A few things stand out already. First, this was a very prestigious group of men, and yet all of them went to find Huldah. If she were a subordinate, they would have just summoned her to the palace. Second, they sought Huldah out to expound on the meaning of a text they had already read (v. 13). This is striking. The high priest and the royal scribe were trained interpreters of Scripture, yet they needed to consult Huldah on the meaning of the law. Third, the author introduces Huldah to the story in an almost nonchalant manner; her gender appears unexceptional.[51] Both Jeremiah and Zephaniah were prophets in Judah at this time, and yet Josiah sent his elite delegation to Huldah.[52] Huldah is not presented as a last resort or as something unusual. Lastly, Huldah gave a prophetic word concerning the impending doom facing Judah and the manner of Josiah's death, and her message ignited the most significant—though short-lived—spiritual revolution in the history of the divided monarchy.[53]

As we saw with Deborah, some scholars distinguish between the public and private ministry of Old Testament prophets and argue that female prophets only engaged in the latter. Huldah "did not publicly proclaim God's word," says Tom Schreiner. "Rather, she explained in

---

50 See Mordecai Cogan and Hayim Tadmor, *Kings II*, Anchor Bible Commentary 11 (Yale University Press, 1988), 281–82, on the identity and significance of these five men.

51 "Huldah's gender is of far more interest to subsequent readers," quips Francesca Stavrakopoulou, "than it appears to have been to the biblical writers." "The Prophet Huldah and the Stuff of State," in *Enemies and Friends of the State: Ancient Prophecy in Context*, ed. Christopher A. Rollston (Eisenbrauns, 2018), 285.

52 There's been a lot of speculation about why Josiah sent his people to her and not to one of the male prophets (see Stavrakopoulou, "Huldah," 285, for various theories). But the text is simply uninterested in this question.

53 Stavrakopoulou sufficiently refutes the notion that Huldah gave a false prophecy ("Huldah," 288).

private the word of the Lord when Josiah sent messengers to her. She exercised her prophetic ministry in a way that did not obstruct male headship."[54]

Tom Schreiner is one of my favorite biblical scholars, so I'm usually prone to agree with him. But in this case, I find his interpretation a bit strained. First, many male prophets gave prophecies to an individual or a small group of people, and this made them neither more nor less significant.[55] The biblical authors don't divide prophecy into categories of public and private—they only distinguish between true prophets and false prophets. Second, there's nothing in the text suggesting that Huldah "exercised her prophetic ministry in a way that did not obstruct male headship," as Schreiner says. Huldah declared God's word to a group of five elite religious and political leaders. The biblical author doesn't seem concerned about preserving male headship. Third, Huldah's message was intended "for me and for the people and for all Judah about what is written in this book that has been found" (v. 13). Though initially given to five men, Huldah's prophecy was ultimately communicated to the masses.

In every way, Huldah is presented similar to how male prophets are presented throughout Scripture. If we were to substitute Huldah's name with a male name, no one would bat an eye. The text doesn't distance her prophetic ministry from that of her male prophetic counterparts.

---

54 Tom Schreiner, "The Valuable Ministries of Women in the Context of Male Leadership: A Survey of Old and New Testament Examples and Teaching," in *Recovering Biblical Manhood and Womanhood: A Response to Evangelical Feminism*, ed. John Piper and Wayne Grudem (Crossway, 1991), 216.

55 Nathan spoke to David individually (2 Sam. 12). Other prophets like Isaiah and Ezekiel were sent delegations of elite men just like we see in the case of Huldah (see Isa. 37:1–7; Ezek. 20:1–3). In fact, we don't see very many male prophets speaking in front of crowds; see Marg Mowczko, "Huldah's Public Prophetic Ministry," *Marg Mowczko* (blog), February 19, 2018, https://margmowczko.com/huldah-prophetess/#_ftnref12.

There might be good reasons to avoid using Huldah as an argument for women in first-century church leadership. Perhaps Old Testament prophets served a different function than New Testament prophets and leaders did. Certainly, ancient Israel's political system was very different from the early church in the New Testament. But I don't think alleging that Huldah's ministry was private rather than public is a good reason for downplaying her prophetic leadership during Josiah's reforms.

Deborah and Huldah, then, were two female prophets who exercised leadership over men in ancient Israel, and the biblical authors don't critique them for doing so. The women communicated God's word to men, who responded in obedience to the message.

But does this mean they were actually *teaching* men?

Wayne Grudem rightly points out that it was Israel's all-male priesthood, not prophets, who were responsible for teaching the law to God's people. According to Grudem, prophets simply passed on the divine message given to them, but they had "no authority ... to do more than that, such as explaining or applying the message." The "role of teaching the people was reserved for the priests," who were all men.[56]

I think this is largely true; Huldah relayed God's message but offered no interpretation of it. It's worth noting, however, that prophets carried more authority than priests or even kings in ancient Israel. Prophets frequently confronted both kings and priests, which was revolutionary in the ancient world. Sometimes their confrontation involved a "thus saith the Lord" message (e.g., Jer. 7:1–11), but other times it was a swift rebuke without direct divine revelation, as in the case of Nathan's confrontation of David (2 Sam. 12:1–10). Prophets were king makers and king

---

56 Grudem, *Evangelical Feminism,* 137.

breakers—they occupied the most authoritative office under the Mosaic covenant.[57]

While it's true, then, that male priests were responsible for instructing the people in the law of Moses, I think it's inaccurate to say prophets weren't leaders or authority figures in the Old Testament.

So why was Israel's priesthood a male-only institution?

## All-Male Priesthood

Indeed, Old Testament priests were the primary religious teachers in Israel (Lev. 10:11; Mal. 2:7), and all priests were male. But what is the rationale for the priesthood being exclusively male? It could be because God didn't design women to be teachers. Thus, male-only teachers are rooted in creation, and the principle is universal and absolute.[58]

There are, however, other possible rationales that have to do with the context of ancient Israel. Some say God wanted to distance Israel's worship practices from those of pagan religions where women served as cultic prostitutes.[59] The problem with this view is that there is hardly any evidence (if any at all) for cultic prostitution in the ancient Near East. It's still a popular theory today, but it's probably more myth than reality.[60]

Another proposed rationale has to do with ritual purity laws in the Old Testament.[61] A woman who was menstruating or who had recently given birth was considered ritually unclean during that time.[62] A priest's

---

57 I thank Sandy Richter for pointing this out to me.

58 Grudem, *Evangelical Feminism*, 137–38.

59 Philip Payne, *The Bible vs. Biblical Womanhood: How God's Word Consistently Affirms Gender Equality* (Zondervan, 2023), 19.

60 The title of Stephanie Budin's book says it all: *The Myth of Sacred Prostitution in Antiquity* (Cambridge University Press, 2010).

61 See William G. Witt, *Icons of Christ: A Biblical and Systematic Theology for Women's Ordination* (Baylor University Press, 2021), 177–80.

62 Leviticus 12:1–8; 15:19–33.

daily duties required ritual purity, which means female priests would have to take a lot of time off. Plus, several key priestly duties fell on specific days of the year. It's not like a woman could push her period back a few days to make sure she was ritually clean to perform her duties on Rosh Hashanah.

I think this argument has some merit, but it does seem speculative.[63] It makes sense in light of the social context, but as far as I'm aware, there's nothing in the actual text of Scripture that implies this rationale for excluding women from the priesthood.

There's another rationale for an all-male priesthood that I find most persuasive: Israel was a patrilineal society, where inheritance was passed on through the male heir.[64] Such is the case of the priesthood. It was a hereditary office passed down through the male descendants of Levi. Even men from non-Levitical tribes could not be priests and therefore teachers—no matter how qualified they might have been. The rationale for excluding women, then, might have to do with social norms surrounding lineage and not theological reasons concerning gender.

At the end of the day, God's rationale for the all-male priesthood doesn't actually contribute much to our debate for one simple reason: Under the new covenant, all believers, men and women, are priests.[65] This doesn't mean all believers are qualified to be pastors and leaders. It just means that we can't appeal directly to Israel's all-male priesthood to exclude women from teaching and leading in churches today.

---

63 Richard Nelson points out that nocturnal emissions would have also rendered male priests unclean (Lev. 15:2–18), and unlike menstruation, these would be impossible to anticipate and plan for. See *Raising Up a Faithful Priest: Community and Priesthood in Biblical Theology* (Westminster John Knox, 1993), 96.

64 I thank Sandy Richter for pointing this out to me. See also Nelson, *Faithful Priest*, 97.

65 Isaiah 61:6; 1 Peter 2:9; Revelation 5:10; cf. Exodus 19:3–6.

## Conclusion

While the Old Testament features far more male leaders than female leaders, quantity should not be confused with quality. Women play heroic roles at critical junctures, and the Bible isn't afraid to commend their righteous behavior against the backdrop of unrighteous and foolish men.

From my vantage point so far, I tend to see the pervasive presence of male leaders in the Old Testament as descriptive rather than prescriptive. God seems to be working with cultural norms rather than creating them. If male-only leadership were God's idea, we wouldn't see divinely approved exceptions to the rule, few though they may be. If God had commanded that only men can lead, then even one deviation from his command wouldn't be just an *exception* to the rule; it would be *immoral*. The biblical writers don't refer to women like Deborah and Huldah this way.

However, I'm very open to the New Testament correcting my perception thus far. Perhaps these few exceptions to male-only leadership were unique allowances during extraordinary circumstances. Or perhaps the female leadership we see in the Old Testament is too different in kind from New Testament church leadership to be relevant for today's debates. It's not like Deborah's superb military skills map neatly onto Paul's requirements for elders. And yet, I don't want to dismiss the countercultural stories of heroic women, some of whom were leaders, and the impact this would have had in shaping the imagination of the early church. Again, these women played key roles in God's story of redemption and are memorialized in the Old Testament—the Bible of first-century Christians.

In any case, it's probably best to hold off on buttoning up any firm conclusions about women in church leadership just yet. All I know is, I'm itching to see what the New Testament has to say.

## Chapter 3

# WOMEN IN THE MINISTRY OF JESUS

I've got to be honest. I've never been impressed with egalitarian arguments from the Gospels. I feel like many of them squeeze things out of the text that aren't clearly there, or they interpret the positive view of women in the Gospels to mean they are leaders. Jesus, no doubt, humanized women in ways that may have been startling in his culture. He addressed women publicly,[1] used women as positive examples in his teaching,[2] and included women in his ministry.[3] Jesus clearly valued women, and women played important roles in his mission. I don't know any complementarian who denies this.[4] Just because Jesus valued women doesn't mean he appointed them to be teachers and leaders over men. And there's the glaring issue

---

1 He spoke directly to the woman caught in adultery (John 8:10–11), the widow at Nain (Luke 7:12–13), the hemorrhaging woman (Luke 8:43–48; cf. Matt. 9:20–22; Mark 5:25–34), and a group of women on his way to the cross (Luke 23:27–31).

2 E.g., the Queen of the South (Matt. 12:42), the widow of Zarephath (Luke 4:26), a widow who was persistent before a corrupt judge (Luke 18:1–5).

3 E.g., Luke 8:2–3.

4 See James A. Borland, "Women in the Life and Teachings of Jesus," in *Recovering Biblical Manhood & Womanhood: A Response to Evangelical Feminism*, ed. John Piper and Wayne Grudem (Crossway, 1991), 114–15.

that all twelve apostles are men, which I've always assumed was a devastating argument for egalitarians. Indeed, it's the primary reason the Catholic Church does not ordain women as priests.[5]

I thought this was going to be a quick and easy chapter. I'd just point out the lack of evidence for women leaders in Jesus' ministry and move on to Paul. But admittedly, I hadn't done much study on women in the Gospels. So I decided to carve out several months in my journey and dive deeper into the Gospels to see if there's more to the story than I had originally thought.

What I found is a picture more complicated than I had previously assumed: passages I hadn't considered, themes I hadn't explored, questions I never thought to raise. I still think the evidence for women in leadership can be stretched further than the Gospel writers intended. And Jesus having all-male apostles seems to offer a strong argument for a complementarian view. But the Gospel writers describe the faith and behavior of women in fascinating ways, marking them out as not just passive recipients of Jesus' kindness but crucial agents in the expansion of Jesus' mission. And, as we'll see, I do think there might be a case for female leaders in the Gospels, albiet a subtle one.

## Women as Model Disciples in Contrast to Men

When we talk about Jesus' disciples, we need to remember that the term "disciples" isn't limited to the twelve apostles. Matthew and Mark do often use "disciple" (*mathētēs*) to refer to the Twelve, but there are some

---

5 See Sara Butler, *The Catholic Priesthood and Women: A Guide to the Teaching of the Church* (Hillenbrand Books, 2007), 46–51. For a thorough analysis of this view, see William Witt, *Icons of Christ: A Biblical and Systematic Theology for Women's Ordination* (Baylor University Press, 2020), 173–291.

exceptions.[6] And Luke and John use "disciple" to refer to followers of Jesus more broadly.[7] In fact, Luke never calls them the Twelve "disciples." He always calls them "apostles," while referring to other believers as "disciples."

We can think of Jesus' disciples as being in three concentric circles.[8] The smallest circle is the Twelve, the next is a larger group of disciples who literally followed Jesus around Palestine, and the widest circle includes anyone who believes in Jesus. Women were not part of the Twelve, but they were part of the other two circles.[9]

I've always known this and didn't think it was particularly noteworthy. But after paying closer attention to the text, I noticed something remarkable. The Gospel writers don't just include women as disciples of Jesus. Rather, they highlight women as exceptional disciples who emulated the kind of radical obedience Jesus expected, often in contrast to the faithlessness of men—*especially the twelve apostles.*[10] Over and over, women exhibited the very discipleship traits that male disciples failed to embody.

I want to explore this further by looking at how each Gospel writer portrays women in their respective narratives.

---

6 See Michael Wilkins, *Following the Master: A Biblical Theology of Discipleship* (Zondervan, 1992), 176–93. Joseph of Arimathea, for instance, is said to have become "a disciple" (Matt. 27:57), even though he's not part of the Twelve.

7 E.g., Luke 6:17; John 6:60, 66.

8 Nijay Gupta, *Tell Her Story: How Women Led, Taught, and Ministered in the Early Church* (IVP Academic, 2023), 62.

9 The only time a woman (Tabitha) is explicitly called a "disciple" is in Acts 9:36.

10 Mark especially likes to highlight the constant failure of the Twelve, who often lacked faith (4:40; 6:50; 9:19; 11:22), doubted Jesus' supernatural abilities (6:50–52; 8:4), misunderstood his messianic vocation (8:31–33), failed to understand his words (7:18; 8:14–21), were unable to cast out demons (9:14–19), deserted him in his greatest hour of need (14:50), and, in the case of Peter, denied that they knew him (14:66–72); see Mary Ann Beavis, "Women as Models of Faith in Mark," *Biblical Theology Bulletin* 18, no. 1 (1988): 7.

## Women in Mark

Mark's Gospel includes many stories of women,[11] but there are four scenes in particular that play a strategic role in the narrative. In fact, "Mark's narrative plot could not succeed without these four narrative roles of women."[12]

The first is Jesus' encounter with the hemorrhaging woman (Mark 5:24–34). This woman was living in impossible circumstances. She'd been bleeding for twelve years, which would have rendered her ceremonially unclean and therefore outcast from society.[13] She had spent all she had on doctors, leaving her poor and alone. Her only hope lay in Jesus, but coming near him would risk further ridicule and ostracism. Courageously, she jeopardized it all. She trusted the power of Jesus, pursued him in a crowd, daringly reached out to touch him, and was instantly healed. Jesus sensed that someone had touched him, and when he asked who it was, the disciples offered a condescending response (v. 31). The woman, however, "with fear and trembling" told Jesus "the whole truth" (v. 33 CSB),[14] which elicited high praise from Jesus: "Your faith has saved you" (v. 34 CSB).

This scene plays a central role in this section in Mark (4:35–6:6), which is bookended by two scenes about a lack of faith from the twelve apostles (4:40) and Jesus' hometown (6:1–6). Sandwiched between these stories, Mark spotlights the hemorrhaging woman as the only

---

11 Mark contains twenty passages (totaling 114 verses) that include women. Fabian Ekwunife Ezenwa, "The Hermeneutics of Women Disciples in Mark's Gospel: An Igbo Contextual Reconstruction" (PhD thesis, Boston College, 2018), 10.

12 W. M. Swartley, "The Role of Women in Mark's Gospel: A Narrative Analysis," *Biblical Theology Bulletin* 27, no. 1 (1997): 17.

13 Swartley, "Role of Women," 18.

14 "The word *truth* is never used in direct reference to anyone else in Mark's work except Jesus." Marla J. Schierling, "Women as Leaders in the Marcan Communities," *Listening* 15 (1980): 254.

person thus far who has demonstrated the kind of radical faith Jesus demands.[15]

Mark's description of the woman also foreshadows the final days of Jesus. He says that she "suffered" (*paschō*) for twelve years (5:25–26); Mark's only other uses of the verb *paschō* describe Jesus and his crucifixion (8:31; 9:12). The woman's illness is described as a "scourge" (*mastix*, 5:29), and Mark uses the same word to depict the scourging of Jesus during his trial (10:34). Faith and suffering are fundamental traits of discipleship in Mark. The woman not only modeled both; she foreshadowed the suffering of Jesus himself.[16]

The second scene that plays an important role in Mark is Jesus' encounter with the Syrophoenician woman (7:24–30).[17] Her daughter was demon-possessed, so she pursued Jesus to find healing for her child. She was a Gentile. She was a woman. She had a demon in her house. The odds were stacked against her, just as they were for the hemorrhaging woman, but she boldly sought out Jesus, a Jewish male leader, in the privacy of a home.[18] And when she begged him for help, he compared her to a dog.[19] Unshaken by the insult, the woman turned Jesus' jab into proof that he should heal her: "Lord ... even the dogs under the table eat the

---

15 Jairus, whose story provides the more immediate bookends for the woman's encounter with Jesus, is viewed much more positively than the Twelve. But he still fell short of the woman's robust faith. "When compared to Jesus' word to Jairus, 'Do no fear, only believe,' it is clear that the woman plays the stronger narrative role, calling the reader to faith in Jesus" (Swartley, "Role of Women," 18).

16 See Schierling, "Women as Leaders," 252.

17 She's probably a Greek woman born in the region of Syrian Phoenicia, while Matthew's description of her as "Canaanite" probably refers to her religious affiliation. Ben Witherington III, *Women and the Genesis of Christianity* (Cambridge University Press, 1995), 74.

18 Mark tells us that Jesus was trying to hide from the crowds, but somehow she found out where he was.

19 Jesus appears to dehumanize the woman by calling her a dog, though there are many interpretations of Jesus' statement. I think the most compelling one is to see Jesus testing her faith by adopting a common Jewish view of Gentile people to see how she would respond. Comparing her to a dog represents the reality of how many in her social context would have viewed her. For a recent proposal that Jesus' statement is not pejorative, see N. Clayton Croy, "Puppies and Pejoratives: Did Jesus Insult the Syrophoenician Woman (Mark 7.24–30)?," *New Testament Studies* 70, no. 3 (2024): 407–20.

children's [bread] crumbs" (v. 28), eliciting Jesus' approval and healing of her daughter.).

Four things are noteworthy about this story. First, while Mark does not use the word *faith* to describe the woman, she clearly demonstrated radical faith in her encounter with Jesus. In fact, the parallel in Matthew has Jesus telling the woman, "You have *great faith*" (15:28)—an accolade used only one other time in the Gospels (Matt. 8:10).

Second, Mark contrasts the woman's faithful response with the apostles' faithlessness. He flanks his account of the woman with two stories where the apostles lack understanding (7:18; 8:17, 21). And in the scene with the Syrophoenician woman, the apostles are nowhere to be found.[20] The persistence, resilience, and great faith of the woman is contrasted with the fragility and fluttering faith of the Twelve.

Third, this is the only story in Mark where someone seems to have rhetorically outmaneuvered Jesus. Jesus verbally sparred with a woman, and to the shock, perhaps offense, of every ancient male reader, she won. "She alone, in contrast to the worsted scribes, Pharisees, and Sadducees, has victory conceded to her, winning an apparent change of stance which brings about the healing of her daughter."[21]

Fourth, like the story of the hemorrhaging woman, this story falls in a crucial position in Mark's narrative, where themes of discipleship, Gentile inclusion, and Jesus' messianic identity are highlighted (6:14–8:30). While the disciples kept missing the deeper spiritual significance of bread (8:14–21), a Gentile woman begged for bread from Jesus' table

---

20 In Matthew's Gospel, the woman's "great faith" contrasts with the disciples, who had "little faith" (Matt. 16:8); they were immediately annoyed at the woman and urged Jesus to "send her away" (15:23). "In Matthew her great faith contrasts with the disciples' great annoyance at her persistent pleading" (Witherington, *Women*, 76).

21 Winsome Munro, "Women Disciples in Mark?," *Catholic Biblical Quarterly* 44, no. 2 (1982): 227.

(7:24–30).[22] Mark's Gentile audience would have looked to this woman as a model of what it meant for a Gentile to overcome sociocultural barriers and embrace a Jewish Messiah.

Another story where a woman takes center stage comes in Mark 12:41–44, where Jesus observed a widow giving her whole life in service to God.

> And he sat down opposite the treasury and watched the people putting money into the offering box. Many rich people put in large sums. And a poor widow came and put in two small copper coins, which make a penny. And he called his disciples to him and said to them, "Truly, I say to you, this poor widow has put in more than all those who are contributing to the offering box. For they all contributed out of their abundance, but she out of her poverty has put in everything she had, all she had to live on." (ESV)

The woman models the radical sacrifice necessary for discipleship, a theme that runs through the latter half of Mark (8:37–16:8). As Mary Ann Beavis notes: "She is the only character, other than Jesus and John the Baptist, who gives 'all her living/life' (*holon ton bion autēs*) in service of God."[23] Mark contrasts this righteous widow with the male scribes who "devour widows' houses" (12:40) and the rich young ruler who was unable to give up all he had to follow Jesus

---

22 There's a "bread motif" running through Mark 6:8–8:19, where the word "bread" (*artos*) occurs eighteen times (it's only used three other times in Mark).

23 Beavis, "Women," 6.

(10:17–22). Letting go of possessions and giving up one's life are key traits of discipleship, and it's an unnamed widow who best emulates such behavior in Mark's Gospel.[24]

The fourth story is about another unnamed woman (14:3–9), who made a great sacrifice by anointing Jesus' head with a jar of very expensive perfume, worth "more than a year's wages" (14:5). Like the Old Testament prophets, who often acted out their message as a sign of things to come, this woman anticipated Jesus' death by preparing his body for burial. Some men in the house, lacking her spiritual acumen, furiously scolded the woman. Jesus, however, praised her by offering "his lengthiest and most positive pronouncement on the words or deeds of any person preserved by the evangelist Mark."[25] It's actually quite rare for Jesus to commend someone for their actions. He did so only twice in Mark's Gospel. And both times, he commended women: the widow, who gave all she had, and this woman, who anointed him.

In addition to these four stories, Mark also notes that women were present at Jesus' crucifixion (15:40) and burial (15:47) and that they were the first witnesses of his resurrection (16:1–8). Once again, Mark contrasts female presence with male absence. Judas betrayed Jesus. Peter denied him. And all the others "deserted him and ran away" (14:50 CSB; cf. 14:27). In this context, Mark makes a seemingly passing comment that "in Galilee" several women "used to *follow* [*ēkolouthoun*] Him and *serve* [*diēkonoun*] Him" (15:41 NASB). This short statement is loaded with theological implications for our question about women in

24 "The willingness to make sacrifices for the sake of the gospel is a necessary characteristic of discipleship—ranging from giving up one's possessions to giving up one's own life." Holly J. Carey, *Women Who Do: Female Disciples in the Gospels* (Eerdmans, 2023), 64–65.

25 Beavis, "Women," 7.

leadership. But before we get there, let's look at the women in the other three Gospels.

## Women in Luke

Luke opens with one of the most commendable depictions of women in all four Gospels. Mary and Elizabeth exemplify the kind of faith and action that Jesus would later demand of his followers, and the prophet Anna displays resilient hope in the coming Messiah.

Zechariah and his wife Elizabeth are both introduced as righteous and blameless (1:6). But as the story unfolds, Zechariah shows a lack of faith, while Elizabeth exhibits faith throughout. Their story echoes the account of Abraham and Sarah (Gen. 18), who also received news of an upcoming miraculous birth. In Genesis, it was Abraham who believed and Sarah who didn't. But in Luke, the roles are reversed: Elizabeth is the "new Abraham" who believes, while Zechariah stands in for disbelieving Sarah.[26]

Mary too is a model disciple in Luke's opening chapters. Like Zechariah, she received a visit from Gabriel, but unlike Zechariah, she believed the angel's report. Her response, "Behold, I am the servant of the Lord" (Luke 1:38 ESV), echoes Samuel's response to God's prophetic call,[27] and her self-designation as "servant" correlates with Abraham,[28] Moses,[29] David,[30] and many other Old Testament heroes.[31]

---

26 Carey, *Women*, 106.
27 1 Samuel 3:4–8.
28 Psalm 105:42.
29 2 Kings 18:12.
30 Psalm 89:3.
31 These include Joshua (Josh. 24:29), Daniel (Dan. 6:20), Jonah (Jon. 1:9 LXX), and Hannah (1 Sam. 1:16). Simeon (Luke 2:29) and those who prophesy and preach the Word throughout Acts are also identified as "servants" (*doulos*, Acts 2:18; 4:29; 16:17). See Barbara E. Reid, "The Gospel of Luke: Friend or Foe of Women Proclaimers of the Word?" *Catholic Biblical Quarterly* 78, no. 1 (2016): 7.

Mary's song of praise (her Magnificat, 1:46–55) is laced with Scripture, drawing on the Old Testament songs of Miriam,[32] Deborah,[33] and Hannah,[34] whose words in 1 Samuel 2 set up the theme of role reversal that shapes the book of Samuel—powerful elites are torn down while the marginalized are lifted up. Mary drew on Hannah's lyrics to capture this same theme in Luke's Gospel. God "looked with favor on the humble condition of his servant" and "toppled the mighty" while "exalt[ing] the lowly. He has satisfied the hungry ... and sent the rich away empty" (Luke 1:48, 52–53 CSB).

Though Luke never calls Elizabeth and Mary prophets, his depiction of their actions paints them as prophetic messengers. They received the divine message, faithfully proclaimed it to others, and are described in similar terms to the prophets of old.[35]

Anna, however, is explicitly called a prophet (2:36). And her situation is truly remarkable. She was married for seven years and then lived the next eighty-four years as a widow, which means she probably was around 105 years old.[36] Living for eighty-four years as a widow in the first century was not for the fainthearted. Instead of remarrying at an early age, Anna chose to dedicate her life to unswerving service to God.[37] When she laid eyes on Mary's child, she did what prophets do—she began

---

32 Exodus 15:1–21.

33 Judges 5.

34 1 Samuel 2:1–10.

35 Carey, *Women*, 104–5. Barbara Reid has argued extensively that Luke portrays Elizabeth, Mary, and Anna "in the mode of powerful prophets" ("Gospel of Luke," 19). See also Barbara Reid, "Women Prophets of God's Alternative Reign," in *Luke–Acts and Empire: Essays in Honor of Robert L. Brawley*, ed. David Rhoads et al., Princeton Theological Monograph Series 151 (Pickwick, 2011), 44–59.

36 The age of Anna is debated. For the view taken here, see Richard Bauckham, *Gospel Women: Studies of the Named Women in the Gospels* (Eerdmans, 2002), 99–100.

37 Carey, *Women*, 103.

to "speak about him to all who were looking forward to the redemption of Jerusalem" (v. 38 CSB).

Anna stands at the end of the birth narrative, which begins with the obedience of Elizabeth and Mary. The story of baby Jesus is thus wrapped with stunning portraits of marginalized women who emulate radical faithfulness and enduring hope.

Luke goes on to tell several more noteworthy stories about women. I'll highlight two.

In Luke 7:36–50, an unnamed woman anoints Jesus' feet and wipes them with her hair.[38] The scene happens inside the house of a Pharisee named Simon, who showed some level of hospitality by inviting Jesus into his home for dinner. But upon seeing the woman's behavior, Simon's true colors were revealed: "[Jesus], if he were a prophet, would know who and what kind of woman this is who is touching him—she's a sinner!" (v. 39 CSB). Jesus then used Simon as a negative foil for the woman's service, faith, and "great love"—quintessential virtues of discipleship (vv. 44–50).

This story sets up the very next scene, where Luke introduces a band of female disciples in Jesus' entourage:

> Soon afterward he went on through cities and villages, proclaiming and bringing the good news of the kingdom of God. And the twelve were with him, and also some women who had been healed of evil spirits and infirmities: Mary, called Magdalene, from whom seven

38 This is probably the same incident recorded at the end of the other three Gospels (Matt. 26:6–13; Mark 14:3–9; John 12:1–8), though Luke's version has several unique features, including its placement in the middle of Jesus' ministry rather than at the end.

> demons had gone out, and Joanna, the wife of Chuza, Herod's household manager, and Susanna, and many others, who provided [*diēkonoun*] for them out of their means. (8:1–3 ESV)

Along with the three named women (Mary Magdalene, Joanna, and Susanna), Luke says there were "many others, who provided for" or served [*diēkonoun*] "them out of their means" (v. 3 ESV). These prominent and apparently wealthy Galilean women were part of Jesus' entourage, traveling with him and the Twelve throughout his ministry. And these women played a vital role in Jesus' mission, since they appear to have been his primary patrons. The Twelve are simply mentioned, but the women are described as *serving*—a key virtue for disciples of Jesus. In fact, this moment marks the first "substantive description of the activity of any of Jesus' followers in the gospel," notes Holly Carey. "Up to this point the focus has been on Jesus' activities, and it is only after this that the actions of the Twelve begin to be included."[39]

Luke highlights these same women again at the end of his Gospel. They were present at the cross (23:27), burial (23:55–56), and resurrection (24:1–10). And like Mark, Luke contrasts their faith with the disbelief of the Twelve (24:11; cf. 24:25). The women were the first to witness Jesus' resurrection, and when they announced it to the apostles, Luke says their "words seemed like nonsense to them, and they did not believe the women" (24:11 CSB).

Luke bookends not only Jesus' birth but also his entire Gospel with women. From cradle to grave and on through the empty tomb, women

---

39 Carey, *Women*, 118.

play substantial roles in the Messiah's ministry and emulate what radical discipleship looks like.[40]

## Women in John

John records several fascinating stories of women that are unique to his Gospel. I'll highlight three in particular: the Samaritan woman's interaction with Jesus (John 4), Martha's confession (John 11), and Mary Magdalene's conversation with the resurrected Jesus (John 20).

Jesus' dialogue with the Samaritan woman is the longest in John's Gospel, intentionally drawing readers' interest. People often assume the woman is promiscuous, with five husbands and all. But considering the historical context, she was probably widowed several times.[41] She was not a rebellious woman, but one who'd been dealt a terrible hand and was doing whatever she could to survive.

Her encounter with Jesus is remarkable. A Jewish male leader speaking openly with a Samaritan woman would have turned some heads, as we see in the disciples' reaction (4:27). Against all odds, the woman confessed she was waiting for the coming Messiah (v. 25), believed Jesus when he said he was the one, and immediately proclaimed his message to the entire town of Sychar, who believed "because of the word of the woman who testified [*marturousēs*]" to them (v. 39 NASB).

John contrasts the woman's loyal response with the disciples' fear and confusion. They were shocked that Jesus was even talking to her but were too scared to ask him why (v. 27). The woman was shocked too, but she

---

40 The crucifixion and resurrection narratives are connected to the birth narratives through many rhetorical echoes, as Barbara Reid points out ("Gospel of Luke," 19–20).

41 See e.g., Lynn Cohick, "The 'Woman at the Well': Was the Samaritan Woman Really an Adulteress?," in *Vindicating the Vixens: Revisiting Sexualized, Vilified, and Marginalized Women of the Bible*, ed. Sandra Glahn (Kregel Academic, 2017), 249–54.

responded with faith instead of fear. While the male disciples went into town to buy literal food, the woman took Jesus' spiritual food into the town and fed them with the gospel.[42] The woman displayed confidence that Jesus was the Messiah and courageously evangelized her hometown. Meanwhile, the disciples were left scratching their heads, still wondering if someone secretly brought Jesus some lunch (v. 33).

John contrasts the woman not only with the disciples but also with Nicodemus in the previous chapter (3:1–21).[43] Nicodemus came to Jesus, but he did so at night, while the woman met Jesus at midday. He was inquisitive like the woman, but his understanding of Jesus' identity was fuzzy at best. He rightly acknowledged that Jesus was a "teacher who has come from God" (v. 2). But after Jesus talked about being born again by water and Spirit, Nicodemus was confused. We're not even sure where he was spiritually at when he left the conversation.

Things played out differently with the woman. She began by not knowing who Jesus was. But after another conversation about water and Spirit, Jesus revealed his identity and the woman immediately believed and obeyed. Nicodemus moved from understanding to misunderstanding, while the woman went from not understanding at all to believing, obeying, and proclaiming that Jesus was the Messiah. "The juxtaposition of these two stories invites us to weigh the responses of both characters, and at this point Nicodemus is found wanting."[44]

---

42 John is very intentional about this contrast: "John's use of 'meanwhile' (*en tō metaxu*, 4:31) has the effect of emphasizing that *while* she is witnessing and calling people to Jesus, the male disciples are preoccupied with food and are confused about the kind of food that sustains Jesus: doing the will of God (4:34)" (Carey, *Women*, 167).

43 Carey, *Women*, 164.

44 Carey, *Women*, 166–67.

With exquisite artistry, John showcases the woman, whose obedient response and gospel proclamation eclipse the failures of the bewildered men around her.

Martha's confession is another fascinating incident (11:1–44). Most Christians are familiar with Peter's confession in Matthew 16:16, where he famously acknowledges that Jesus is "the Christ, the Son of the living God" (ESV). What often goes unnoticed is that Martha makes a similar confession in John 11:27: "I believe that you are the Christ, the Son of God, who is coming into the world" (ESV).

John places Martha's confession at the last and most significant of Jesus' seven signs—the raising of Lazarus from the dead. John tells us that Jesus wanted to raise Lazarus from the dead so that the Twelve would "believe" (v. 15). But the Twelve aren't even mentioned in the rest of the story. Instead, John showcases Martha, and her confession takes center stage. She's the first and only person in John's Gospel to confess that Jesus is both the Messiah and the Son of God. And she followed her confession with immediate action (v. 28; cf. 12:2).[45] It's striking that "Messiah" and "Son of God" are combined only one other time in John—at the end when he summarizes the purpose of his book: "These are written that you may believe that Jesus is the Messiah, the Son of God" (20:31).[46] Martha is the only character who perfectly models the main reason why John wrote his entire Gospel.

Finally, let's look at Mary Magdalene's encounter with Jesus (20:1–18). Mary is mentioned more frequently than any other woman in the Gospels, and she's always listed first when others are named. Indeed,

---

45 Peter's confession, however, was short-lived, as he received an immediate and scathing rebuke from Jesus (Matt. 16:22–23; Mark 8:32–33).

46 Carey, *Women*, 171.

Mary plays a leading role in all four Gospels' resurrection stories.[47] In John's account, Mary is the only woman named at the tomb on Easter morning (v. 1). After she arrived at the tomb and found it empty, she immediately ran to tell Peter and John that "they have taken the Lord out of the tomb" (v. 2). Already the scene is remarkable. The apostles were hiding behind locked doors "because they feared the Jews" (v. 19 CSB), while Mary wasn't afraid to visit the tomb of a man just executed for allegedly starting a revolution.

After they rushed to the tomb, Peter and John returned to their safehouse. Meanwhile, Mary lingered in the garden and became the first person to witness the resurrected Jesus and enjoyed one of the most intimate encounters with her Lord (vv. 11–18). Though she didn't recognize him at first, his identity became clear when he called out her name: "Mary" (v. 16). She responded, "Rabboni," or "Teacher" (v. 16), implying that she was his student, alongside the male disciples (who were still hiding).

Jesus told Mary to "go to my brothers and tell them that I am ascending to my Father" (v. 17 CSB). She obeyed and was the first person to carry the message of Jesus' resurrection to the eleven apostles, proclaiming: "I have seen the Lord!" (v. 18).

I used to think Mary did nothing more than pass on information to men, which is unexceptional for our topic. But the early church ascribed much more significance to Mary's proclamation. The resurrection became the turning point in the life of the church, and its validity

---

47 Her name "Magdalene" is sometimes believed to indicate the village (Magdala) where she was from. But there's little evidence for this. Mary's name always occurs with the definite article ("*the* Magdalene"), which literally means "the tower." According to Jerome, Mary was named as such because of her outstanding faith. See Joan Taylor and Helen Bond, *Women Remembered: Jesus' Female Disciples* (Hodder & Stoughton, 2022), 70–71.

hangs on the credibility of its witnesses. It's no wonder that Mary was hailed "the apostle to the apostles" by the early church.[48] Even Celsus, a second-century critic of Christianity, tried to discredit the resurrection by mocking Mary as a "hysterical female" who supposedly witnessed it.[49] The fact that Celsus even knew about Mary's witness shows the prominent role she played in the stories Christians told about the resurrection of Jesus.[50]

This doesn't mean Mary was part of the Twelve, nor does it necessarily mean she was a leader or teacher of men. Again, the story isn't intended to directly answer questions about women in church leadership. But Mary clearly did more than simply pass on information to other men. The Gospel writers all highlight the witness of women—especially Mary Magdalene—in their resurrection narratives, marking them as essential agents in the most important event in Christianity. She and other women "are given priority by God as recipients of revelation and thereby the role of mediators of that revelation to men."[51]

48 As far as I can tell, the first writer to label the women at the tomb (including Mary) "apostles" was the third-century writer Hippolytus of Rome. *De Cantico* 24–26, in Gérard Garitte, ed., *Traités d'Hippolyte sur David et Goliath, sur le Cantique des Cantiques et sur L'Antéchrist*, Corpus Scriptorum Christianorum Orientalium 264 (Sécretariat du Corpus SCO, 1965), 43–49. This later developed into Mary Magdalene being called *apostola apostolorum*, or "apostle of the apostles." On the reception of Mary in the early church, see Gerald O'Collins and Daniel Kendall, "Mary Magdalene as Major Witness to Jesus' Resurrection," *Theological Studies* 48, no. 4 (1987): 631–46; Taylor and Bond, *Women Remembered*, 59–73.

49 Origen, *Contra Celsum* 2.55, trans. H. Chadwick (Cambridge University Press, 1980), 109–10. Interestingly, the same Celsus mentions a certain group of Christians who "derive their name from Mariamme" (Origen, *Contra Celsum* 5.62), which could refer to Mary Magdalene. Ancient evidence of such a group is also found in the second-century (possibly Gnostic) text *The Gospel of Mary*. Mary's importance in the early church is also highlighted in the second-century mainstream (i.e., non-Gnostic) text *The Gospel of Peter*, which refers to her as a "disciple" (see Taylor and Bond, *Women Remembered*, 60–63).

50 Bauckham, *Gospel Women*, 271.

51 Bauckham, *Gospel Women*, 275.

## Women in Matthew

Our discussion of Matthew can be brief, since his Gospel doesn't add much to the picture we've already studied. But he contributes one striking feature that's not in the other Gospels: He includes four women (five, if we count Mary) in Jesus' genealogy (Matt. 1:1–17).

Genealogies in the Bible are not random pieces of information. They are profoundly theological. They tell the story about God's commitment to raise up the seed of Eve (Gen. 3:15) through the line of Abraham to crush the serpent and rescue the world from sin and death. Matthew's Gospel—and the entire New Testament—begins with a spotlight shining brightly on women, who are woven into the genealogical line that carried God's promises to fruition.

Jesus' genealogy in Matthew also tells a story about Jesus' past, which would inform his future ministry. Matthew's inclusion of Tamar, Rahab, Ruth, and Bathsheba is both intentional and instructive. Three of the four women were non-Jewish, and all four were socially marginalized and (except possibly for Ruth) mixed up in some kind of sexual scandal. These were the kinds of people God worked through to send his Son, and they were the type he would attract and mobilize in his earthly ministry.

It wasn't unheard of for Jewish writers to includes wives of significant men to genealogies. The book of Jubilees (second century BC), for instance, lists all the wives from Adam to Abraham and the wives of Jacob's sons. Pseudo-Philo's first-century work names all the wives from Adam to Noah. But Matthew's genealogy doesn't include just the wives of famous men. He highlights four women who played strategic roles in God's story of Israel's redemption.[52] And they all demonstrated

---

52 See Bauckham, *Gospel Women*, 18.

some level of persistence against all social odds and were used by God in mighty ways.[53] "It is not coincidental," writes Holly Carey, "that all four of the women named in Matthew's list of Jesus' ancestors have stories that emphasize their active roles in bringing about God's purposes, often in contrast to the men who are present in their stories and with whom they interact."[54] Matthew's genealogy points ahead to a kingdom where women are not bystanders but bearers of the mission.[55]

## Are Women in the Ministry of Jesus Considered Leaders?

I find all this interesting, and I hope you've enjoyed the tour. But we've only danced around our question at hand: Do the Gospels portray women as leaders over men?

Part of the problem is that the Gospel writers weren't directly focused on our question. It's not like they designed their narratives to navigate the egalitarian and complementarian debates. It worth noting, however, that while the Gospels record events that happened before Pentecost, they were written much later—even later than Paul's letters—and were therefore intended to instruct the New Testament church. We shouldn't force the Gospels to address our question with more clarity than they do, but we also shouldn't discount the subtle and powerful ways they might contribute to our conversation.

---

53 Carey, *Women*, 81. Bauckham argues that Bathsheba is the one exception, since she was entirely passive in her affair with David (*Gospel Women*, 27). Maybe this is why she alone is given a passive description as "the wife of Uriah" (Matt. 1:6 ESV). However, Bathsheba did play an active role in ensuring that Solomon would carry on David's dynasty (1 Kings 1:11–40).

54 Carey, *Women*, 82.

55 Debates abound over Matthew's rationale for including these four women (see the thorough analysis in Bauckham, *Gospel Women*, 17–46).

So what can we say about women and leadership in the Gospels? The women in the Gospels certainly exhibited many of the virtues Jesus expects from his followers—faithfulness, courage, hope, sacrifice, suffering, generosity, hospitality—and they even heralded the good news that Jesus was the Messiah. This alone doesn't mean they were leaders. After all, someone can be a faithful disciple without being a leader. All leaders should be faithful disciples, but not all faithful disciples are leaders.

I'm still struck by the way the Gospel writers contrast the women's faithfulness with the faithlessness of the Twelve—especially if we assume that the Twelve were being trained to be leaders in the early church. The women in the Gospels modeled the kind of radical commitment, unswerving faith, and Christlike suffering that Jesus demands of his followers. Think about how this would've landed for the original male readers of the Gospels, who swam in a male-dominated culture where women were considered less significant, less moral, less wise, and less virtuous than men. It's in this social context that early readers were given several examples of women who demonstrated the kind of discipleship that men—some of whom would be church *leaders*—were to pattern their lives after. Imagine the apostles reading the Gospels and seeing women exemplify the leadership qualities that they failed to embody.

I also think it's safe to say that the Gospels depict women as exemplary preachers of the divine word to men. Elizabeth, Mary, Anna, the Samaritan woman, and the women who witnessed the resurrection of Jesus (especially Mary Magdalene) all proclaimed messages about Jesus to a community of—often fragile and faithless—men. I don't think this is determinative, but it is at least suggestive of women proclaiming messages about Jesus to a community of men gathered in a house on Sunday.

Does this mean the Gospel writers considered such women to be leaders? Perhaps a more important question is: What does it mean to be a *leader* according to Jesus?

The Gospels don't contain a detailed delineation of who's a leader and who's not. But they're not completely silent on the issue. In fact, Jesus came pretty close to offering a definition of leadership in Mark 10, when James and John requested (or demanded) to sit at Jesus' right and left when he came to rule over the kingdom (v. 37). These sons of thunder wanted to occupy a position of authority in Jesus' kingdom, so he upended their understanding of authority with one of the most revolutionary statements in his entire ministry—one that is central to Mark's Gospel as a whole:

> You know that those who are considered rulers of the Gentiles lord it over [*katakurieuousin*] them, and their great ones exercise authority [*katexousiazousin*] over them. But it shall not be so among you. But whoever would be great among you must be your servant [*diakonos*], and whoever would be first among you must be slave [*doulos*] of all. For even the Son of Man came not to be served [*diakonēthēnai*] but to serve [*diakonēsai*], and to give his life as a ransom for many. (Mark 10:42–45 ESV; cf. Matt. 20:25–28; Luke 22:25–27)

Jesus overturns a secular understanding of hierarchical rulership. In his kingdom, it's the "servant," the "slave," and the one who "serves" who are "great among you"—not the one who acts like a pagan ruler wielding power over people.[56]

As we search for leaders in Jesus' ministry, then, we need to have a Christian definition of leadership, not a secular one. We need to know what kinds of people we're even looking for.

Significantly, the only people Mark describes with the verb *diakoneō* ("to serve"), which is Jesus' key leadership trait, are angels (1:13), Jesus (10:45), and women—Peter's mother-in-law who "began to *serve*" Jesus and the disciples (1:31 ESV), and several women who "followed" and "*served*" Jesus (15:41 MSG).[57] Thus, Mark bookends his central statement about Jesus' mission (10:42–45) with two stories of women, and only women, who displayed this fundamental leadership trait: service. Mark never describes a man as living out Jesus' Mark 10 vision of Christian leadership.

Luke too records Jesus' redefinition of leadership (22:24–27), and like Mark, he shows Peter's mother-in-law and the Galilean women offering such service (Luke 4:39; 8:3). Luke also includes a parable unique to his Gospel that describes servants being ready for their master's return, just as Jesus' followers are to be ready for his return (12:35–40). Jesus challenged the ancient hierarchies of master-slave relations by saying that, when the master in the parable returned, he would "get ready, have [his servants] recline at the table, then come and *serve them* [*diakonēsei*

---

56 In the Gospels, whenever the apostles are said to exercise some kind of "authority" (*exousia*), it always refers to their authority over nonhuman entities like demons or dark forces (Matt. 10:1, 8; Mark 3:14–15; 6:7–30; Luke 9:1), never to their authority over other human beings.

57 The verb *diakoneō* occurs four times in Mark (1:13, 31; 10:45; 15:41). The noun *diakonos* occurs in 9:35 and 10:43.

*autois*]" (v. 37 CSB). Jesus turned the social order on its head: The master would serve the servants.

In John's Gospel, Jesus' famous foot-washing incident (13:1–20) also redefines leadership as service. The Master served the servants by washing their feet. And Jesus directly correlated such service to his identity as "Teacher and Lord" (vv. 13–14 ESV) and commanded his followers to imitate his behavior. In the previous chapter, Mary had already washed Jesus' feet with her hair after sacrificing her expensive perfume (12:1–8). The two scenes are clearly connected. Mary's foot-washing anticipated Jesus' foot-washing. Mary and Jesus both showed what it means to be a servant and, according to Jesus, a leader.

In the Gospels, women don't wield modern CEO-like authority. But they are the only disciples who act as *servants*—the key leadership trait of Christianity.

## What About the Twelve Male Apostles?

Some see Jesus' choice of twelve male apostles as proof of male-only leadership in the church. "Christ not only valued women very highly, but also demonstrated a clear role distinction between men and women," writes James Borland. "Nowhere is this issue seen more clearly than in Jesus' selection of only men for the role of apostle."[58] The twelve apostles served as a foundation for the church (Rev. 21:14; cf. Eph. 2:20; 4:11), and some are highlighted as leaders in Acts.[59] It's noteworthy that when Judas needed to be replaced, the Eleven specified that they needed to

---

58 Borland, "Women," 120.

59 See Acts 2:14; 5:12, 18, 40, 42; 6:2–4; 9:29; 15:2; Galatians 1:17 (Borland, "Women," 121). Only five (or six if we count Judas) of the original Twelve are explicitly named in Acts: Peter, John, James, Philip, and Bartholomew.

choose a replacement from among the "men" (*andrōn*, Acts 1:21), even though there were many faithful women available.[60]

I used to think this was a slam-dunk argument for complementarians, and I still think it has some merit. But there are two pushbacks worth considering.

First, some say that Jesus could have chosen twelve men for social reasons. The Jewish culture at that time might not have tolerated a rabbi surrounding himself with female disciples as part of the Twelve. Thus, Jesus was being sensitive to his cultural context.

I don't find this argument very compelling, though. Jesus *did* surround himself with many female disciples, who traveled around with him and even funded his ministry (Luke 8:2–3). Even though they weren't part of the Twelve, Jesus wasn't afraid to travel around with these women as key participants in his mission. I don't think Jesus was nervous about challenging social customs, like when he talked openly with the Samaritan woman (John 4) or went in to dine with Mary and Martha in their house (Luke 10:38–42). If Jesus had a female apostle or two, it wouldn't have been much more socially outlandish than what we already see in the Gospels.

A second argument points out the symbolic nature of the twelve apostles: They represent the reconstituted twelve tribes of Israel. Since the *twelve* tribes derive from *twelve* male patriarchs (sons of Jacob), the *twelve* apostles had to be male for the symbolism to work.[61] The sex of the Twelve, then, is irrelevant for the sex of future leaders of the church.

60 See Borland, "Women," 122.
61 Witt, *Icons*, 265.

I think this argument makes a lot of theological sense. The twelve apostles are clearly mapped onto the twelve tribes of Israel,[62] so it's plausible that the sex of the Twelve is integral to the analogy. If so, the absence of women among the Twelve isn't designed to forever exclude women from church leadership. It just tells us that Jacob's twelve sons were male and therefore the twelve apostles had to be male as well. The choice of males, then, is intended to be symbolic of Israel's past, not determinative of the church's future leaders.

I wonder if we can raise a more fundamental question: Are the twelve apostles intended to be a paradigm for future church leaders? If so, they certainly aren't very good examples of what leadership should look like. Not only do they often serve as a negative foil for genuine discipleship, but in the Gospels, it's women more than men who serve as examples of the leadership virtues Jesus talked about (e.g., Mark 10:42–45).

I don't want to get too far ahead of myself, but I couldn't help but peek over at Titus 1, where Paul lists qualifications for elders, who must be

> blameless—not overbearing, not quick-tempered, not given to drunkenness, not violent, not pursuing dishonest gain. Rather, he must be hospitable, one who loves what is good, who is self-controlled, upright, holy and disciplined. He must hold firmly to the trustworthy message as it has been taught, so that he can encourage others by sound doctrine and refute those who oppose it. (vv. 7–9)

---

62 Matthew 19:28; Luke 22:30; Revelation 21:12–14.

I find it interesting that female disciples in Jesus' ministry displayed these traits much more than the Twelve. Many women in the Gospels are depicted as "blameless"[63] and are never "quick-tempered" or "violent," while some of the twelve apostles certainly are.[64] Women are constantly portrayed as "not pursuing dishonored gain"[65] and as showing hospitality.[66] In all the stories we've looked at, women are the ones who "[love] what is good" and are "self-controlled, upright, holy and disciplined." Elizabeth, Mary, the Samaritan woman, and the faithful women at the cross, burial, and resurrection "hold firmly to the trustworthy message."[67]

I don't think this proves that women can hold all leadership roles in churches today. The rest of the New Testament could still establish other theological reasons why only men should occupy all levels of leadership. But for now, I'm suspicious of the argument that the sex of the Twelve proves that church leadership is reserved for men.

## Conclusion

In many ways, the Gospel accounts of women in Jesus' ministry pick up where the Old Testament leaves off. The Gospels contain more stories about men than women, just like the Old Testament. But the portrait in both is complicated. Women show up at strategic points in the Old Testament and embody covenant faithfulness in contrast to men, and this theme becomes even more pronounced in the Gospels, where women, far more than men, exemplify the kind of radical discipleship

63 See Luke 1:6.
64 See Mark 10:35–45; Luke 9:51–56.
65 See Mark 12:41–44; Luke 8:3.
66 See Mark 1:31; Luke 7:36–50; 10:38–42.
67 See Luke 24:9–11; John 20:18.

Jesus demands from his aspiring followers. This alone doesn't end our debate. We should not treat the Gospels as a detailed list of qualifications for later church leaders. But I do think it's significant that in the few places where Jesus focuses explicitly on leadership traits (e.g., Mark 10:42–45), the women involved in Jesus' ministry emulated these qualities far more than the men.

Chapter 4

# LEADERS AND LEADERSHIP IN THE EARLY CHURCH

Once I worked through the Gospels, I was eager to jump straight into Paul's letters to see if he described any women as leaders. But after seeing how Jesus reconfigures leadership in Mark 10, I started to wonder if we've been wearing secular-colored lenses in our search for women leaders. If we take Jesus' words seriously, then we're not looking for women who have ascended to the top like some CEO who climbed the corporate ladder. Perhaps we're not even looking for women with badges and titles, or ones who have been "ordained" to a clear ministry position. According to Jesus, if we want to find someone exercising true authority, we should be looking for a servant with a towel in hand. And I suspect that the kind of person Jesus had in mind wouldn't be worried about having a leadership title.

So how did the first-century church think of leadership? How did they even think of church? These are crucial questions for a study on women in *church leadership*. It's natural to assume that our current church structures, led by pastors and elders and bishops and priests, are biblical and then ask the New Testament if women can fill these roles. But we need to first understand "church" and "leadership" according to a first-century perspective. We can't just assume the early Christians were working with the same categories and values we have today.

So I want to venture back to the first century to ascertain what leadership and church looked like for early Christians and explore how women might have fit in to their understanding. Let's start by revisiting Jesus' revolutionary statement about leadership in Mark 10. As we'll see, these words left their mark on other New Testament writers, especially Paul:

> You know that those who are considered rulers of the Gentiles lord it over [*katakurieuousin*] them, and their great ones exercise authority [*katexousiazousin*] over them. But it shall not be so among you. But whoever would be great among you must be your servant [*diakonos*], and whoever would be first among you must be slave [*doulos*] of all. For even the Son of Man came not to be served [*diakonēthēnai*] but to serve [*diakonēsai*], and to give his life as a ransom for many. (vv. 42–45 ESV)

Notice the density of "serving" terms here: *diakonos*, *doulos*, *diakonēthēnai*, *diakonēsai*. Such words are actually quite rare in the Gospels, but they're clustered here when Jesus reshapes our understanding of true authority.[1] Similar statements permeate Jesus' teaching and ministry: "Many who are first will be last, and the last first";[2] "whoever exalts himself shall be humbled, and whoever humbles himself shall be exalted";[3] greater is "the one who serves" at the table than "the one who is at the table."[4] Jesus, of course, embodied this revolution of leadership and power when he took "the form of a slave" (Phil. 2:7 CEB) and washed the disciples' feet (John 13:1–17)—a radical reconfiguration of what it means to be "Teacher and Lord" (John 13:13–14 ESV).

Such "kingdom reversals" shape the New Testament's view of leadership.[5] Paul in particular viewed leadership through a Mark 10 lens, which is why "servant"—*diakonos*—became one of his favorite monikers for Christian leaders.

The word *diakonos* ("servant") has a variety of meanings across Greek literature, but throughout the New Testament, it often refers to a servant or someone doing servant-like work.[6] Paul uses *diakonos* nineteen times in all his letters, often to describe his own apostolic ministry

---

1 In Mark, for instance, the verb *diakoneō* occurs only five times, two of which are in Mark 10:45. In Matthew, it occurs six times, two of which are in Matthew 20:28, the parallel to Mark 10:45. The noun *diakonos* occurs only two times in Mark (9:35; 10:45); in both passages, Jesus redefines greatness in the kingdom.

2 Mark 10:31; see also Matthew 20:16; Mark 9:35; Luke 13:30.

3 Matthew 23:12 NASB; see also Luke 14:11; 18:14; cf. Matt. 18:4.

4 Luke 22:27.

5 See the excellent discussion in Michelle Lee-Barnewall, *Neither Complementarian nor Egalitarian: A Kingdom Corrective to the Evangelical Gender Debate* (Baker, 2016), 103–19.

6 See Andrew Clarke, *A Pauline Theology of Church Leadership*, Library of New Testament Studies (T&T Clark, 2008), 60–71. John N. Collins argues that *diakonos/diakonia* does not primarily refer to menial service. See *Diakonia: Re-Interpreting the Ancient Sources* (Oxford University Press, 2009). Clarke, however, rightly points out that Collins doesn't fully appreciate the significance of Jesus' use of *diakonos* in Mark 10:42–45 or Paul's typical use of the term (*Pauline Theology*, 65).

(seven times) or the ministry of his coworkers (five times).[7] Many of these contexts are similar to Mark 10, where Jesus uses servant language to upend secular notions of authority. Paul too had to wrench the church away from a secular understanding of leadership, and he reached for servant language to do so.[8]

First Corinthians 1–4, for instance, is a classic example of this clash between secular and Christian leadership values.[9] It appears that "so many of the church's leaders continued to imbibe the culture of their surrounding society,"[10] where "the more prominent individuals in the church were regarded within the community as its leading figures."[11] "'I am with Paul' … 'I am with Apollos' … 'I am with Cephas'" (1 Cor. 1:12 NASB; cf. 3:4). The Corinthians praised certain people based on the secular values of honor and status, and Paul sought to dismantle their hierarchical view of leadership.

It's here where Paul describes both Apollos and himself as "servants" (*diakonoi*) to downplay their status: "What, after all, is Apollos? And what is Paul? Only servants [*diakonoi*], through whom you came to believe" (3:5). Paul oddly says, "*What*" (not *who*) "is Apollos?" and "*What* is Paul?" The Greek word literally means "what"—it describes a mere object, not a person. The Corinthians tried to put Paul and Apollos

---

7 Paul also used *diakonos* to refer to Christ (Rom. 15:8; Gal. 2:17), governing authorities (Rom. 13:1), and false apostles, whom Paul called "servants" of Satan (2 Cor. 11:15). On three occasions, Paul used *diakonos* in a way that might refer to a kind of "office" or established position in the church (Rom. 16:1; Phil. 1:1; 1 Tim. 3:8, 12), though this is widely disputed.

8 While the verb *diakoneō* applies to Christians serving one another in general (Rom. 15:25; 1 Pet. 4:10), Paul almost always uses the noun *diakonos* to describe his own apostolic ministry (2 Cor. 6:4; 11:23; Eph. 3:7: Col. 1:23, 25) or that of his coworkers (Rom. 16:1; Col. 4:7, 12; cf. Col. 1:7 HCSB, "fellow *slave* [*sundoulos*]").

9 Andrew Clarke, *Secular and Christian Leadership in Corinth: A Socio-Historical and Exegetical Study of 1 Corinthians 1–6* (Wipf & Stock, 2006).

10 Clarke, *Pauline Theology*, 185.

11 Clarke, *Pauline Theology*, 176.

on a pedestal, so Paul turned the Corinthian view of leadership on its head by saying that he and Apollos were "only servants [*diakonoi*]." Paul then compared their apostolic ministry to the menial tasks of building, planting, and watering a garden (vv. 5–15). Such "blue-collar" work was carried out by low-status people and considered shameful to first-century elites. What, then, were Apollos and Paul? Paul says that they were nothing (v. 7). "So then, no more boasting about human leaders!" (v. 21).

Like Jesus before him, Paul upended the Corinthians' view of leadership with a steady dose of kingdom reversals. "God has chosen what is foolish in the world to shame the wise, and God has chosen what is weak in the world to shame the strong" (1:27 CSB). Even though Paul was an apostle and a Roman citizen, he came to the Corinthians "in weakness, in fear, and in much trembling" (2:3 CSB). Secular leaders flaunt their high status and wield power over their subordinates. But in God's kingdom, apostles are "in last place," "condemned to die," "fools," "weak," "dishonored," "poorly clothed," "homeless," "like the world's garbage, like the dirt everyone scrapes off their sandals" (4:9–13 HCSB).

Paul therefore legitimized his apostolic authority by inverting the significance of social status, honor, and prestige.[12] Like Jesus before him, Paul described Christian leaders as servants first and foremost, vastly unlike the "rulers of the Gentiles" who "lord it over" their people (Mark 10:42 CSB).[13]

Not only did Paul love to use servant language to describe leaders, but he also avoided the common terminology applied to authority

---

12 Clarke, *Pauline Theology*, 216.

13 Peter also exhorted elders to be "eager to serve" and not "*lording it over* [*katakurieuontes*] those entrusted to you" (1 Pet. 5:1–3).

figures in his day.[14] The word *archōn* ("ruler"), for instance, was a typical term for leaders in Paul's world. In the New Testament, it refers to imperial rulers, synagogue leaders, other Jewish and secular leaders, and Satan, but Paul never describes Christian leaders with it.[15] Other New Testament writers use the cognate noun *archēgos* ("ruler") to refer to the exalted Christ in Acts and Hebrews but never for Christian leaders, and Paul never uses the term.[16]

One of the most common Greek words for "authority" is *exousia*. Paul uses it to refer to secular rulers, demonic powers, and, on two occasions, his own apostolic authority.[17] It's worth noting, though, that every time Paul defends his apostolic authority, he highlights his weakness, suffering, and slave-like behavior. And Paul never describes any other Christian leader with *exousia*.[18] Not elders, not pastors, not overseers, not any other apostle. The only time Paul employs *exousia* language to describe a believer's relationship toward another believer is when he says wives and husbands have mutual authority over each other's bodies (1 Cor. 7:4)—a rather startling thing to say in the first century.[19]

Paul's avoidance of typical "authority" language doesn't mean he didn't have authority. He calls his instructions "command[s]" that the church should "obey" (2 Thess. 3:4, 14), and he asserts his authority throughout his letter to the Galatians. Indeed, the very nature of his letters is shaped by apostolic authority, derived, of course, from God. Yet Paul also seems hesitant at times to insist on his authority. "As

---

14 See Andrew Clarke, *Serve the Community of the Church: Christians as Leaders and Ministers* (Eerdmans, 2000), 75.

15 E.g., Romans 13:3; 1 Corinthians 2:6, 8; Ephesians 2:2; cf. Matthew 9:18, 23; Luke 8:41.

16 Acts 3:15; 5:31; Hebrews 2:10; 12:2.

17 2 Corinthians 10:8; 13:10.

18 E.g., Romans 13:1–3; 1 Corinthians 15:24; Ephesians 1:21; 2:2; 3:10; 6:12.

19 Paul also uses *exousia* in 1 Corinthians 11:10, which we'll look at in chapter 8.

apostles of Christ we could have asserted our authority," he tells the Thessalonians, but "instead, we were like young children among you" (1 Thess. 2:6–7). Even with the unruly Corinthians who could use "a rod of discipline," Paul contemplates visiting them with "love and a gentle spirit" (1 Cor. 4:21).

Paul clearly held authority over the church, but it was a Christian kind of authority distinguished from the top-down, superior-over-inferior authority that permeated his culture (and ours). So too with other Christian leaders. In our quest to find out whether women were leaders in the early church, then, we need to make sure we use a Christian lens, not a secular one. We're not looking for women who climb to the top rung of a hierarchical ladder of authority and lord it over those below them. Rather, we're looking for women who model true Christian authority—servants who stoop to wash grungy feet.

So who were the early church leaders, and how do we know?

## Paul's Leadership Terminology

One of the simplest ways to identify leaders is to look up all the places where Christians are described as such. But we have to keep in mind that Paul and other New Testament writers use a range of leadership terminology. Some terms are quite familiar, like "elder," "overseer," and "pastor." But Paul also uses other terms and phrases to discuss leaders—some of whom functioned like elders and overseers without being named as such. The New Testament doesn't give us an ironed-out hierarchy of leadership terminology, where a senior pastor or bishop heads the list, followed by a team of elders, possibly some other pastors, and finally a group of deacons who assist the more senior leaders in their tasks. This kind of structure began to emerge in the second century, but the New

Testament paints a variegated picture of leadership and uses a variety of terms to do so.[20]

Paul, in fact, includes the words "elder" and "overseer" in only three of his thirteen letters. Despite its popularity in churches today, "pastor" (*poimēn*) only occurs once (as part of "pastor-teacher" in Ephesians 4:11 MSG).[21] This doesn't mean church leaders go unmentioned in his other letters. It just means the terms "elder," "overseer," and "pastor-teacher" aren't the only ways Paul designates church leadership. These titles—if we should even think of them as titles—represent only a slice of Paul's ecclesiological pie.

In the Greco-Roman and Jewish social context, elders were older members who were respected in the community and therefore exercised local leadership.[22] Throughout the book of Acts, "elders" refers both to non-Christian Jewish leaders and to Christian leaders, though the specific church role of the latter group isn't always clear.[23] R. A. Campbell, who has written the most definitive study on elders in the ancient world, sees "elder" as primarily a title of honor rather than a church "office" as we find depicted in later Christian writings.[24] The term "elder" is "*more of a way of speaking about leaders, than an office of leadership itself.*"[25]

---

20 Ignatius of Antioch (early second century) is the first writer to refer to three tiers of leadership, with a single overseer/bishop over a plurality of elders, who are over a plurality of deacons. See e.g., Ignatius, Ephesians 1:3; 4:1; Magnesians 2:1; Trallians 1:1; Philadelphians 1:1; Smyrnaeans 8:1; and the discussion in John H. Elliott, "Elders as Leaders in 1 Peter and the Early Church," *HTS Theological Studies* 64, no. 2 (2008): 689.

21 The verb *poimainō* ("to pastor, shepherd") is used three times in the New Testament to refer to the work of ministry (John 21:16; Acts 20:28; 1 Pet. 5:2).

22 Elliott, "Elders," 686.

23 Acts 11:30; 14:23; 15:2, 4, 6, 22–23; 16:4; 20:17; cf. non-Christian Jewish elders in Acts 4:5, 8, 23; 6:12; 23:14; 24:1; 25:15.

24 R. A. Campbell, *The Elders: Seniority Within Earliest Christianity* (T&T Clark, 1994). Roger Gehring largely agrees, though he sees the term "elder" developing into a kind of office in the Pastoral Epistles, which he doesn't appear to think are Pauline. See Roger Gehring, *House Church and Mission: The Importance of Household Structures in Early Christianity* (Hendrickson, 2004), 279–80.

25 Campbell, *The Elders*, 140 (italics in original).

"Overseer" is a rather fluid term used frequently in the Septuagint and in extrabiblical Greek literature. It sometimes refers to a designated office, while in other places it describes the function or role of a person (that is, one who offers oversight).[26] Most "overseers" in ancient literature were men, but in some cases women are also described as "overseers."[27] Paul uses "overseer" in discussing a formal leadership role in 1 Timothy 3:1–2 and Titus 1:7, and he may have assumed that men would occupy this position, but we'll address this in chapter 10. Paul mentions overseers one other time, in Philippians 1:1, and it's not clear whether he's referring to a formal leadership position or simply describing how some believers functioned in the church.[28] There's nothing in Philippians 1:1 that indicates whether men and women were overseers or whether only men filled this role.[29]

Paul and other New Testament writers seem to use "elder" and "overseer" synonymously: Elders were mature and prominent members of the community who oversaw the church.[30] While the phrase "pastor-teacher" is used only once (Eph. 4:11 MSG), the verb "to pastor" is applied to the ministry work of elders and overseers,[31] which suggests that the

26 Korinna Zamfir, "Once More: About the Origins and Background of the New Testament *Episkopos*," *Sacra Scripta* 10 (2012): 206.

27 Plato, for instance, describes women as "overseers" of young married couples and at athletic events (*Laws* 6.784A, 7.795D); see Raymond F. Collins, "Bishop," in *The New Interpreter's Dictionary of the Bible*, ed. Katharine Doob Sakenfeld, vol. 1 (Abingdon, 2009), 472.

28 Clarke also notes that "The phrase is anarthrous, 'with overseers and deacons,' and may not, therefore, refer to a formalized group" (*Pauline Theology*, 49).

29 It's possible that Lydia functioned as an overseer in the church, and some suggest that Euodia and Syntyche (Phil. 4:2–3) did as well, though the text doesn't explicitly say this.

30 The "elders" of Ephesus (Acts 20:17) are tasked as "overseers" of the church (Acts 20:28); see also Titus 1:5, 7; Zamfir, "Once More," 217. Clarke, however, suggests that overseers were a select group of leaders drawn from among the elders—all overseers are elders, but not every elder is an overseer. Overseers, according to Clarke, were responsible for teaching and led the house church, while elders who were not overseers were "an authoritative group, whose role was predominantly to make decisions and pass judgements from a community-wide perspective" (Clarke, *Pauline Theology*, 60). See Gehring, *House Church*, 269–81 for a discussion of the different views.

31 Acts 20:28; 1 Peter 5:2.

terms "elder," "overseer," and "pastor" were probably used to describe similar leadership roles.

Even though Paul rarely mentions elders and overseers, he describes leaders in other ways that resemble his descriptions of elders and overseers.[32] Paul's earliest mention of Christian leaders, for instance, comes in 1 Thessalonians 5, where he writes:

> Acknowledge those who *work hard* [*kopiōntas*] among you and *lead/manage* [*proistamenous*] you in the Lord and who admonish you. (v. 12, my translation)

Paul clearly identifies the leaders of the Thessalonian church, but he doesn't use the words "elder," "pastor," or "overseer." Instead, he uses other leadership terms to describe the work they were doing. *Proistēmi* is the clearest one. This term only occurs in Paul (eight times), and he uses it elsewhere to describe the leadership of overseers (1 Tim. 3:5), elders (1 Tim. 5:17), Christians gifted at leading (Rom. 12:8), and deacons who manage their household (1 Tim. 3:12).[33] *Proistēmi* means "lead" or "manage," but it also carries a sense of "care for."[34] Both senses are probably intended here, since "leading" and "caring" collectively capture the pastoral work of Christian leadership. The noun form of this word (*prostatis*) refers to financial benefaction, which suggests that part of "caring for" included financially providing for those in need—a key virtue among well-to-do house-church hosts. There's nothing gender-specific about the

32 See Vincent Branick, *The House Church in the Writings of Paul* (Michael Glazier, 1989), 78–96.

33 Paul's two other uses in Titus 3:8, 14 have a different meaning.

34 See the thorough discussion in Allan Chapple, "Local Leadership in the Pauline Churches: Theological and Social Factors in Its Development—a Study Based on 1 Thessalonians, 1 Corinthians and Philippians" (PhD diss., Durham University, 1984), 217–32.

word *proistēmi*; in fact, Paul calls Phoebe a *prostatis* (Rom. 16:2). If Paul excluded women from "leading" and "caring for" the church, this prohibition must be derived from elsewhere, not from the word *proistēmi*.

Paul also says the leaders in Thessalonica "work hard" (*kopiōntas*). The Greek word *kopiaō* is one of Paul's favorite ways to describe ministry work.[35] The term itself is a general one and does not *mean* "leadership."[36] But Paul frequently applies it to the work of leaders, including his own apostolic ministry,[37] and to elders who "work hard" (*hoi kopiōntes*) at "preaching and teaching" (1 Tim. 5:17). Paul also uses *kopiaō* to describe the leaders in Corinth who deserved submission (1 Cor. 16:16), which we'll look at later. In all these cases, Paul employs *kopiaō* in connection to the work of leaders in the church. This might be significant for our question about women in church leadership, because Paul also uses *kopiaō* to describe the ministry work of four women in Romans 16: Tryphena, Tryphosa, Mary, and Persis—the latter two worked "*very* hard" (Rom. 16:6, 12). If these women were not leaders, then this is the only time Paul uses *kopiaō* to describe the ministry work of non-leaders.

First Thessalonians 5 indicates leaders performed roles similar to the work of elders and overseers. It's likely that Paul was addressing the house-church hosts in Thessalonica who functioned as the elders/overseers of this church, even if these terms aren't used.

The same is true of the leaders of the Corinthian church. Again, the terms "elder," "overseer," and "pastor" don't occur in Paul's Corinthian letters, yet Paul still identifies leaders in this church:

---

35 See Clarke, *Pauline Theology*, 71–72.

36 Paul used it to refer to manual labor on three occasions (1 Cor. 4:12; Eph. 4:28; 2 Tim. 2:6).

37 1 Corinthians 15:10; Galatians 4:11; Philippians 2:16; Colossians 1:29; 1 Timothy 4:10; see Clarke, *Pauline Theology*, 71–72.

> Recognize the household of Stephanas were the firstfruits in Achaia, and they have devoted themselves to *the service* [*diakonian*] of the Lord's people. I urge you, brothers and sisters, to *submit* to [*hupotassēsthe*] such people and to everyone *who joins in the work* [*tō sunergyounti*] and *labors at it* [*kopiōnti*]. I was glad when Stephanas, Fortunatus and Achaicus arrived, because they have supplied what was lacking from you. (1 Cor. 16:15–17, my modification of the NIV)

Stephanas and his household were among the first converts (that is, "firstfruits") in Corinth, whom Paul himself baptized when he evangelized the city (1 Cor. 1:16). Stephanas was a man of high social standing and wealth, who served as a host and patron for one of the Corinthian house churches. Paul did not call Stephanas an elder. But as an older man and senior in the faith, it's almost certain that he would have been viewed as such.[38]

Stephanas wasn't the only leader, though. Paul tells the Corinthians "to submit to" the "*household* of Stephanas." Who exactly did Paul have in mind, and were women included? The text doesn't explicitly say. It's likely that Fortunatus and Achaicus were part of his household, either as slaves or freed slaves.[39] If Stephanas's wife was still alive, she would have certainly been part of his "household," along with his adult children (if he had any) and others under Stephanas's care.[40]

---

38 Chapple, "Local Leadership," 423.

39 Gordon Fee, *The First Epistle to the Corinthians*, New International Commentary on the New Testament (Eerdmans, 2014), 919.

40 Roy Ciampa and Brian Rosner, *The First Letter to the Corinthians*, Pillar New Testament Commentary (Eerdmans, 2010), 858.

Paul goes on to identify "*everyone* who joins in the work and labors at it" as leaders (16:16). Again, we're not sure who "everyone" refers to. But the term is not gender-specific. Unless Paul had already laid down a theology of male-only leadership in Corinth, his use of "everyone" would seem to include women.

Paul describes the work of these Corinthian leaders with three different words. "Service" (*diakonian*), as we've seen, is the hallmark of Christian leadership, and "labor" (*kopiōnti*) is the same word Paul used in 1 Thessalonians 5:12, noted earlier. The phrase "joins in the work" (*tō sunergounti*) is particularly relevant to our investigation. Paul doesn't employ this verb very often, but he uses the noun form, *sunergos* ("coworker"), twelve times to identify sixteen different partners in his apostolic ministry—three of whom are women.[41] *Sunergos* refers to some kind of partnership or collaboration in ministry work.[42] While the term does not *mean* "leadership," Paul often applies it to fellow leaders in the church. Paul's "coworkers" are other apostles (like Apollos) or leaders who ran in apostolic circles (like Luke, Mark, Timothy, and Titus). He also calls house-church leaders, such as Philemon and Aquila, his "coworkers." And here in 1 Corinthians 16, the verb form *sunergounti* clearly describes the work of leaders.

Significantly for our topic, Paul calls three women "coworkers" in his letters: Priscilla, Euodia, and Syntyche (Rom. 16:3; Phil. 4:2–3). "Coworker" doesn't lexically mean "leader." But the fact that Paul uses the term to describe leaders and three female ministry partners is

---

41 Men: Aquila (Rom. 16:3), Urbanus (Rom. 16:9), Timothy (Rom. 16:21; 1 Thess. 3:2), Apollos (1 Cor. 3:9), Titus (2 Cor. 8:23), Epaphroditus (Phil. 2:25), Clement (Phil. 4:3), Justus (Col. 4:11), Philemon (Philem. 1), and Mark, Aristarchus, Demas, and Luke (Philem. 24). Women: Priscilla (Rom. 16:3) and Euodia and Syntyche (Phil. 4:3).

42 See Clarke, *Pauline Theology*, 93–94; Chapple, "Local Leadership," 406–7; Victor Paul Furnish, "Fellow Workers in God's Service," *Journal of Biblical Literature* 80 (1961): 364–70.

nothing to sniff at. This may not prove that Paul considered them to be leaders, but I think it might suggest it.

We'll look closely at Priscilla in the next chapter. For now, I simply want to note that Paul identifies leaders with a variety of terms and phrases, not just "elder," "overseer," and "pastor." It would be wrongheaded, therefore, to say "no women are identified as elders, overseers, or pastors" and conclude "no women are leaders."

Aside from using leadership terminology, Paul might have identified leaders when he singled out certain people as recipients of his letters. Paul usually addressed his letters to entire churches without naming their leaders, while some letters are addressed to individual leaders like Timothy and Titus. Paul's letter to Philemon is interesting since it's not only addressed to Philemon, the host of a house church, but also to two other people—one of whom is a woman:

> Paul, a prisoner of Christ Jesus, and Timothy our brother:
>
> To Philemon our dear friend and coworker, to Apphia our sister, to Archippus our fellow soldier, and to the church that meets in your home. (vv. 1–2 CSB)

The five named people (Paul, Timothy, Philemon, Apphia, and Archippus) were all united together in ministry and mission. Philemon was probably the homeowner and host of the church.[43] Paul and

---

43 The "your" in the final phrase is singular and probably refers to Philemon. See Joseph A. Fitzmyer, *The Letter to Philemon: A New Translation with Introduction and Commentary*, Anchor Bible (Doubleday, 2000), 89. Scot McKnight says it's possible that Archippus is the antecedent of "your" but still lands on Philemon being the homeowner. See Scot McKnight, *The Letter to Philemon*, New International Commentary on the New Testament (Eerdmans, 2017), 58–59. Nicholas Quient argues that "your" refers collectively to Philemon, Apphius, and Archippus. See Nicholas Quient, "Was Apphia an Early Christian Leader?," *Priscilla Papers* 31, no. 2 (2017), www.cbeinternational.org/resource/was-apphia-early-christian-leader.

Timothy refer to him as "*our* dear friend" and our "*coworker*," connecting Philemon to their ministry work. Same with Archippus, whom Paul calls "*our* fellow soldier" and elsewhere exhorts to "complete the ministry you have received in the Lord" (Col. 4:17). Paul describes Timothy as "our brother" and Apphia as "our sister," correlating the two on some level.[44] (The only other woman Paul calls "sister" is Phoebe [Rom. 16:1], who was clearly a prominent and influential woman in the early church, as we'll see in chapter 5.) All five of these named people seem to have been colleagues in the ministry of the gospel. Does this mean these five, including Apphia, were leaders?

Some have suggested that Apphia was Philemon's wife,[45] but this is unlikely, since Paul calls her "our sister" (or "the sister," *tē adelphē*) and not "your wife" (*sou gunē* or *tē gunē*). Plus, Paul's description here doesn't reflect how he refers to other husband-wife partners, like Aquila and Priscilla or Andronicus and Junia (1 Cor. 16:19; Rom. 16:7). Apphia was probably not Archippus's wife for the same reason. Regardless, she was likely a prominent person in the church, since she's one of the three named recipients of the letter.

Since Paul, Timothy, and Philemon were church leaders, it's certainly possible, if not probable, that Apphia and Archippus were as well. At the very least, if Paul had wanted to distance Apphia from a leading role in the church that met in Philemon's home, I think he could have done a much better job.

---

44 "'Brother' (*adelphos*) and 'sister' (*adelphē*) are two of a variety of terms sometimes designating special leadership roles" in Paul's letters. Carolyn Osiek and Margaret MacDonald, *A Woman's Place: House Churches in Earliest Christianity* (Fortress Press, 2006), 27.

45 Douglas J. Moo, *The Letters to the Colossians and to Philemon*, Pillar New Testament Commentary (Eerdmans, 2008), 382–83; James D. G. Dunn, *The Epistles to the Colossians and to Philemon* (Eerdmans, 1996), 312.

I want to explore one more way in which we might identify leaders in the first-century church. This one is more implied from the historical context than explicitly stated in the text. Though, as we'll see, I don't think the text is completely silent. Let's look at church in its first-century context—specifically, house churches and the homeowners who hosted them.

## Were the Hosts of House Churches Leaders?

When we think of "church," we shouldn't imagine a building, a large gathering, or an order of service where a senior pastor delivers a monologue while everyone else passively looks on. The first Christians gathered in the homes of wealthy Christians who could afford a house large enough to host a church.[46] By "large enough," I mean it could fit twenty to thirty people (fifty at most), which would have been the typical size of a house church.[47]

It's important to note that the house was more than just a physical space for believers to gather. The concepts of home and household shaped the way early Christians conceived of church. In his groundbreaking book on house churches, Roger Gehring notes: "In the ancient world the *oikos* [house] not only consisted of physical space but also was a clearly defined social environment. For the church to meet in this context meant allowing itself to be more or less influenced by this environment."[48] Christians didn't just gather for church in a home. They believed the church was a home, which is why the New Testament so often describes church as

---

46 Paul directly refers to house churches on at least four occasions: Romans 16:3–5; 1 Corinthians 16:19; Colossians 4:15; Philemon 2. See also Acts 2:46; 5:42.

47 James Jeffers, *The Greco-Roman World of the New Testament Era: Exploring the Background of Early Christianity* (IVP Academic, 1999), 81; Branick, *House Church*, 37–42.

48 Gehring, *House Church*, 193.

a family. Sisters, brothers, fathers, mothers—the early Christians didn't think church is *like* a family. They believed it *is* a family. It is, as Paul says, "the household of God" (1 Tim. 3:15 ESV).

Houses not only shaped the early Christian imagination of church; they were also the engine that empowered the spread of Christianity. The Spirit birthed the church in a house (Acts 2:2). Believers broke bread and shared goods in a house (Acts 2:42, 46). Ethnical barriers were broken down in a house (Acts 10:1–48). Houses became the base of operations in cities throughout the Mediterranean world: in Jerusalem, Antioch, Caesarea, Philippi, Corinth, Thessalonica, and everywhere else the gospel took root.[49] It's no wonder that when Saul was trying to "destroy the church" (NIV) prior to his conversion, he "would enter house after house" to "drag off men and women, and put them in prison" (Acts 8:3 CSB). These weren't houses of random believers. Saul was targeting house churches, since these were the command centers of the early Christian movement.

Houses, therefore, "served as the basic foundation for all church life" and became "the operational base for the missional outreach" in the ministries of both Jesus and Paul.[50]

What does this have to do with our question about women in church leadership? I want to make two observations.

First, in the first century, women played prominent roles in the home. Their influence wasn't limited to the home; some women occupied

---

49 See e.g., Acts 12:12–14; 16:31, 40; 17:7; 21:8–9; Romans 16:23; and the incisive discussion in Gehring, *House Church*, 62–228.

50 Gehring, *House Church*, 295. Houses played a significant role in the ministry of Jesus as well. Houses were the places where he taught (Matt. 13:36; Mark 2:1; 7:14–27; 9:33; 10:2–12), was received as a guest (Luke 5:29; 7:36–50), and even hosted gatherings (Mark 2:15; cf. Mark 6:34–44; 8:1–10; Luke 12:37); see Branick, *House Church*, 20.

leadership roles in civic, religious, and even political spheres of the Roman Empire.[51] But the home was the woman's primary domain.[52] This point might seem trivial, or even offensive, to our modern society, where the idea of "domestic prowess" conjures up images of a woman cooking, cleaning, and waiting hand and foot on a husband who works a "real" job outside the home. But in the first century, the home was the center of production, business, and education, and for those living in cities, household duties often included managing the family's shop.[53] Several Greco-Roman writers testify to the significant part wives played in the household.[54] Xenophon, for instance, compares the wife to a queen bee, who supervised all the household activities.[55] Plutarch refers to the wife as the "manager of the house" (*oikodespoinē*) on several occasions.[56] The husband was still the *paterfamilias* ("father of the household"), which meant he had authority over the property. But in terms of household relationships, the *materfamilias* ("mother of the household") often served as the primary manager—alongside or even in the place of her husband.[57]

Here's the upshot: Since the home "served as the basic foundation for all church life" and "the operational base for the missional outreach," then "to step into a Christian house church" in the first century "was to

---

51 See e.g., Emily A. Hemelrijk, *Hidden Lives, Public Personae: Women and Civic Life in the Roman West* (Oxford University Press, 2015).

52 "The mother in many ways was the manager of the household" (Branick, *House Church*, 21).

53 Susan E. Hylen, *Women in the New Testament World* (Oxford University Press, 2019), 32–35.

54 See Osiek and MacDonald, *Woman's Place*, 146–57.

55 Xenophon, *Oeconomicus* 7.36–43; cf. 9.15.

56 Plutarch, *Advice to Bride and Groom* 140C, 141D, 141F, 142B.

57 See Richard Saller, "*Pater Familias, Mater Familias*, and the Gendered Semantics of the Roman Household," *Classical Philology* 94 (1999): 182–97. In some cases, female property owners brought their property into the marriage and continued to manage it jointly with or even independently from their husbands (see Osiek and MacDonald, *Woman's Place*, 155, who say this arrangement was "quite common"). The New Testament also testifies to the important role that women played in the home (see e.g., Acts 12:12; 1 Tim. 5:14; 2 Tim. 1:5).

step into women's world."[58] This alone doesn't mean they were leaders in the house churches. But it does mean that women played vital roles in first-century house churches and therefore the Christian mission as a whole.

A second observation is more directly relevant for our question about women in church leadership: Some women owned the homes where Christians gathered, which suggests that as the host, they might have been leaders of that church.

As we've seen, the social environment of the home shaped the way Christians viewed the church. This applied especially to leadership in the church. "The leadership structures of the house church did not have to be created out of nothing," notes Roger Gehring. "The church in the house came with its leadership so to speak 'built in.'"[59] Therefore, the homeowner—usually a man—who hosted the gathering would be looked upon as the natural leader of that gathering.

Such hosts were typically older, mature, and educated and had good administrative skills. These skills carried over into the life of the church, which is why Paul correlates "managing" the church with how homeowners "managed" their household (1 Tim. 3:4–5; Titus 1:7). As a wealthy (often the wealthiest) member, the householder served as a patron of the church. They not only hosted the church but also provided room and board for traveling Christians, sponsored missionary activities, gave material support to poor believers, and offered legal aid to those they hosted.[60] Such hospitality was not an optional add-on to Christian

58 Osiek and MacDonald, *Woman's Place*, 163; cf. 33–34.

59 Gehring, *House Church*, 194, quoted in R. Alastair Campbell, *The Elders: Seniority Within Earliest Christianity* (T&T, 2004), 126.

60 Gehring, *House Church*, 200.

service; it was vital for the advancement of the gospel and the mission of the early church.[61]

The host also provided for, and probably presided over, the common meal—the significance of which can hardly be overstated.[62] This meal was not a small cracker and a dose of grape juice, nor was it a potluck believers had after church. In the first century, the meal was "the central act of worship in the household meetings."[63] The meal broke down social barriers and enacted the unity of the church (1 Cor. 10:17).[64] Jew and Gentile, slave and free, male and female all gathered around the same table to celebrate the Lord who abolished social barriers and brought salvation to all. As a "marker of communal solidarity," the common meal was a profoundly theological event.[65] The one who oversaw the meal carried tremendous responsibility in creating and leading this "central act of worship" in first-century house churches.[66]

Many scholars therefore argue that hosts of house churches were de facto leaders in the church.[67] This doesn't mean they were the only leaders. Certainly, if an apostle, teacher, or prophet was present, they would take on a leadership role as well in the gathering. We also can't

---

61 "Hospitality ... meant sharing in [Paul's] work" (Branick, *House Church*, 18).

62 See Dennis E. Smith, "Food and Dining in Early Christianity," in *A Companion to Food in the Ancient World*, ed. John Wilkins and Robin Nadeau (Wiley-Blackwell, 2015), 543–54.

63 Brian Capper, "Apostles, Householders and Honoured Household Servants: The Transition of Christian Worship from Domestic to Public Space and the Origins of the Threefold Ministry in the Social Pattern of New Testament Church," *The Polish Journal of Biblical Research* 12, no. 1 (2013): 16. Paul even uses "eating" and "gathering" interchangeably: "when you come to together to eat" (see 1 Cor. 11:17, 18, 20, 33); "when you come together to gather" (see 1 Cor. 14:26); see Smith, "Food and Dining," 543.

64 Smith, "Food and Dining," 544.

65 This is why Paul rebuked Peter for "not acting in line with the truth of the gospel" when he stopped sharing meals with Gentiles (Gal. 2:14).

66 Capper, "Apostles," 16.

67 Gehring, *House Church*, 190–96, 225–28; Capper, "Apostles," 16; Branick, *House Church*, 21, 91.

say with certainty what specific leadership responsibilities the host would have held. Did they teach? Did they counsel? Did they offer pastoral oversight? I don't think we can know for sure. What we can say is that the host almost certainly would have been viewed as a leader on some level.

This is significant for our question since the New Testament names four different women who were heads of their households and hosted a church in their home: Mary (Acts 12:12), Nympha (Col. 4:15), Lydia (Acts 16:15, 40), and Priscilla with her husband Aquila (Rom. 16:3–5; 1 Cor. 16:19).[68] Given the role that hosts played in first-century house churches, it's historically plausible, if not probable, that these women were viewed as leaders.

Some think it's "grasping at straws" and "simply wild speculation" to suggest that female household hosts might have been leaders.[69] But this seems overly dismissive to me. We certainly shouldn't go beyond the text, but we also must interpret the text in light of its cultural context and not our own.

Plus, we're not simply relying on assumptions based on the historical context. The text itself does color in the picture. While we don't know much else about Mary and Nympha other than that they hosted a church in their home, we have a lot more information about Priscilla, whom we'll look at in the next chapter, and Lydia—the first European convert and host of the church in Philippi (Acts 16:11–40).

---

68 We could possibly add Chloe of Corinth to this list (1 Cor. 1:11), along with Phoebe in Cenchreae (Rom. 16:1–2), although these are less clear. We're not sure if Chloe hosted a gathering, or whether she was even a Christian (see Fee, *Corinthians*, 55). We'll look at Phoebe in the next chapter.

69 Wayne Grudem, *Evangelical Feminism & Biblical Truth: An Analysis of More Than 100 Disputed Questions* (Crossway, 2012), 262.

Lydia was probably a wealthy widow who owned a successful business, and she was the head of her household (16:14–15).[70] Luke calls her a "worshiper of God" (*sebomenē*), which means she was a Gentile who followed the Jewish way and revered Israel's God (v. 14).[71] When she responded to Paul's gospel, she and her entire household were baptized (v. 15).[72] She immediately insisted that Paul and his companions "come and stay at my house" (v. 15) and "prevailed [*parebiasato*] upon" them (v. 15 ESV). Her home became the base of Paul's ongoing mission in Philippi.[73] After Paul and Silas got out of jail, they went to Lydia's home, where believers were gathered (v. 40).[74] In a short time, a house church had formed in Philippi, and it was Lydia who hosted it in her house.

Three things are worth noting about Lydia. First, Lydia's generosity and hospitality played a key role in Paul's mission in Philippi. In fact, Luke highlights two converts in the narrative, the jailer and Lydia, but Lydia is the only one he names. This suggests that she was a key figure in the Christian community in Philippi. Second, Lydia's previous commitment to Judaism meant she was already acquainted with the Old Testament—the church's Bible. She would have had way more biblical knowledge than, say, the Philippian jailer, who was a pagan convert with

---

70 For a thorough discussion of her business and social status, see Teresa Calpino, "The Lord Opened Her Heart: Women, Work, and Leadership in Acts of the Apostles" (PhD diss., Loyola University Chicago, 2012), 258–63.

71 Calpino, "Lord Opened Her Heart," 268.

72 Household baptism "conforms to the classic ideology of the subordinate household fully obedient to its head" and implies that "the authority of the head of the household ... extends to their religious practices" (Osiek and MacDonald, *Woman's Place*, 157–58). For other household conversions, see Acts 10:2; 16:33; 18:8; 1 Corinthians 1:16; cf. John 4:53.

73 We're not sure how long Paul and his companions were in Philippi, but Luke described them as traveling repeatedly between Lydia's home, where they stayed, and the place of prayer by the river (Acts 16:16) (Calpino, "Lord Opened Her Heart," 250–51).

74 Apparently, Luke departed from Philippi before all this happened, since he stopped using *we/us* after Acts 16:17.

no prior commitment to the Jewish faith. Third, we know from inscriptions found at Philippi that women occupied leading roles in both the religious and civic life in the city.[75] As a wealthy business owner and head of her household, Lydia would have been a respected person in the city with a relatively high social status. This doesn't mean she must have been a leader in the church. But it does mean it would have been natural for the Philippian converts to recognize her as such.

Though she's not identified as an "elder" or "pastor" or "overseer," it's likely that Lydia played a key leadership role in the nascent house church in Philippi. Not only does her role as the house-church host suggest this, but other details in the text add weight to this conclusion.

## Revisiting "Leadership" in First-Century House Churches

This may be a good place to revisit the general definition of *leadership* that I sketched out in the introduction to this book, where I said that a leader is a person who (1) holds a recognized title or position of authority (such as "king" or "elder"), (2) guides and directs a group of people toward a specific goal or mission, or (3) speaks or acts in a way that expects others to follow their direction.

This definition still works, but we should refine it through several things we've learned in this chapter.

First, we need to make sure we're looking for leaders through a *Christian* lens, not a secular one. New Testament leadership is not a prestigious position of power and privilege but one of service and sacrifice, fit only for those eager to wash feet.

75 See Calpino, "Lord Opened Her Heart," 240–42.

Second, Paul's leadership terminology is diverse. While he uses terms like "elder," "overseer," and "pastor-teacher" in a few letters, he elsewhere employs a range of terms and phrases to describe leaders—those who manage, work hard, serve, and work with him.

Third, when we pay close attention to social and historical context, we find many people whose leadership role may be implied rather than explicitly stated, such as house-church hosts and named recipients of Paul's letters. Such people may not be called "elders," "pastor-teachers," or "overseers," but it's plausible that they functioned in similar ways.

Fourth, we should identify "leadership" activities according to a first-century context, even if modern churches might not think of them as such. For instance, Protestant churches today typically view teaching as the primary (sometimes only) leadership activity in the gathering, while those who pass around the wafers and thimbles filled with grape juice for Communion aren't considered leaders. Teaching was a vital part of the first-century house-church gathering, but so were activities like prayer, the distribution of goods to the poor, and the common meal—the "central act of worship."[76] It would be anachronistic to downplay the theological significance of the house-church host's role in overseeing these vital activities. If a female household host with five years of Christian faith under her belt told some adult men fresh in the faith to make preparations for the common meal, gave them money to buy the goods, then presided over the meal at the gathering, this may have been understood by the early church as an important form of leadership, even if today's churches might dismiss it as little more than kitchen duty.

---

76 Capper, "Apostles," 16.

In terms of our debate about women leaders in the early church, then, it would be wrong to limit our quest to the question, Are women described as "elders," "overseers," or "pastor-teachers"? This is a good question to include in our search, but it's not the only one. Instead, we should ask, Are women described with explicit leadership terminology, associated with other terms and phrases that may signify leadership, or identified in a way that would have been understood as leadership according to the first-century context of early Christians who met in homes? I know that's a mouthful, but it's more historically and biblically accurate. According to my study thus far, it seems that some women played leadership roles in the early church, even though the specific nature of their leadership role isn't always clear.

## Conclusion

Thus far, I think there's a case for female leaders in the New Testament church. But I want to be cautious at this point in my study. I still have a long way to go. There are some passages that might restrict certain leadership roles to men, and others could suggest that women may teach and preach but only under the authority of certain male leaders. Some passages may even forbid women from teaching altogether. I want to hold my tentative conclusions with an open hand until I study these other passages.

What we can say for sure is that women played a vital role in the early church's mission and Paul's ministry in particular. And no chapter of the New Testament captures this more stunningly than Romans 16.

Chapter 5

# WOMEN IN THE MINISTRY OF PAUL (ROM. 16)

I've always loved Paul's letter to the Romans—in fact, I spent a good deal of time in it for my PhD dissertation. But I have to admit, I'd hardly even looked at chapter 16 until I started researching for this book. I thought the end of the letter was just a bunch of greetings with little theological importance. But I've now learned that nothing could be further from the truth. Ancient letters often end by highlighting some of the most important themes in the letter itself.[1] And such is the case with Romans 16.

Romans contains many theological themes—justification by faith, the gift of the Spirit, the role of Israel in God's plan. But there is a steady emphasis on the unity of believers amid social and ethnic differences throughout the letter (see especially Rom. 14–15), and chapter 16, where Paul greets a plethora of Christians of various social strata, reinforces this message. Slaves and free, Jews and Gentiles, men and

1 Mark Reasoner, "Chapter 16 in Paul's Letter to the Romans: Dispensable Tagalong or Valuable Envelope?," *Priscilla Papers* 20, no. 4 (2006): 11–16; Steven Croft, "Text Messages: The Ministry of Women and Romans 16," *Anvil* 21, no. 2 (2004): 87–94.

women—they're all unified by their common faith in Christ, and Paul's final greetings drive home this essential theological point. Romans 16 is like Paul's personal commentary on his famous statement in Galatians: "There is neither Jew nor Gentile, neither slave nor free, nor is there male and female, for you are all one in Christ Jesus" (Gal. 3:28).[2] Whatever social hierarchies resided in the minds of the Roman believers, if they hadn't been corrected already, they would be shattered by the time their community finished listening to the final pages of Paul's letter.

It really is remarkable that Paul names so many people in this chapter. He typically just closes his letters with a general greeting to "all God's people in Christ Jesus" (e.g., Phil. 4:21). Why greet so many people in Rome? Paul probably wanted to show that, even though he had never personally visited the Roman church, he had done ministry with many of its key people. Since Paul was looking to establish Rome as the base of his future missionary aspirations in Spain, his extensive greetings to the Roman church would have strengthened his rapport with Christians there. Romans 16 served an essential purpose, not only for the letter itself but for Paul's ministry as a whole.

Paul mentions twenty-six people by name in this chapter, in addition to many who are unnamed (like "those in the household of Narcissus" in v. 11). Of the twenty-six people named, ten are female and sixteen are male.[3] Although more men are named than women, Paul "uses com-

---

2 For my take on Galatians 3:28 as it pertains to our topic, see Preston Sprinkle, "Galatians 3:28 and the Women in Leadership Debate," available at theologyintheraw.com/womeninleadership.

3 The ten named women are Phoebe, Priscilla, Junia, Persis, Mary, Tryphena, Tryphosa, Julia, Nereus's sister, and Rufus's mother.

mendatory speech for more women than for men."[4] Specifically, Paul singles out five men and seven women who were particularly "active in the service of the gospel."[5]

For instance, Paul describes four women as ones who "work hard" (Tryphena and Tryphosa, v. 12) or "worked very hard" in the Lord (Mary, v. 6, and Persis, v. 12). As we saw in the last chapter, Paul always uses *kopiaō* ("work hard") in connection to the work of leaders—elders "who work hard [*hoi kopiōntes*] at preaching and teaching" (1 Tim. 5:17 CSB) and the leaders in Thessalonica (1 Thess. 5:12) and Corinth (1 Cor. 16:16)—as well as his own apostolic ministry (e.g., 1 Cor. 15:10; Gal. 4:11). In every case, *kopiaō* describes the work of leaders in the church. Does this mean Tryphena, Tryphosa, Mary, and Persis were leaders?

I want to avoid hasty conclusions based simply on word associations, and we still need to work through other passages that might exclude women from leadership (like 1 Tim. 2:8–15). But my complementarian seminary professors under the leadership of John MacArthur always taught me to figure out a Greek word's meaning by looking at how it's used elsewhere in the Bible, *especially* by the same writer. The fact that Paul uses *kopiaō* throughout the rest of the New Testament to describe the ministry of church leaders—and never once to describe the ministry of non-leaders—is significant. Following the rules of good exegesis,

4 Nijay Gupta, *Tell Her Story: How Women Led, Taught, and Ministered in the Early Church* (IVP Academic, 2023), 99.

5 J. A. Fitzmyer, *Romans: A New Translation with Introduction and Commentary*, Anchor Bible Commentary 33 (Yale University Press, 2008), 734. The women described this way are Priscilla, Mary, Junia, Tryphena, Tryphosa, Persis, and the mother of Rufus. The men are Aquila, Andronicus, Urbanus, Apelles, and Rufus.

this sure looks like strong textual support for women leaders in Paul's ministry.

Aside from the four women who *kopiaō* in the Lord, Paul mentions three other women in Romans 16 who deserve extended reflection: Phoebe, Priscilla, and Junia. Paul's depiction of these three women has stirred much interest—and much debate. We'll discuss them in the order they are listed.

## Phoebe: Servant, Patron, and Letter Performer

Paul opens Romans 16 with a commendation of a woman named Phoebe:

> I commend to you our sister Phoebe, a deacon [*diakonon*] of the church in Cenchreae. I ask you to receive her in the Lord in a way worthy of his people and to give her any help she may need from you, for she has been the benefactor [*prostatis*] of many people, including me. (vv. 1–2)

Two facts about Phoebe immediately jump out. First, Paul calls her a "deacon [or servant, *diakonon*] of the church in Cenchreae." Second, she was a "benefactor [*prostatis*] of many people, including" Paul. A third significant point isn't explicitly stated, but it's strongly implied: Phoebe carried Paul's letter to the Romans, which may also mean she was the one who read, and perhaps interpreted, Paul's words to the Christians in Rome.

Let's explore each of these aspects of Phoebe's story in depth, starting with her status as a patron.

## Phoebe the Patron

Paul describes Phoebe as a "patron" or "benefactor" (*prostatis*) of "many people," including Paul himself.[6] Some Bibles translate *prostatis* as "helper" (e.g., NASB, RSV), but this is too generic and fails to capture what the term meant in Paul's world. A *prostatis* was a high-status person who usually had considerable wealth and power, funded various building projects, and served as a guardian of other individuals and groups.[7] Some patron-client relationships existed along the lines of a rigid social hierarchy—the patron at top and the client down below. But other benefactors simply gifted their money with no expectation that the receiver would grovel at their feet. It's likely that Phoebe was among the latter.[8]

It's natural to assume that men were the ones who held such prestigious positions in the first century. But scholars have now shown that a striking number of women were benefactors as well.[9] For instance, several first-century inscriptions praise a woman named Junia Theodora, a wealthy Roman citizen and key benefactor of the city of Corinth—just a few miles away from Cenchreae, where Phoebe lived. Junia "accomplished numerous ... benefits for the federation" in Corinth, "welcome[d] in her own house ... travelers and citizens," and "bestowed numerous benefits

---

6 On the meaning of *prostatis*, see E. D. MacGillivray, "Romans 16:2, *Prostatis/Prostatēs*, and the Application of Reciprocal Relationships to New Testament Texts," *Novum Testamentum* 53 (2011): 183–99; E. A. Judge, "Cultural Conformity and Innovation in Paul: Some Clues from Contemporary Documents," *Tyndale Bulletin* 35 (1984): 20–24; Robert Jewett, *Romans: A Commentary* (Fortress Press, 2006), 946–48.

7 Gupta, *Tell Her Story*, 119.

8 See MacGillivray, "Romans 16:2," 183–99.

9 See Carolyn Osiek and Margaret MacDonald, *A Woman's Place: House Churches in Earliest Christianity* (Fortress Press, 2006), 194–219.

also on many of our citizens," earning her the moniker "a woman of the greatest honour."[10]

It's likely that Phoebe, a *prostatis*, played a similar role. (Remember: The noun *prostatis* is closely related to the verb *proistemi*, another word Paul uses to describe church leadership.) Phoebe generously supported Christians in need and funded Paul's own ministry. The text doesn't explicitly say she hosted a church in her home, but given her wealth and generosity—and the fact that Paul calls her a *diakonos* of the church at Cenchreae—it's likely that she did. Either way, her role as a *prostatis* to Paul and many others indicates that she exerted considerable influence in the early church's mission.

Does this alone mean she was considered a leader? She certainly would have been from a cultural perspective. Anyone wealthy enough to be a *prostatis* to many people was considered a leading figure in the city. But the Greco-Roman view of status and authority—the stuff Jesus denounced in Mark 10—doesn't in itself qualify a person as a leader in God's upside-down kingdom. If Paul considered Phoebe a Christian leader in the church, it wasn't simply because she was a wealthy elite but because she generously used her wealth to fuel the mission and thus became a "servant" to many.[11]

## Phoebe the Servant

Phoebe has unfortunately found herself in a tug-of-war between egalitarians and complementarians over the meaning of *diakonos* ("servant," "deacon"). Egalitarians often protest interpretations that label Phoebe a

10 Cited in Gupta, *Tell Her Story*, 119–20.
11 See Judge, "Cultural Conformity," 20–23.

mere *servant* and *not* a leader.[12] Complementarians disagree: *Diakonos* is not a leadership title. It simply describes people who *served*, *not* people who led.[13]

Phoebe was clearly a generous woman of integrity who served Paul and many others. I almost wonder if she would be annoyed at modern attempts to drag her into leadership or keep her out of it. She probably took seriously Jesus' words in Mark 10 and didn't need to wield power and authority like the Gentile leaders of the secular kingdom.

Speculations aside—what does "[*diakonos*] of the church in Cenchreae" mean?

Paul will later use *diakonos* to refer to a kind of office or official ministry role that appears to be distinguished from the leadership of overseers (1 Tim. 3:8–13). Whether these "deacons" occupied leadership roles in the church is widely disputed.[14] Either way, it's unlikely that Paul was thinking of this latter office—if we should even call it an office—when he called Phoebe a servant. As noted in the previous chapter, Paul uses *diakonos* in a variety of ways to describe ministry work.

Perhaps most significant for our investigation is this: Every other *named* person that Paul calls a *diakonos* is a church leader. Paul uses

---

12 See e.g., Linda Belleville, "An Egalitarian Perspective," in *Two Views on Women in Ministry*, rev. ed., ed. James R. Beck (Zondervan, 2005), 60–61.

13 Wayne Grudem argues that as a *diakonos*, Phoebe did not have "any teaching or governing authority in the church." *Evangelical Feminism & Biblical Truth: An Analysis of More Than 100 Disputed Questions* (Crossway, 2012), 264.

14 On the one hand, only overseers (not deacons) are described as "able to teach" (1 Tim. 3:2), suggesting that overseers and not deacons were the leaders. On the other hand, both overseers and deacons are called to manage their households well (1 Tim. 3:4–5, 12), which suggests that both "have a duty to lead (*proistamenoi*) within the house-church." Andrew Clarke, *A Pauline Theology of Church Leadership*, Library of New Testament Studies (T&T Clark, 2008), 70. I think Andrew Clarke is probably correct when he says that "it may reasonably be deduced that the overseer had greater responsibilities than the deacon, but that there is a measure of overlap in their spheres of duty" (*Pauline Theology*, 70).

*diakonos* to describe both himself and Apollos, specifically in relation to their apostolic ministry (1 Cor. 3:5; 2 Cor. 6:4; 11:23). Timothy too is called a "good servant [*diakonos*]" (1 Tim. 4:6 CSB). Epaphras, who first brought the gospel to Colossae and instructed them in the faith, is called "our dear fellow servant [*diakonos*]" (Col. 1:7; 4:12).[15] Paul calls Tychicus a "faithful servant [*diakonos*], and fellow slave" (Col. 4:7 HCSB; cf. Eph. 6:21), connecting him to Paul, Timothy, and Epaphras. Tychicus, in fact, appears to have been one of Paul's most faithful and trusted emissaries, since Paul commends him in several letters.[16]

As far as I can tell, Paul never applies the singular noun *diakonos* to another named Christian who is not a church leader.[17] If Phoebe is not a leader, this is the only place where Paul uses *diakonos* for a named person who is a non-leader. As with the verb *kopiaō*, I'm tempted to follow the advice of my hermeneutics professors and say that Paul probably considered Phoebe to be a church leader.

As a wealthy benefactor, Phoebe could have used her social status to exercise secular authority—wielding her power and bossing people around. But instead, she embodied Jesus' Mark 10 paradigm of true greatness. If Phoebe was a leader, it would have been because, even as a high-status person, she chose to do the work fit for servants.[18]

---

15 James D. G. Dunn, *The Epistles to the Colossians and to Philemon: A Commentary on the Greek Text*, New International Greek Testament Commentary (Eerdmans, 1996), 64.

16 Ephesians 6:21; Colossians 4:7; 2 Timothy 4:12; Titus 3:12; cf. Acts 20:4. "If number of mentions is significant, this would make Tychicus, along with Silvanus, one of Paul's closest associates after Timothy and Titus" (Dunn, *Epistles*, 271–72).

17 The word *diakonos* occurs in two other passages in Romans. Paul calls governing authorities "God's servant" (Rom. 13:4) and Christ "a servant of the Jews" (Rom. 15:8).

18 Bruce Winter, *Roman Wives, Roman Widows: The Appearance of New Women and the Pauline Communities* (Eerdmans, 2003), 203.

## Phoebe the Letter Performer

Virtually all scholars agree that Phoebe carried Paul's letter to Rome.[19] Customarily, the person who carried a letter would also read it to its recipient(s).[20] This too is widely agreed upon by scholars.[21]

But "reading" a letter in the ancient world wasn't just reading out loud, as we might think of it today. Most experts in ancient letter writing use the word *perform* rather than *read* to describe how a letter carrier conveyed its message. "Ancient authorities on rhetoric dating to Paul's time considered the reader's voice, gestures and even his face to be an essential part of effective communication."[22] Cicero, for instance, goes into great detail about the various emotions and body parts involved in an effective delivery.[23]

Letter carriers commonly provided additional information, personal comments, and (if necessary) further explanations of what was written in the letter.[24] Because of this, it "was advantageous to both Paul and his recipients to have an informed carrier read the letter so as to provide

---

19 Every commentary I've looked at agrees that Phoebe was the letter carrier. See e.g., C. E. B. Cranfield, *A Critical and Exegetical Commentary on the Epistle to the Romans: Introduction and Commentary on Romans IX-XVI*, vol. 2, International Critical Commentary (T&T Clark, 2000), 780; Jewett, *Romans*, 943.

20 E. Randolph Richards, *Paul and First-Century Letter Writing: Secretaries, Composition and Collection* (IVP Academic, 2004), 185.

21 Jewett, however, offers a divergent perspective. He argues that Phoebe certainly carried the letter and even helped interpret it for the Roman audience but that it was Tertius (Rom. 16:22) who actually read it (*Romans*, 23, 979). For a counterargument, see Allan Chapple, "Getting *Romans* to the Right Romans: Phoebe and the Delivery of Paul's Letter," *Tyndale Bulletin* 62, no. 2 (2011): 213.

22 Richards, *Letter Writing*, 202; cf. 184–85. See also, among others, David Rhoads, "Biblical Performance Criticism: Performance as Research," *Oral Tradition* 25, no. 1 (2010): 157–98; Pieter J. J. Botha, "The Verbal Art of the Pauline Letters: Rhetoric, Performance and Presence," in *Rhetoric and the New Testament: Essays from the 1992 Heidelberg Conference*, ed. Stanley Porter and Thomas Olbricht, Journal for the Study of the New Testament Series 90 (JSOT Press, 1993), 417–19.

23 Cicero, *De Oratore* 3.57.216; see also Cicero, *Sermo Corporis* 3.59.222; Botha, "Verbal Art," 418.

24 Richards, *Letter Writing*, 202.

the proper inflections and nuances."[25] Letter carriers often received prior coaching from the author in how the letter was to be read. Some even memorized its contents. Those who didn't memorize it would have at least a thorough knowledge of the letter, helping to ensure that their performance would capture both the content and the presence of the author.[26]

The character and skill of a letter's carrier and performer were paramount in ancient correspondence. "Private carriers had to be trustworthy, for their reports were believed. It was expected that private carriers would have added information."[27] Cicero notes it was common for there to be substantial interaction between the letter writer and the letter carrier.[28]

In light of letter carriers' significance in the ancient world, some scholars describe Phoebe not only as the carrier and performer of Paul's letter to the Romans but also as its first interpreter. Allan Chapple writes:

> The bearer of the letter was also its interpreter—when it was being read out for the first time, the letter was also receiving its first public interpretation.... With so much riding on the positive reception of Romans, there is thus little doubt that Paul would have gone through it carefully with Phoebe so that she was able to communicate its contents as he wanted. Her reading of the

---

25 Richards, *Letter Writing*, 202.
26 Botha, "Verbal Art," 417.
27 Richards, *Letter Writing*, 184. One ancient letter describes the author's profound trust in the carrier/performer this way: "Please learn from the man who brings you this letter. He is no stranger to us" (P.Coll. 3.6, cited in Richards, *Letter Writing*, 183).
28 Cicero, *Ad Quintum Fratrem* 3.1.23, 3.7.1; *Ad Familiares* 15.17.1–2.

> letter can thus be seen as an authorised interpretation of its contents.[29]

Randy Richards agrees that ancient letter carriers often served as interpreters who were "expected to elaborate further the contents of the letter. In fact, there are many examples of letters that describe the situation briefly and give the writer's conclusion. The carrier was then expected to elaborate all the details for the recipient."[30] The line between a letter and its carrier was a fuzzy one.

In short, Phoebe was more than just an ancient postwoman. She likely played a significant role in helping the *meaning* of Paul's letter reach the hearts and minds of the first Christians who heard it.

What does this contribute to our question of women in church leadership? I want to be cautious not to squeeze too much out of this historical reconstruction. We don't actually know for sure how Phoebe read Paul's letter or if she offered any authoritative interpretation or explanation of his words. These things are historically plausible, maybe even likely, but they're not certain.

What we can say with certainty is that Paul trusted Phoebe with a letter vital to his ministry—and indeed, the history of Christianity—and he didn't have a problem putting a woman in a position where she might be expected to expand upon, interpret, and explain the contents of the letter. Paul could have found a man from the church at Corinth (a church that he was well acquainted with) to deliver the letter if he wanted to. Or he could have had Gaius, his wealthy host (Rom. 16:23),

---

29 Chapple, "Getting *Romans*," 213.
30 Richards, *Letter Writing*, 183.

send one of his male servants or clients to carry the letter. Instead, Paul chose a woman—his patron and fellow *diakonos* of the gospel.

In sum, Phoebe was a servant and a patron, and she was entrusted to perform Paul's letter to the Roman church. These three roles individually suggest that it's possible that Phoebe was a leader. Taken cumulatively, however, it's not just possible—it's probable. Again, I don't want to draw firm conclusions until I've wrapped my mind around the rest of Paul's theology about women and leadership. But Phoebe offers another strong piece of evidence for women in leadership.

## Priscilla: Coworker and House-Church Leader? (16:3–5)

Priscilla[31] and Aquila are the most prominent and frequently mentioned married couple in the mission of the early church.[32] They appear six times in the New Testament: three times in Acts 18 (vv. 1–3, 18–19, 26) and three times in Paul (Rom. 16:3–4; 1 Cor. 16:19; 2 Tim. 4:19). Early church fathers, regardless of their views on women in leadership, almost universally held high praise for Priscilla.[33]

We can piece together Priscilla's ministry life as follows. She and her husband, Aquila, were living in Rome when the Emperor Claudius

---

31 The name Priscilla (used throughout Acts 18) is a diminutive of the more formal Prisca (used by Paul in Rom. 16:3; 1 Cor. 16:19; 2 Tim. 4:19).

32 Jerome Murphy-O'Connor, "Prisca and Aquila: Traveling Tentmakers and Church Builders," *Bible Review* 8 (1992): 40–51, 62 (40); C. W. Stenschke, "Married Women and the Spread of Early Christianity," *Neotestamentica* 43, no. 1 (2009): 145–94.

33 John Chrysostom's description of Priscilla is particularly gushing. See Catherine Clark Kroeger, "John Chrysostom's First Homily on the Greetings to Priscilla and Aquila," *Priscilla Papers* 5, no. 3 (1991): 16–20. Some Christian scribes, however, seemed to diminish her influence. For instance, while the best and most reliable manuscripts list Priscilla first in Acts 18:26, some later manuscripts switch the order, listing Aquila first; see Dominika A. Kurek-Chomycz, "Is There an 'Anti-Priscan' Tendency in the Manuscripts? Some Textual Problems with Prisca and Aquila," *Journal of Biblical Literature* 125, no. 1 (2006): 124.

expelled all Jews from the city, landing them in Corinth (Acts 18:1–2). They were tentmakers like Paul, and so their common vocation brought them together when Paul first visited Corinth (Acts 18:3). When Paul left for Ephesus, Priscilla and Aquila went with him (Acts 18:18). Paul stayed there for eighteen months, during which Priscilla and Aquila opened their new home to host a church in Ephesus (1 Cor. 16:19). On one occasion, Priscilla and Aquila attended a synagogue service in Ephesus, and they noticed a teacher named Apollos misrepresenting the gospel. They pulled him aside and "explained to him the way of God more adequately" (Acts 18:26). The next time we see Priscilla and Aquila is in Romans 16:3–5, which means they had returned to Rome and were hosting another house church. Finally, they must have moved back to Ephesus, since Paul sent his greetings to them via Timothy, a leader of the Ephesian church, in his final letter (2 Tim. 4:19).

Here is Paul's greeting to this dynamic duo in Romans 16:

> Greet Priscilla and Aquila, my co-workers in Christ Jesus. They risked their lives for me. Not only I but all the churches of the Gentiles are grateful to them.
>
> Greet also the church that meets at their house. (vv. 3–5)

Four issues surround the ministry of Priscilla and Aquila: (1) the order of their names, (2) the nature of their house-church ministry, (3) their instruction of Apollos, and (4) their description as "co-workers in Christ Jesus" who "risked their lives" for Paul.

First, the order of their names. On two occasions, Aquila is mentioned first (Acts 18:1–3; 1 Cor. 16:19), but in the other four, Priscilla is mentioned first (Acts 18:18, 26; Rom. 16:3; 2 Tim. 4:19).[34] Speculations abound over why this is. One thing is certain: It was rare in the Greco-Roman world for a wife to be mentioned first, unless the wife was a citizen while the husband was a slave.[35] Some suggest, therefore, that Priscilla held a higher social status than her husband.[36] But Jerome Murphy-O'Connor points out that both held the same occupation (tentmakers) and argues that it would have been unlikely for a high-status person to work in such a blue-collar trade.[37] Moreover, Paul resists secular attitudes about social hierarchy; it would seem strange for him to reinforce that hierarchy by naming a high-status wife before her low-status husband *simply* because of class difference. This has led some scholars to suggest that Priscilla played a more prominent role in the church than her husband, explaining why Paul and Luke list her first.[38] Lack of further evidence prevents us from arriving at a firm conclusion. But I think the latter view makes more sense, from the little we know.

Second, let's consider Priscilla and Aquila's role as house-church hosts (Rom. 16:5). It's not clear if they were hosting the entire body of Roman believers in their home, which would require a rather large house, or if they hosted one of several Roman house churches. Either way, Priscilla and Aquila are prominent figures, since they head Paul's list of greetings in chapter 16.

---

34 Paul mentions three other male-female pairs in Romans 16, and in each case the man is listed first: Andronicus and Junia (v. 7), Rufus and his mother (v. 13), and Nereus and his sister (v. 15). "This suggests that placing Prisca before Aquila in Romans was not absolutely accidental," notes Kurek-Chomycz ("Prisca and Aquila," 114n18), though she concludes that we simply don't know why. Luke describes two other husband-wife couples, and in both cases the husband is listed first (Acts 5:1; 24:24).

35 See Marleen Boudreau Flory, "Where Women Precede Men: Factors Influencing the Order of Names in Roman Epitaphs," *The Classical Journal* 79, no. 3 (1984): 216–24.

36 Jewett, *Romans*, 955.

37 Murphy-O'Connor, "Prisca and Aquila," 40–51.

38 Gupta, *Tell Her Story*, 130.

As we saw in the previous chapter, house-church hosts were probably considered leaders. There's a certain level of historically informed speculation that goes into this assumption, making it tough to determine the precise role that hosts like Mary and Nympha played in their churches. But with Priscilla and Aquila, things are different. We have much more information about their ministry work. Luke's and Paul's venerable descriptions of Priscilla and Aquila's theological acumen, boldness for the gospel, and close proximity to Paul make it especially likely that they exercised leadership in their house churches. And there's no indication from the text alone that Aquila carried more authority than Priscilla simply because he was a man. If anything, Priscilla seems to have been the more notable minister.

Third, let's consider how Priscilla and Aquila instructed Apollos. While attending a synagogue service in Ephesus, they "took him and explained the way of God more accurately to him" (Acts 18:26, my translation). This raises two questions: Did Priscilla "teach" Apollos? and, Did Priscilla and Aquila address Apollos publicly or privately?

Let's start with the question of privacy. The phrase "took him" (*proselabonto auton*) could imply a private conversation. The same words are used when Peter "took [Jesus] aside" to rebuke him (Matt. 16:22).[39] The phrase can also mean "to receive" or "welcome" someone into the community or a home (Rom. 15:7; Philem. 17), which would mean that Priscilla and Aquila received Apollos into their home for "'in house' instruction."[40] As such, their instruction wouldn't necessarily be private, since their home was a house church and not simply a private abode.

---

39 See also Acts 17:5; 18:26; 27:33; 27:36; 28:2; Romans 14:1, 3; 15:7; Philemon 17.

40 Osiek and MacDonald, *Woman's Place*, 30; cf. 226–27. Some translations say they invited Apollos into their home (NIV), while others say they took him aside (NASB, NET). The Greek word *proslambanō* can mean both. Frederick William Danker, ed., *A Greek-English Lexicon of the New Testament and Other Early Christian Literature*, 3rd ed. (University of Chicago Press, 2000), 883.

But let's assume it was private instruction. If so, why the privacy? That depends on who you ask.

For complementarian scholars like Wayne Grudem, this privacy was important because the "example of Priscilla and Aquila instructing Apollos privately … does not contradict" Paul's teaching elsewhere that only men can govern and teach in the assembled church.[41] Other scholars, including both egalitarians and complementarians, suggest that Priscilla and Aquila chose privacy because they didn't want to shame Apollos by publicly correcting him.[42]

Both explanations are speculative; the text doesn't say why they took him aside. I think the context of Acts 18 could suggest that they wouldn't correct Apollos in the middle of the synagogue service, since the Christian mission was already on fragile terms with the Jews (vv. 6–16). Socially, it certainly would have been shameful to correct a teacher in the middle of the service, especially if they wanted Apollos to remain credible as a public preacher in Corinth. I don't see anything in the text suggesting that they took Apollos aside to ensure Priscilla wouldn't violate Paul's (alleged) instructions about women not teaching men in public.

What about the nature of their instruction? Did Priscilla teach Apollos? Wayne Grudem says no. He points out that the verbs "to teach" (*didaskō*) and "to preach" (*kerrusō*) are not used here. The verb that is used, *ektithēmi*, simply means "to convey information by careful elaboration" or "to explain, expound."[43] Priscilla was simply involved in

41 Grudem, *Evangelical Feminism*, 178–79.

42 Bruce, *Acts*, 360; Peterson, *Acts*, 526.

43 Danker, *Greek-English Lexicon*, 310, cited in Grudem, *Evangelical Feminism*, 179.

explaining the full gospel to Apollos in a private encounter. This doesn't mean, Grudem argues, that she was formally "teaching" him.

Grudem rightly defines *ektithēmi*, but I think he underappreciates how it's used in Acts.[44] Whether *ektithēmi* includes "teaching" depends on the content and nature of what's being explained. In Acts 28:23, for instance, Paul was "explaining [*exetitheto*] about the kingdom of God, and from the Law of Moses and from the Prophets he tried to persuade them about Jesus." This "explaining" certainly involved some level of teaching from Scripture. The same is probably true with Priscilla and Aquila. When they "explained" to Apollos "the way of God more accurately" (18:26), it seems arbitrary to say they were merely relaying information to Apollos and not teaching him.[45]

Plus, notice how Priscilla and Aquila's "explaining" directly parallels Apollos's own teaching in the previous verse:

> [Apollos] had been **instructed** [*katēxēmenos*] **in the way of the Lord** [*tēn hodon tou kuriou*] ... and taught [*edidasken*] about Jesus **accurately** [*akribōs*]. (v. 25)
>
> Priscilla and Aquila ... took him aside and **explained** [*exethento*] to him **the way of God** [*tēn hodon tou theou*] **more accurately** [*akribesteron*]. (v. 26 ESV)

---

44 Luke is the only New Testament author to use this verb, which he does in four places, all in Acts (7:21; 11:4; 18:26; 28:23).

45 Marg Mowczko points out that during Paul's three-month ministry in Ephesus, Luke describes him as "speaking boldly" (*parrēsiazomai*), "reasoning/discussing" (*dialegomai*), and "persuading" (*peithō*) in the synagogue (Acts 19:8). The main word for teaching (*didaskō*) is not used here, but it's hard to imagine that Paul wasn't teaching (cf. Acts 19:9–10); Marg Mowczko, "Did Priscilla Teach Apollos?," *Marg Mowczko* (blog), September 11, 2010, https://margmowczko.com/did-priscilla-teach-apollos.

Luke describes Apollos with two words that convey teaching (*katēxēmenos* and *edidasken*). He then describes Priscilla and Aquila's correction in a way that mirrors the wording of Apollos's own teaching (*akribesteron* and *tēn hodon tou theou*). It doesn't appear that Luke's use of *exethento* is intended to distance Priscilla from any kind of teaching.[46]

Fourth, Paul describes Priscilla and Aquila as "co-workers in Christ Jesus" who "risked their lives" for him (Rom. 16:3–4). As noted in the previous chapter, Paul uses the term "coworker" (*sunergos*) twelve times to describe sixteen different people, three of whom are women (including Priscilla).[47] Almost all the people Paul identifies as coworkers were clearly leaders in the church. I'm not basing this assessment simply on the term "coworker" but on what we know about these people from other passages. I've only found two or three "coworkers" about whom we don't have sufficient evidence to confidently conclude that they were leaders, and even these two or three still could be leaders.[48]

---

46 See Daniel Wallace's incisive study, "Did Priscilla 'Teach' Apollos? An Examination of the Meaning of *Ektithēmi* in Acts 18:26," Bible.org, June 29, 2004, https://bible.org/article/did-priscilla-teach-apollos. Wallace concludes that *ektithēmi* does not carry the notion of exhortation but does include the sense of "instruction" in Acts 18:26. Priscilla and Aquila's instruction "was not, of course, a mere history lesson" but "a historical-doctrinal explanation of the Christian faith."

47 The two other women are Euodia and Syntyche (Phil. 4:3). It's impossible to say for sure that they were leaders. I think the strongest evidence that they were is their description as "co-workers" who "contended at [Paul's] side in the cause of the gospel" (Phil. 4:3), along with the fact that Paul calls them out publicly for their disunity (see Gupta, *Tell Her Story*, 104–7).

48 Coworkers who are clearly leaders include Luke, Mark, Timothy, Titus, and Philemon. I think complementarians would be happy to add Aquila to this list. Aristarchus (Philem. 24) should probably also be considered a leader; he was a traveling minister with Paul (Acts 19:29; 20:4; 27:2), and the two were in prison together (Col. 4:10). Paul's description of Epaphroditus (Phil. 2:25–30) is glowing: Paul calls him "my brother, co-worker and fellow soldier," "your messenger [*apostolon*]" and servant, who should be considered highly "honor[ed]" since he "risked his life" for "the work of Christ." The cumulative weight of all these terms and phrases suggests he was a leader. We know less about Demas (Philem. 24), who's mentioned in passing in Colossians 4:14 and ended up leaving the faith toward the end of Paul's ministry (2 Tim. 4:10). We also know little about Clement (Phil. 4:3), who's only mentioned once. (Several early church fathers identified him as "Clement of Rome," the third bishop of the Roman church, but there is no biblical evidence for this.) He was a coworker with Paul who "contended at [Paul's] side" along with Euodia and Syntyche (Phil. 4:2–3). We know the least about Justus (Col. 4:11), who's simply called a coworker of Paul.

As for Priscilla, we have a much larger window into her "coworking" activities. She's often mentioned before her husband, cohosted a house church with him, instructed the mighty Apollos in the faith, and, together with her husband, risked her life for Paul, which garnered gratitude from "all the churches of the Gentiles" (Rom. 16:4). The Greek phrase *trachēlon hupethēkan* ("risked their lives") literally means "lay down one's neck" and is "a colloquialism for risking execution," but it can be used figuratively for risking one's life in general.[49] Whatever Priscilla and Aquila did for Paul, it certainly came with the threat of serious consequences. We know that Paul's ministry in Ephesus caused quite a stir (Acts 18) and that Priscilla and Aquila hosted a house church in Ephesus after Paul left. Perhaps their connection to Paul was a source of ongoing opposition to their ministry—so much so that they almost died for the sake of the gospel. Their courageous stance for the gospel gave them public notoriety and a target on their backs.

Priscilla, then, wasn't just a coworker. She was a particularly notable one who played a vital role in the mission of the early church. I do wonder, If Priscilla were never mentioned and all these glowing descriptions were applied only to Aquila, would anyone doubt that he was a leader?

The fact is, Priscilla and Aquila are always mentioned together, with Priscilla often mentioned first. Their work is never distinguished. Whatever they did, they did it together.

As with Phoebe, I think sound exegesis suggests that Priscilla was a recognized early church leader. But—and I hope you don't get sick

---

49 Jewett, *Romans*, 957–98.

of me saying this—I want to hold off making definitive claims about women's church leadership until I've considered everything Paul has to say on the issue.

## Junia the Apostle?

The last woman we'll discuss in this chapter is Junia, who's listed alongside a man named Andronicus (probably her husband) in Romans 16:7. Paul writes:

> Greet Andronicus and Junia, my fellow Jews who have been in prison with me. They are outstanding among [or *to*] the apostles, and they were in Christ before I was.

There are three main interpretive issues in the discussion surrounding Junia: (1) whether Junia (or Junias) is even a woman, (2) whether she is called an "apostle," and (3) if Junia is an apostle, what kind of apostle?

The scholarly literature devoted to these three questions is legion. When I turned my attention to researching Junia, I thought I'd just read a few commentaries and articles to help me figure out if she was a leader. I didn't think I'd have to devote weeks of study to comb through dozens of tedious books and articles, examining parallel phrases in ancient Greek texts and inscriptions. It took Matt Hamilton forty-five pages to summarize all the literature devoted to Junia, and his survey spanned only twelve years (2010–2022)![50]

---

50 Matt Hamilton, "Junia as a Female Apostle in Romans 16:7: A Literature Review of Relevant Sources from 2010 to Present," *Reconciliation* 6, no. 1 (2022): 31–77.

Wrestling with Romans 16:7 became one of the most arduous tasks in my journey through this debate. I'll share my findings as concisely as I can, but I have to warn you, there's no way to do justice to the issue without discussing nitty-gritty issues of Greek grammar and ancient inscriptions.

Fortunately, our first interpretive issue won't take long. Even though some late manuscripts write her name as "Junias" (which would be a man's name in Greek), it's now all but settled among scholars that her real name was the female "Junia."[51] A few people will always argue otherwise, but almost everyone—complementarians and egalitarians alike—now agrees that Junia was a woman.[52]

The second issue is way more complicated and extremely technical. Scholars disagree over whether Paul calls Junia an apostle. His phrase "outstanding among/to the apostles" (*episēmoi en tois apostolois*) could mean that Junia *was* an apostle or simply that she was outstanding *in the eyes of* the apostles. It all rests on how we interpret the Greek word *episēmoi* ("outstanding") alongside the phrase *en tois apostolois* ("among/ to the apostles").

Up until 2001, most scholars interpreted the phrase to mean "among the apostles," meaning that Junia was an apostle. But in 2001, two New Testament scholars, Daniel Wallace and Michael Burer, did a computer search of similar constructions in ancient Greek literature where *episēmoi* (or another form of the word *episēmos*) was used in

---

51 This became a live debate after Bernadette Brooten's seminal essay back in 1977, "'Junia ... Outstanding Among the Apostles' (Romans 16:7)," in *Women Priests*, ed. Leonard Swidler and Arlene Swidler (Paulist Press, 1977), 141–44. But the debate more or less ended in 2006 with Eldon Jay Epp's game-changing book, *Junia: The First Woman Apostle* (Fortress Press, 2006).

52 The only recent scholar I've found who argues otherwise is Al Wolters, "*IOYNIAN* (Romans 16:7) and the Hebrew Name *Yĕḥunnī*," *Journal of Biblical Literature* (2008): 397–408.

similar grammatical constructions (*en* + the dative plural). They said they had found "several dozens" of examples in Greek literature and inscriptions where the phrase almost always means "outstanding to," not "outstanding among." Thus, Junia was most likely not an apostle.

Their article, however, elicited a number of scathing critiques.[53] So, a decade later, Burer published a lengthy response to his critics.[54] Burer not only argued that his original thesis holds weight but that several more Greek texts (not mentioned in his first study) further prove his view.

When I first read Burer's second article, I thought the case was closed: Junia is not an apostle. But then I took a closer look at Burer's evidence, and the case reopened.

Burer lists thirty-six Greek constructions similar to Paul's (*episēmos* with *en* + a dative plural) and argues that thirty-five of them should be translated "to," not "among." But when I combed through his references for myself, I discovered that only ten of the thirty-five contain the Greek word *en* before the dative plural. I know it's a small word, but it's enormously significant. Without the word *en*, the phrase would much more likely mean "to," not "among." No one disputes this. Of Burer's thirty-six references, then, only ten are relevant to the point he's trying to prove.

Then I looked closely at the ten examples that do reflect Paul's actual wording in Romans 16:7 by including the word *en*. In all but one case,

---

53 See Richard Bauckham, *Gospel Women: Studies of the Named Women in the Gospels* (Eerdmans, 2002), 172–80; Eldon Jay Epp, "Text-Critical, Exegetical, and Socio-Cultural Factors Affecting the Junia/Junias Variation in Romans 16,7," in *New Testament Textual Criticism and Exegesis: Festschrift J. Delobel*, ed. A. Denaux, Bibliotheca Ephemeridum Theologicarum Lovaniensium 161 (Leuven University/Peeters, 2002), 227–91; Linda L. Belleville, "*Iounian ... episēmoi en tois apostolois:* A Re-Examination of Romans 16.7 in Light of Primary Source Materials," *New Testament Studies* 51 (2005): 231–49.

54 Michael Burer, "*Episēmoi en tois apostolois* in Rom 16:7 as 'Well-Known to the Apostles': Further Defense and New Evidence," *Journal of the Evangelical Theological Society* 58, no. 4 (2015): 731–55.

contrary to Burer's thesis, the phrase almost certainly means "among" and not "to."[55] Here are two examples so you can see for yourself:

> **Example 1**
> Now this man [Thales of Miletus] became most well-known to/among the Greeks [*episēmotatos en tois Hellēsi*].[56]

Burer cites this passage as an example of an "exclusive sense" of our phrase (*episēmos* with *en* + a dative plural); that is, the person in question, Thales of Miletus, is *not* part of the group he's being compared to (the Greeks). But this is almost certainly wrong for one simple reason: Thales of Miletus was a renowned *Greek* sage. He was well-known among his own people, the Greeks, not well-known to some other group he wasn't part of, so *en* must mean "among" here.[57]

> **Example 2**
> For indeed he was present in glory, prominent to/among angels [*episēmos en angelois*], and manifest to all powers above, just as the morning star also is careless among the stars [*en tois astrois*].[58]

---

55 I came to this conclusion after working through Burer's texts on my own, but I later came across an incisive article by Yii-Jan Lin offering a similar criticism of Burer: "Junia: An Apostle Before Paul," *Journal of Biblical Literature* 139, no. 1 (2020): 191–209.

56 Eusebius, *Praeparatio evangelica* 10.14.11.1, cited in Burer, "Well-Known," 752.

57 See too Lin, "Junia," 196n25.

58 Cyrillus Alexandrinus Theol. (AD 4th–5th centuries), *Commentarius in Isaiam prophetam*, vol. 70, p. 377, line 33, cited in Burer, "Well-Known," 751.

At first I thought Burer was correct about *en* meaning "to" in this passage, since I assumed it was talking about Jesus (or God). But when I read the larger context of the passage, I realized the "he" it's talking about is actually Satan. As an angelic being, Satan is not "prominent *to* angels," but "prominent *among* angels," since he's one of them. This is confirmed by the very next line, which uses the same construction: "The morning star is also careless *among the stars* [*en tois astrois*]." The "morning star" is not "careless to" but "careless among" the stars.[59]

In summary, nine of Burer's ten references that parallel Romans 16:7 are better translated as "among" not "to," which actually lends support for Junia being among the apostles.

To be clear, there are some references listed in Burer's two articles that do mean "to," not "among."[60] So it's possible to interpret Romans 16:7 this way; namely, that Junia is not an apostle. But this is a less likely meaning. "Among" is far more often the better translation. Based on the examples we have, then, I think the scales tip in favor of seeing Junia as outstanding *among* the apostles, not simply *to* the apostles.

One way to scrutinize this interpretation is to look at how native Greek speakers in the early church understood Romans 16:7. If the phrase *could* go either way, their opinion should mean something. It's significant, then, that Chrysostom, Theodoret, and (possibly) Origen—native Greek speakers—all take Romans 16:7 to include Junia as a member of the apostles.[61] "Indeed, how great the wisdom of this woman must have been

---

59 Lin, "Junia," 196n25.

60 From my vantage point, the following texts/inscriptions should probably be taken to mean "to," not "among": Euripides, *Hipp.* 103; Lucian, *Harm.* 1.17; *TAM* 2.905.1; *TAM* 2.1–3.838; *TAM* 2.1–3.905; *FdXanth* 7.76.1.1.1.4; and possibly Psalms of Solomon 2:6.

61 For a survey of patristic interpretations of Andronicus and Junia, see David Huttar, "Did Paul Call Andronicus an Apostle in Romans 16:7?," *Journal of the Evangelical Theological Society* 52, no. 4 (2009): 760–78.

that she was even deemed worthy of the title apostle," says Chrysostom.[62] Theodoret agrees: Andronicus and Junia "are notable, not just among the disciples, but among the teachers, and not even among the common teachers, but among the apostles."[63]

Chrysostom's view of Junia is significant not only because he was a native Greek speaker but also because he didn't believe women should be leaders or preachers in the church. He wasn't as misogynistic as many church fathers, but he certainly would have been happy to read Romans 16:7 as "to" rather than "among" if he thought the Greek allowed for it. And yet, even though he was shocked that Paul called Junia an apostle, he never seemed to doubt that this was what the text said.

Junia's apostleship is supported by two other phrases in the same verse. First, since Paul himself was an apostle, it makes more sense to interpret our debated phrase as "among the apostles" rather than "to the apostles." Why would Paul say that two non-apostles are "outstanding to the apostles," as if he weren't one of those apostles? That would be like Mookie Betts saying Shohei Ohtani is "outstanding to the Dodgers," when Mookie himself is a Dodger. (Sorry, it's a baseball thing. Go blue!)

Second, Paul's phrase "were also in Christ before me" likewise suggests that Andronicus and Junia were apostles (v. 7 CSB). The only other time Paul uses the phrase "before me" (*pro emou*) is when he's defending his apostleship. In Galatians 1:17, he writes, "I did not go up to Jerusalem to those who had become apostles *before me* [*pro emou*]; instead I went to Arabia and came back to Damascus" (CSB). It's important to note that Paul was the last of the apostles (1 Cor. 15:8–9), so chronology helps

62 *Hom. Rom.* 31.2, in Epp, *Junia*, 32.
63 *PG* 82.220, cited in Huttar, "Did Paul?," 761.

determine who's an apostle and who is not. Anyone claiming to be an apostle *after* Paul is a fraud. Only those who were in Christ *before* Paul could claim to be legitimate apostles. So then, Paul's comment that Andronicus and Junia were "in Christ before me" could support their apostolic status. Otherwise, why would he add this otherwise unnecessary detail?[64]

From my best reading of the evidence, Paul most likely considered Junia to be an apostle. But what *kind* of apostle?

This is our third interpretive issue, and it opens up a whole new flurry of scholarly discussion. In the New Testament, the Greek word *apostolos* ("apostle") can mean (1) a member of the Twelve; (2) a broader group of key figures in the early church, including but not limited to the Twelve, such as Barnabas, Apollos, and Paul himself,[65] or (3) messengers sent from particular churches (2 Cor. 8:23; Phil. 2:25). Each of these three options carries different implications for the potential leadership roles of an "apostle."

Junia was clearly not part of the Twelve, so this leaves us with the last two options. How likely is it that she was part of the third group: a messenger sent from a particular church? Paul uses *apostolos* to mean "messenger" on two other occasions: to describe Epaphroditus ("your

---

64 Noted by Lin, "Junia," 208. Esther Ng doesn't see this as significant, since the phrase "and they were in Christ before I was" is "dealing with a new attribute of the two individuals ... rather than their calling as apostles." Esther Yue L. Ng, "Was Junia(s) in Rom 16:7 a Female Apostle? And So What?," *Journal of the Evangelical Theological Society* 63, no. 3 (2020): 527. But I don't think this final phrase needs to directly modify the term "apostles" for it to be relevant. Paul mentions their prior conversion in the same breath that he mentions their apostolic status.

65 Barnabas (Acts 14:4, 14; 1 Cor. 9:6), Apollos (1 Cor. 4:9), the brothers of Christ (1 Cor. 9:5; Gal. 1:19), and possibly Silas and Timothy (1 Thess. 2:6–7; cf. 1:1). Paul also refers to "all the apostles" alongside the Twelve (1 Cor. 15:5, 7), which may include other unnamed apostles (see Bauckham, *Gospel Women*, 180).

messenger," Phil. 2:25) and some unnamed "brothers" who are "messengers of the churches" (2 Cor. 8:23 CSB). But Paul describes these "messengers" as being connected to specific churches; he doesn't depict Andronicus and Junia this way. He does not depict them as messengers of the church at Rome. Plus, Paul uses the definite article "the" (*tois*) with "apostles" (*apostolois*), which suggests a particular group—*the* apostles—rather than a generic group of messengers sent out from various churches.[66] "It is hard to see," writes Richard Bauckham, how messengers of different churches "could form a known body of people among whom Andronicus and Junia could be said to be outstanding."[67]

Since Andronicus and Junia weren't part of the Twelve and probably aren't messengers sent out from the Roman church, this leaves the second group as the most likely category for Junia's apostleship.

The apostles in this group are clearly leaders in the early church. They are sometimes distinguished from the Twelve (Acts 15:2, 4), but in other passages both are grouped together as "apostles" (1 Cor. 9:5–6; 12:28).[68] Paul, who's part of this second group of apostles, recognized that Peter, James, and John (members of the Twelve) were "esteemed as pillars" in the Jerusalem church (Gal. 2:9), but he also relativized their unique importance (Gal. 2:6) and even rebuked Peter to his face (Gal. 2:11–14). Thus, there doesn't appear to be a hierarchy of authority of the

---

66 Lynn H. Cohick, *Women in the World of the Earliest Christians: Illuminating Ancient Ways of Life* (Baker, 2009), 216–17.

67 Bauckham, *Gospel Women*, 180.

68 For the nature and work of these apostles, see H. D. Betz, "Apostle," in *The Anchor Yale Bible Dictionary*, ed. David Noel Freedman, vol. 1 (Doubleday, 1992), 309–11; C. L. Westfall, "Apostle," in *Dictionary of Paul and His Letters: A Compendium of Contemporary Biblical Scholarship*, ed. Scot McKnight (IVP Academic, 2023), 49–53.

Twelve over this other category of apostles. Both groups played a fundamental role in building the early church (1 Cor. 12:28; Eph. 2:20).[69]

Throughout the New Testament, we see apostles preaching the gospel in synagogues (Acts 14:1–6) and in public places (Acts 14:15–17); planting churches (1 Cor. 3:5–15), sometimes alongside and with the same authority as Paul (1 Thess. 2:5–6; cf. 1:1);[70] performing "signs, wonders and miracles" (2 Cor. 12:12; cf. Acts 5:12); and guarding and transmitting key doctrinal traditions about the Christian faith (1 Cor. 15:3–5; cf. 2 Tim. 1:13–14). Their roles "could vary but they seem to be centered in the proclamation of the gospel and the founding and administering of new churches."[71] *Apostolos*, in this sense, is about as close to a formal leadership term as we find in the New Testament.

There were also a number of self-proclaimed "super-apostles" (2 Cor. 11:5) in the first century, whom Paul calls "false apostles ... masquerading as apostles of Christ" (2 Cor. 11:13). One way to distinguish a true apostle from a false one is to ask, Are they suffering? When Paul defends his apostleship, he doesn't flash a badge or flaunt a title. Instead, he boasts about all the times he's been beaten, tortured, and thrown into prison (2 Cor. 11:23–29; cf. 1 Cor. 4:6–13).

It's interesting that Paul also highlights the suffering of Junia and Andronicus: They "have been in prison with me" (Rom. 16:7).[72]

---

69 Ephesians 2:20 ("built on the foundation of the apostles and prophets") is not limited to the Twelve. "Apostles" includes at least Paul himself and other key figures in the church (cf. 1 Cor. 3:5–15, where both Paul and Apollos are described as building the church).

70 First Thessalonians 2:6 appears to include Paul, Silas, and Timothy (cf. 1 Thess. 1:1) when it says, "Even though as apostles of Christ we could have asserted our authority."

71 Betz, "Apostle," 310.

72 See the incisive study by Nijay K. Gupta, "Reconstructing Junia's Imprisonment: Examining a Neglected Pauline Comment in Romans 16:7," *Perspectives in Religious Studies* 47 (2020): 385–97.

Several things could land you in a Roman prison in the first century: theft, murder, attempted murder, temple robbery. But it's unlikely that such sinful activities would earn Paul's praise. So what kind of crime did Andronicus and Junia commit?

Romans also imprisoned people for civil disturbance and inciting riots—and this was why some early Christians wound up in Roman prisons. Paul himself was accused of these crimes when he preached the gospel (Acts 19:40). Whether Andronicus and Junia went to prison together with Paul then or on a different occasion, it's likely they were jailed for the same reason. Perhaps this couple also "turned the world upside down" (Acts 17:6 CSB) by "defying Caesar's decrees, saying that there is another king, one called Jesus" (v. 7). Whatever they did to get themselves in so much trouble, it must have been something public and recognizably disruptive.

The conditions of Roman prisons were horrid: dark, dangerous, crowded, and noisy. "A stench so terrible assailed anyone who drew near that it could scarcely be endured."[73] Prisoners were beaten, tortured, and often held in heavy chains that left deep wounds and deadly infections. Food was scarce in prisons, and people scarcely made it out alive.[74] If they didn't die from the beatings and torture, diseases spawned by rotting corpses might do the trick.[75]

It was very rare for women to be thrown in prison. Those who were imprisoned stayed in the same cells as men, where they faced the constant

73 Diodorus Siculus 31.9.1–2.

74 Libanius, *Orations* 45.8.

75 Thucydides 7.87.1–2.

threat of sexual assault and rape.[76] To avoid this brutality, some women took their own lives.[77]

It's remarkable that Junia not only endured such a hellhole but also continued her apostolic duties after she was released. Paul's use of the present tense in Romans 16:7, "*are* outstanding among the apostles," suggests that Junia and Andronicus continued their apostolic work after they got out of prison.[78]

We may never know the exact nature of Junia's ministry. Whatever it was, it had to be very public and substantial enough for Rome to respond with punitive force. Junia, as Nijay Gupta points out, "must have been regarded as a threat to public order."[79]

Does this mean Junia was a leader? Even if you're not convinced, surely we can all agree that today's churches would be set ablaze were they led by Christians who embodied a glimmer of Junia's courageous resilience and fierce devotion to the gospel.

The textual evidence, though, does seem overwhelming to me. I think Junia was a leader in the early church.

## Conclusion

Romans 16 showcases the extensive role women played in Paul's ministry. Unless we read this chapter in light of a particular interpretation of 1 Corinthians 14 and 1 Timothy 2, several women seem to play leadership roles in the early church. If all we had were one or two debated

76 Suetonius, *Life of Tiberius* 61.5.
77 Plutarch, *Mor.* 253C–E.
78 Noted by Gupta, "Reconstructing," 396.
79 Gupta, *Tell Her Story*, 152.

words, I would be much more hesitant to draw this conclusion. But the cumulative case seems overwhelming.

If Phoebe were only called a *prostatis*, then perhaps she could be interpreted as a generous wealthy woman who wasn't a leader. This reading would still border on anachronism—failing to appreciate the significance of *prostatis* in the first century. But Paul also describes her with one of his favorite leadership terms, *diakonos*, and entrusts her with carrying and performing his most important letter at the crux of his ministry.

There's no evidence that Priscilla played a supporting role to Aquila, as if he were the only real leader between the two. Priscilla and Aquila are indistinguishable in their extensive ministry ventures—hosting house churches, instructing leaders, working with Paul, and risking their lives for the gospel.

And then there's Junia. This woman probably had no idea how much attention she would receive from later scholars. But I'm confident she would be able to handle all the fuss and fear. I mean, she made it out of a first-century Roman prison and kept on *apostle-ing* the church! Imagine the hush that filled the room when Junia, fresh from a grimy dungeon, stepped through the doors of her first house-church gathering with apostolic fire still burning in her eyes.

Chapter 6

# FEMALE PROPHETS IN THE NEW TESTAMENT

In 2010, I invited Tom Schreiner to teach a winter course on Women in Ministry at Eternity Bible College, where I was a professor at the time. Tom gave a compelling case for a complementarian view. One day after class, I asked what he thought was the strongest case for the egalitarian view. He answered without hiccup or hesitation: "Female prophets."

That's what I love about Tom. He's been a complementarian for nearly as long as I've been alive, and he's very firm in his convictions. Yet he has the humility to acknowledge the strongest arguments for a view he disagrees with.

Tom, of course, went on to give several reasons why he still doesn't believe the presence of female prophets in the New Testament supports the egalitarian view. But I'll never forget thinking: *If I ever study this topic in detail, I'll need to do a deep dive into New Testament prophecy and its implications for women in church leadership.*

And here we are. Though more than a decade after Tom first piqued my interest, I've finally wrapped my mind around New Testament prophecy as it relates to our debate.

## New Testament Prophecy and Women in Leadership

Women were clearly prophets and prophesied in the New Testament. Luke mentions "a prophet, Anna" who "spoke about the child [Jesus] to all who were looking forward to the redemption of Jerusalem" (Luke 2:36–38). Her sex appears unexceptional to Luke, just as Deborah and Huldah's sex does to the Old Testament writers. Luke also describes Pentecost as the fulfillment of Joel's promise that "sons and daughters ... men and women ... will prophesy" (Acts 2:17–18; cf. Joel 2:28–32). When Paul writes to the church in Corinth, he assumes women are prophesying in their gatherings (1 Cor. 11:5). Luke mentions almost in passing that Philip had "four unmarried daughters *who prophesied* [*prophēteuousai*]" (Acts 21:9). The present tense of the verb suggests an ongoing role for these prophets.[1] Once again, Luke doesn't seem surprised that they are female. In fact, both Anna and Philip's daughters are mentioned side by side with male prophets: Simeon (Luke 2:25–35) and Agabus (Acts 21:10–11).[2]

There's no debate about whether women were prophets in the New Testament. There is a debate, however, over the *nature* of New Testament prophecy. Not everyone agrees that prophets were leaders

1 See Craig S. Keener, *Acts 15:1–23:55, Volume 3 of a Cultural and Contextual Exegesis of the Acts of the Apostles* (Baker, 2014), 3090.

2 Keener, *Acts*, 3091.

or that prophecy was similar to teaching and preaching.[3] Part of the problem is that not all New Testament descriptions of prophets and prophecy fit the same mold. Some passages seem to identify a specific group of prophets who played a role distinct from those with the spiritual gift of prophecy.[4] The former seem to be itinerant preachers ministering to multiple churches, while others prophesy to their own local church when a revelation spontaneously comes upon them.[5]

Not all prophecies seem to carry the same authority. Paul tells the Corinthians to "weigh carefully" prophecies, and the Thessalonians are to "test them all."[6] This seems to mean that not every prophecy is trustworthy or bears unchecked authority. But the book of Revelation, which is called a "prophecy" (Rev. 1:3), warns those who don't obey the book and threatens anyone who adds or takes away from its words.[7] I don't think John, the author, would fancy someone weighing or testing his prophecy to see if it were true.

Some prophecies are weighed; others are obeyed. "Christian prophecy was exceedingly varied," writes Max Turner.[8] This is why we shouldn't base our understanding of New Testament prophecy on one passage alone.

---

3 Some of the more significant studies on prophecy in the New Testament are David Hill, *New Testament Prophecy* (John Knox, 1979); E. Earle Ellis, *Prophecy and Hermeneutic in Early Christianity* (Eerdmans, 1978); David Aune, *Prophecy in Early Christianity and the Ancient Mediterranean World* (Eerdmans, 1991); Thomas Gillespie, *The First Theologians: A Study in Early Christian Prophecy* (Eerdmans, 1994); and Wayne Grudem, *The Gift of Prophecy in the New Testament and Today*, rev. ed. (Crossway, 2000). For a recent overview of the issues, see Richard Blaylock, "Towards a Definition of New Testament Prophecy," *Themelios* 44 (2019): 41–60.

4 1 Corinthians 12:28; Ephesians 2:20; 3:5; cf. Romans 12:6; see Hill, *New Testament Prophecy*, 137–38. We probably shouldn't think of prophets as occupying an "office" (see Aune, *Prophecy*, 204), but there does seem to be a group of prophets distinct from those who prophesied spontaneously in the churches.

5 Acts 11:27; 21:8–11; cf. 1 Corinthians 14:30. For itinerant prophets, see Aune, *Prophecy*, 211–17.

6 1 Corinthians 12:10; 14:29; 1 Thessalonians 5:21.

7 Revelation 1:3; 22:7, 10, 18–19.

8 Max Turner, "Spiritual Gifts Then and Now," *Vox Evangelica* 15 (1985): 16.

Instead, we should let the New Testament's varied descriptions provide us with broad parameters for what constitutes "prophecy."

Of all the definitions scholars have proposed, I like Daniel Hill's best:

> A Christian prophet is a Christian who functions within the Church, occasionally or regularly, as a divinely called and divinely inspired speaker who receives intelligible and authoritative revelations or messages which he is impelled to deliver publicly, in oral or written form, to Christian individuals and/or the Christian community.[9]

Fortunately for us, we don't need to figure out everything the New Testament says about prophecy. We only need to address two questions: Is New Testament prophecy akin to teaching and preaching? and, Did prophets and prophecy play an authoritative role in the church?

Egalitarians answer yes to both questions, while a range of responses exists among complementarians. No complementarian has done more work on the issue than Wayne Grudem, who wrote his Cambridge PhD thesis on the topic and has published well-researched works arguing for his view.[10] As we'll see, he answers no to both questions. "Soft complementarians" typically say yes to the first question;

---

9 Hill, *New Testament Prophecy*, 8–9.

10 Grudem's dissertation was published as *The Gift of Prophecy in 1 Corinthians* (Wipf and Stock, 1981). I'll interact with his more recent book, *The Gift of Prophecy in the New Testament and Today*, rev. ed. (Crossway, 2000).

thus, they believe women can teach and preach. But whatever authority prophets held in the early church, they argue, it fell under the authority of male elders.

I've wrestled with these questions for some time now, considering them from different angles and weighing scholarly opinions on the matter. The issues are complex, no doubt, and I don't hold my conclusion with absolute certainty. But I do think there's good evidence that New Testament prophecy had a function similar to teaching and preaching and that prophets did play an authoritative role in the church. Let's explore why.

## Is New Testament Prophecy Akin to Teaching and Preaching?

My understanding of New Testament prophecy's similarity to teaching and preaching is based on two main pieces of evidence. Let's look closely at both.

First, New Testament prophecy can have an exhortative function similar to the function of teaching and preaching. This overlap is laid out in 1 Corinthians 14:3, which might be the New Testament's most explicit description of prophecy's function: "The one who prophesies speaks edification [*oikodomēn*], exhortation [*paraklēsin*], and consolation [*paramuthian*] to people" (my translation).[11]

The term "exhortation" (*paraklēsin*) is particularly noteworthy, since according to complementarian scholar Claire Smith, it's "one of the most

11 Daniel Hill says of *oikodomēn*, *paraklēsin*, and *paramuthian* that "the three when taken together provide the nearest approach in Paul's letters to a definition of the prophetic function," even if the three words are difficult to distinguish (*New Testament Prophecy*, 122–23).

important NT verbs for speaking and influencing."[12] Paul uses this term forty-four times as one of his primary "commanding words."[13] While the noun *paraklēsis* and its verb form *parakaleō* have a range of possible meanings, Paul typically uses them to convey some kind of exhortation, expecting an obedient response.[14] In the Pastoral Epistles, *parakaleō* occurs in connection to teaching (1 Tim. 6:2; 2 Tim. 4:2; Titus 1:9), and in 1 Timothy 4:13, Paul uses *paraklēsis* alongside the public reading and teaching of Scripture: "Until I come, devote yourself to the public reading of Scripture, to preaching [*tē paraklēsei*, literally "the exhortation"] and to teaching."[15] In her extensive study of every occurrence of *parakaleō/paraklēsis* in 1 Corinthians and the Pastoral Epistles, Claire Smith concludes that of the fourteen uses in these four books, a "didactic sense is present in all but two texts."[16]

This same word is used elsewhere to describe the exhortation of prophetic leaders, like John the Baptist who "exhorted the people and proclaimed the good news to them" (Luke 3:18). The prophet Barnabas "exhorted" the Antioch Christians "to remain faithful to the Lord with steadfast purpose" (Acts 11:23 ESV). Paul and Barnabas "exhorted" the disciples "to persevere in the faith" (Acts 14:22 NABRE). Such

---

12 Claire Smith, *Pauline Communities as "Scholasti c Communities": A Study of the Vocabulary of "Teaching" in 1 Corinthians, 1 and 2 Timothy and Titus*, Wissenschaftliche Untersuchungen zum Neuen Testament 2 335 (Mohr Siebeck, 2012), 275. The verb *parakaleō* occurs 109 times, and the noun *paraklēsis* 29 times in the New Testament. Smith points out that there's no substantial difference in meaning between the noun and the verb.

13 Smith, *Pauline Communities*, 274–312.

14 *Paraklēsis/parakaleō* can mean "comfort," "urge," "encourage," "plea," "ask," "exhort." See Romans 12:1; 1 Corinthians 1:10; 4:16; 14:31; 16:12, 16; 2 Corinthians 10:1; Ephesians 4:1; Philippians 4:2; 1 Thessalonians 4:1; 1 Timothy 1:3; 2:1; 5:1; 6:2; 2 Timothy 4:2; Titus 1:9; 2:6, 15. See also 1 Peter 2:11; 5:1; Jude 3.

15 "The definite article with each noun indicates that they were 'recognized items in the congregational meeting for worship'" (Smith, *Pauline Communities*, 286n122, citing Philip H. Towner, "The Function of the Public Reading of Scripture in 1 Timothy 4:13 and in the Biblical Tradition," *Southern Baptist Journal of Theology* 7, no. 3 [2003]: 44–45).

16 1 Corinthians 4:13; 16:12. Smith, *Pauline Communities*, 287.

exhortations are not simply words of encouragement. They are commands to be obeyed.

The entire letter of Hebrews, in fact, is called a "word of exhortation" (*tou logou tēs paraklēseōs*, Heb. 13:22). Hebrews was most likely a well-crafted sermon, rich in theological exegesis and essential Christian doctrine, which was later written down in the form we now have. It's no wonder Paul considered Scripture itself to be the ultimate source of *paraklēsis* (Rom. 15:4–5). *Paraklēsis* is "not the bland communication of information as such," writes Anthony Thiselton. Instead, to engage in *paraklēsis* means to "plead, exhort, encourage, challenge, brace, console, or provide comfort on the basis of ... [the] covenant promises mediated by human agents called and gifted by God for this task through the Holy Spirit."[17]

*Oikodomē* ("build up," "edify") is another word connected to prophecy in 1 Corinthians 14:3. Paul uses this word in a variety of ways. He sometimes uses *oikodomē* to describe something all Christians are to do toward one another (Rom. 14:19; 1 Thess. 5:11). For example, when believers sing psalms, speak in tongues, interpret a tongue, and share wholesome words, they build up, or edify, fellow believers (1 Cor. 14:26; Eph. 4:29).

But when Paul connects *oikodomē* (and its verb form *oikodomeō*) with the work of apostles or prophets, the word refers to planting churches and raising up disciples. Paul describes his apostolic church-planting work with forms of the word *oikodomē* throughout 1 Corinthians 3:9–15. Similarly,

---

17 Anthony C. Thiselton, *The First Epistle to the Corinthians: A Commentary on the Greek Text*, New International Greek Testament Commentary (Eerdmans, 2000), 1088. E. Earle Ellis surveys several passages where *paraklēsis* is used and concludes that it captures "the specific ministry of a prophet" (Ellis, *Prophecy and Hermeneutic*, 130–31).

he writes in Romans 15:20, "It has always been my ambition to preach the gospel where Christ was not known, so that I would not be *building* [*oikodomeō*] on someone else's foundation." In 2 Corinthians 10:8, Paul uses *oikodomē* to describe the goal of his apostolic authority: "Our [apostolic] authority" is something "the Lord gave for building [*oikodomēn*] you up" (CSB; see also 2 Cor. 12:19; 13:10).

Paul also uses *oikodomē* to describe the foundational role prophets played in the early church. In Ephesians 2:20–22, he writes about the church being "built [*epoikodomethentes*] on the foundation of the apostles and prophets, with Christ Jesus himself as the chief cornerstone. In him the whole building [*oikodomē*] is joined together and rises to become a holy temple in the Lord. And in him you too are being built together [*sunoikodomeisthe*] to become a dwelling in which God lives by his Spirit." Ephesians 4:11–12 again connects *oikodomē* to the foundational work of apostles, prophets, and pastor-teachers, who "equip his people for works of service, so that the body of Christ may be built up." Indeed, Jesus himself promised to "build" his church upon Peter (or Peter's confession; Matt. 16:18), and throughout Acts, Luke describes the growing church by saying it is being "built" (Acts 9:31; 15:16; 20:32).

Thus, while Paul can use *oikodomē* in a general sense of believers edifying each other, it appears to convey a more specific meaning of building up the church as a whole when connected to the work of apostles and prophets.

The third word Paul uses in 1 Corinthians 14:3 is *paramuthian* ("consolation," "comfort"). Various forms of this word occur only three other times in Paul (Phil. 2:1; 1 Thess. 2:12; 5:14). All believers are commanded to "comfort" (*paramutheisthe*) one another (1 Thess. 5:14 CSB) and find "comfort" in Christ (Phil. 2:1). The word *paramuthian* is therefore not limited to the work of leaders or teachers. Paul does, however, use the word to describe his apostolic care as a father over his children: "We dealt with each of you as a father deals with his own children, encouraging [*parakalountes*], comforting [*paramuthoumenoi*] and urging you to live lives worthy of God" (1 Thess. 2:11–12). This has led scholars like Abraham Malherbe and Anthony Thiselton to connect *paramuthian* "with the attitude and activity of pastoral care."[18] Malherbe draws on Greco-Roman writers (Seneca, Plutarch, and Philodemus) who argued that exhortation (*paraklēsis*) should be coupled with sensitivity to the personal circumstances of the audience.[19] Paul likewise exhorts and comforts the churches he's writing to. This balance "gives his pastoral preaching and pastoral care a distinctive touch not exhausted by either term alone."[20] Like Paul, the prophets who prophesy (1 Cor. 14:3) are also called to embody this holistic approach toward the church.

There's a danger in slinging around all these parallels and making too much of how each word is used in other contexts. These three words are not used exclusively to describe the ministry work of leaders, and if only one of them were used in connection to prophecy, it might not tell us very much. But the combination of these three words—especially *paraklēsis*—implies that the function of prophecy is similar to teaching.

---

18 A. J. Malherbe, "'Pastoral Care' in the Thessalonian Church," *New Testament Studies* 36, no. 3 (1990): 375–91; Thiselton, *Corinthians*, 1089–90.

19 Seneca, *De Ira* 1.6.3; *Epistulae* 64.7–10, 82.23; Plutarch, *Quomodo adulator* 67B, 73A–C, 74D–E; Philodemus, *Peri parrēsias* 38.

20 Thiselton, *Corinthians*, 1089–90.

This doesn't mean prophecy is the same thing as teaching; the two are clearly distinct gifts. But it does suggest a functional overlap between the two.[21]

More evidence for this functional overlap comes later in 1 Corinthians 14, where Paul connects prophecy with instruction:

> I thank God that I speak in tongues more than all of you. But in the church I would rather speak five intelligible words to *instruct* [*katēchēsō*] others than ten thousand words in a tongue. (vv. 18–19)

The word *prophecy* doesn't appear in these verses, but it's almost certain that Paul has prophecy in mind. These verses occur in a context where Paul is contrasting prophecy with tongues. Prophecy is the greater gift, he says, since people can understand it, while tongues are unintelligible without an interpreter. When Paul contrasts unintelligible words (tongues) with intelligible words, then, the latter almost certainly refers to prophecy.[22] If this is the case, prophecy includes some kind of "instruction" (*katēchēsō*)—one of the words for

21 Chris Knights, "Prophecy and Preaching: Does What Paul Calls 'Prophecy' in 1 Corinthians 14 Include What We Would Today Call 'Preaching'?," *Expository Times* 130, no. 2 (2018): 77. John Calvin goes even further: Those with the gift of prophecy were "outstanding interpreters of Scripture" and "men endowed with extraordinary wisdom and aptitude for grasping what the immediate need of the Church is and speaking the right word to meet it." *The First Epistle of Paul the Apostle to the Corinthians*, Calvin's New Testament Commentaries 9 (Eerdmans, 1996), 271.

22 See Knights, "Prophecy and Preaching," 75–76. Richard Hays believes that "'prophecy' should be read throughout chapter 14 as synecdoche for all forms of intelligible speech gifts that edify the church." *First Corinthians*, Interpretation (Westminster John Knox, 2011), 237.

"teaching" in the New Testament.[23] Despite some scholars' claims that New Testament prophecy is "not intelligent Christian teaching,"[24] the text suggests that intelligent Christian teaching is an important part of prophecy.

Paul also says that people will "learn" from prophecy, suggesting that prophecy can include a teaching component:

> For you can all prophesy one by one, so that everyone may learn [*manthanōsin*] and everyone may be encouraged [*parakalōntai*]. (1 Cor. 14:31 CSB)

Wayne Grudem argues that this doesn't mean prophecy includes teaching: "People can 'learn' from many things in addition to formal Bible teaching or doctrinal instruction."[25] I agree with Grudem about this—teaching isn't the only means by which people can learn. But the spiritual "learning" in this verse is directly connected to the contents of what is prophesied. It seems unlikely that the "learning" that believers gain from prophecy categorically excludes doctrinal instruction,

---

23 The verb *katēcheō* occurs eight times in the New Testament: four times by Paul (Rom. 2:18; 1 Cor. 14:9; two times in Gal. 6:6) and four times in Luke–Acts (Luke 1:4; Acts 18:25; 21:21, 24). The word has two senses: (1) a weaker sense meaning "to inform" or "to recount" and (2) a stronger sense meaning "'to instruct' or 'to teach' someone the basics of a subject or skill" (Smith, *Pauline Communities*, 78). Paul's three other uses outside 1 Corinthians 14 clearly have this latter sense, where the word refers to those "instructed by the law" (Rom. 2:18) and "instruction in the word" (Gal. 6:6). Luke uses *katēcheō* in parallel with *didaskō* ("to teach") in Acts 18:25. Claire Smith argues that "the context" of 1 Corinthians 14 "demands it too has a didactic meaning" (*Pauline Communities*, 79). See also H. W. Beyer, who says that Paul uses *katēcheō* "as a technical term for Christian instruction." "*Katēcheō*" in *Theological Dictionary of the New Testament*, ed. Gerhard Kittel and Gerhard Friedrich, vol. 3 (Eerdmans, 1964), 638–39.

24 Grudem, *Gift of Prophecy*, 115.

25 Grudem, *Gift of Prophecy*, 129.

especially in light of how Paul describes prophecy in 1 Corinthians 14:3 and 14:18–19. Certainly, we can learn doctrine from the prophecy that John wrote down while exiled in Patmos.

A second piece of evidence for New Testament prophecy being akin to teaching and preaching is the fact that prophecy can include interpretation of Scripture.[26]

In Luke 1, for instance, Zechariah "was filled with the Holy Spirit and prophesied" (v. 67), and his prophecy is saturated with over two dozen echoes and allusions to scriptural passages testifying to the coming Messiah (vv. 68–79).[27] God's revelation to Zechariah was enmeshed with scriptural interpretation. I think Richard Blaylock makes a false dichotomy when he says, "Zechariah was demonstrating that his prophetic word ... was the fulfillment of God's promises of old; it does not seem to be the case that the prophecy itself consisted of the interpretation of the OT."[28] Can't it be both? I don't think any first-century reader would have thought, *Zechariah's prophecy is about the fulfillment of God's promise and therefore not an interpretation of God's Word.*

The book of Revelation is the clearest example of a prophecy incorporating scriptural interpretation. Revelation is called a "prophecy" (Rev. 1:3; 22:7, 10, 18–19) and is the most Scripture-saturated book in the New Testament. Various studies have identified up to one thousand references to the Old Testament in just twenty-two chapters. If you squeeze

---

26 Earle Ellis has argued for this point in his book *Prophecy and Hermeneutic*.

27 See J. B. Green, *The Gospel of Luke*, New International Commentary on the New Testament (Eerdmans, 1997), 115–20.

28 Blaylock, "Towards a Definition," 42n5.

the book, Scripture pours out.[29] This doesn't fit Wayne Grudem's more narrow understanding of prophecy as "subordinate to the authoritative *teaching* of Scripture"[30] or something that "should not be considered divine obligations."[31] The Scripture-packed prophecy of Revelation comes with a severe threat to anyone who adds or takes away from its words (22:18–19).

Not every prophecy contains scriptural interpretation, and not everyone who teaches Scripture is prophesying. But prophecy sometimes includes scriptural interpretation; the two should not be categorically distinguished.

Again, New Testament prophecy seems to have a functional overlap with teaching.[32] It doesn't appear limited to "the speaking of merely human words to report something God brings to mind,"[33] as Wayne Grudem suggests, nor does it seem to be true that in the early church "*teaching* based on the written Word of God had far greater authority than occasional prophecies which the speaker *thought* were from God."[34] Distinctions like these don't capture the varied descriptions of New Testament prophecy, which included exhortation, instruction, and scriptural interpretation.

This brings us to our second question about the nature of New Testament prophets and prophecy.

---

29 See G. K. Beale, *The Book of Revelation*, New International Greek Testament Commentary (Eerdmans, 1998), 76–99; cf. 77n16 for various studies that document the number of Old Testament references.

30 Grudem, *Gift of Prophecy*, 122 (italics in original).

31 Grudem, *Gift of Prophecy*, 141.

32 This may be why Luke mentions five leaders in Antioch who were "prophets and teachers" (Acts 13:1) but doesn't tell us which ones were "prophets" and which ones were "teachers." Perhaps all five were prophet-teachers.

33 Grudem, *Gift of Prophecy*, 141.

34 Grudem, *Gift of Prophecy*, 122 (italics in original).

## Did Prophets and Prophecy Play Authoritative Roles in the Early Church?

I think it's hard to deny that New Testament prophets and prophecy carried authority in the early church. The book of Revelation, again, is an example of this. Revelation is certainly unique among New Testament prophecies, since it was written down and accepted into the canon as Scripture. But according to its author, John, the authority of Revelation is derived from the fact that it is a prophecy, not from the fact that it was written and later recognized as Scripture. David Aune, in fact, notes that the letters to churches in Revelation 2–3 "not only contain fragments of prophetic speech ... but also represent a typical form of prophetic speech."[35] Aune goes so far as to say that John is "*representative*" of "*an early Christian prophet*."[36]

Wayne Grudem argues against using Revelation to help define *prophecy*, since this prophecy was written by an apostle. The book of Revelation, Grudem says,

> is not a prophecy given by some ordinary Christian but rather by a very prominent apostle of Jesus Christ. Moreover, this was not a prophecy given in the worship service of some local group of Christians, but to John in exile on the island of Patmos for the benefit of seven churches in Asia Minor (Rev. 1:4), and ultimately for the benefit of the entire Christian church.[37]

35 See Aune, *Prophecy*, 275.
36 Aune, *Prophecy*, 207 (italics in original).
37 Grudem, *Gift of Prophecy*, 44.

I see two problems with this argument. First, it's questionable whether the author is John *the apostle*. The author never calls himself an apostle, and many scholars believe the John who wrote Revelation is not the apostle John. Second, even if the author was John the apostle, he never appeals to his apostleship as the source of the book's authority. Rather, he explicitly appeals to the fact that he received a revelation from Christ and wrote it down *as a prophecy*.[38] John simply refers to himself as a "servant," "brother," and "companion" of the seven churches he's writing to (Rev. 1:1, 9). Whatever status the author held in the church, he never refers to it as the source of the book's authority. John's prophecy has authority not because of who speaks or writes it but because of what it is: a true prophecy.

In addition to the evidence of Revelation, Paul mentions "prophets" and "apostles" in tandem throughout the book of Ephesians. Apostles were leaders and authority figures in the early church, and Paul describes them right alongside prophets as forming the foundation of the church:

> So then you are no longer foreigners and strangers, but fellow citizens with the saints, and members of God's household, built on the foundation of the *apostles and prophets*, with Christ Jesus Himself as the cornerstone. (Eph. 2:19–20 HCSB)

38 David Aune notes that "John intended the Apocalypse to be read aloud in a service of worship (1:3; 22:18), and it is very possible that this public reading would replace a prophetic address to the congregations by one or more of their local prophets" (*Prophecy*, 275).

> This [mystery of the Messiah] was not made known to people in other generations as it is now revealed to His holy *apostles and prophets* by the Spirit. (Eph. 3:5 HCSB)

> And He personally gave some to be *apostles*, some *prophets*, some evangelists, some pastors and teachers. (Eph. 4:11 HCSB)

I think it's difficult to say, as Grudem does, that prophets did not assume "functions of leadership or governing authority" in the church.[39] The apostles certainly did. And Paul lists apostles and prophets together as having foundational significance for building the church.[40] In fact, the Greek construction in Ephesians 2:20 and 3:5 suggests a close relationship between the apostles and prophets. (The definite article joins "apostles" and "prophets," *ton apostolōn kai prophētōn*, in 2:20.) Grudem notes this connection, but he uses it to erase prophets from these passages altogether. He says Paul is not referring to two different groups (apostles *and* prophets) but to one group: apostles who are also prophets, or apostle-prophets. According to Grudem, then, Ephesians doesn't mention prophets prior to 4:11.

Grudem has been reading Greek longer than I've been speaking English, so I was tempted to take his word for it. But when I cracked open several Greek grammars to see if they agreed with Grudem, I found

39 Grudem, *Gift of Prophecy*, 123.
40 The word order ("apostles" coming before "prophets") makes it very unlikely that Paul was thinking of Old Testament prophets here. And Ephesians 3:5, which refers to the same group of "apostles and prophets," clearly means New Testament prophets. See P. T. O'Brien, *The Letter to the Ephesians*, Pillar New Testament Commentary (Eerdmans, 1999), 214–15.

that they didn't. The Greek construction (*ton apostolōn kai prophētōn*) almost certainly refers to two different groups—apostles and prophets—not to apostle-prophets. Renowned Greek grammarian Dan Wallace (who wrote his PhD dissertation on this very Greek construction) makes this argument thoroughly, and every single commentary I've checked disagrees with Grudem and agrees with Wallace.[41] Clinton Arnold even says that he's "not aware of any commentators who have accepted" Grudem's view.[42]

Scholarly consensus aside, it's beyond dispute (and Grudem agrees) that Paul's third mention of apostles and prophets in Ephesians 4:11 certainly refers to two different groups of people—apostles and prophets. This makes it unlikely that Paul had one group in mind in 2:20 and 3:5 (apostle-prophets) but not in 4:11 (apostles and prophets).

In other words, Paul almost certainly refers to apostles and prophets as both playing a fundamental role in building up the church, and he doesn't bother to say that one group plays a more prominent role than the other.[43]

On another occasion, Paul lists prophets before teachers in a way that suggests prophets held some kind of prominence over teachers in the early church:

> God has placed in the church first of all apostles, second prophets, third teachers, then miracles, then gifts

---

41 I looked at eight different commentaries, including several by complementarians. See e.g., Clinton E. Arnold, *Ephesians*, Zondervan Exegetical Commentary on the New Testament 10 (Zondervan, 2010), 170; O'Brien, *Ephesians*, 214.

42 Arnold, *Ephesians*, 169n73.

43 Ellis, *Prophecy*, 141.

> of healing, of helping, of guidance, and of different kinds of tongues. (1 Cor. 12:28)

Paul lists the first three in numerical order ("first ... apostles, second prophets, third teachers"), then loses the numbers and simply says "then ... then ..." to imply that these latter gifts do not bear the same significance as the first three. Paul doesn't explain his rationale for ascribing numbers to the first three, but the order can't be chronological. At least some New Testament prophets (like John the Baptist and Anna) came before the apostles and teachers Paul has in mind.

Many scholars believe the order reflects the unique importance that apostles, prophets, and teachers played in the building of the church.[44] David Garland, for instance, says the gifts "appear to be ranked in order of importance.... Apostles, prophets, and teachers, with their threefold ministry of the word, are essential for both the founding and the continued edification of the church."[45] David Aune agrees that "prophets occupied a special role in the leadership of the Christian community."[46] At the very least, this passage does not suggest that teachers—who are ranked after prophets—are more authoritative than prophets in the early church.[47] It's unlikely that teachers assumed

44 This seems to be the view of most scholars (see the discussion in Thiselton, *Corinthians*, 1013–15). Gordon Fee argues that Paul "certainly intends the first three to be ranked" but wrestles with whether such ranking has to do with authority, importance, or something else. He concludes: "It is not so much that one is more important than the other, nor that this is necessarily their order of authority, but that one has precedence over the other in the founding and building up of the local assembly." *The First Epistle to the Corinthians*, New International Commentary on the New Testament (Eerdmans, 2014), 685–86.

45 David Garland, *1 Corinthians*, Baker Exegetical Commentary on the New Testament (Baker, 2003), 598.

46 Aune, *Prophecy*, 201.

47 In Acts 15, Luke describes Judas and Silas as both "prophets" (Acts 15:32) and "leaders" (*hēgoumenoi*, Acts 15:22) a few verses apart.

"functions of leadership or governing authority"[48] while prophets did not or that teaching had "far greater authority" than prophecy. The text does not support this logic.

But what about prophecies being weighed and tested by the rest of the church (1 Cor. 14:29–32; 1 Thess. 5:20–21)? Doesn't this mean prophecy isn't authoritative? I think this is possible. But Paul could be referring to certain kinds of prophecy and not every kind. After all, some prophecies don't appear to need testing, like Anna's (Luke 2:36–38), Agabus's (Acts 21:10–14), or the book of Revelation. Plus, I'm not sure that testing prophecies necessarily means they're not authoritative. The Bereans tested Paul's authoritative teaching as well, and Luke praises them for it (Acts 17:11). Shouldn't we do the same today with teachers and preachers who exposit the text of Scripture?

In short, I think there's good evidence that prophets carried authority in the early church. This doesn't mean prophets played the same role as apostles or teachers, nor does it mean that every prophet or prophecy was equally authoritative. But the New Testament never makes a distinction between male prophets who carried authority and female ones who did not.

## Conclusion

The New Testament shows us a broad spectrum of roles and functions filled by prophets and their prophetic words in the early church. New Testament prophecy could include (1) some notion of leadership and authority and (2) some didactic and exhortative elements that

48 Grudem, *Gift of Prophecy*, 123.

functionally overlapped with teaching. The New Testament also makes it clear that women were prophets and prophesied, and it doesn't say that women were only gifted with certain non-authoritative kinds of prophecy. We see some women occupying ongoing prophetic roles (Luke 2:36–38; Acts 21:9), while other women might have prophesied more sporadically (1 Cor. 11:5). I don't see any reason to say that women prophets could not have been among the "prophets" who "equip his people for works of service" (Eph. 4:11–12) or among those who exhorted other believers when they prophesied (1 Cor. 14:3). Thus, the presence of female prophets in the New Testament provides evidence for women engaging in ministries that carried a functional overlap with teaching—what we might call "preaching" in church today.

Could it be that women prophets were acting under the authority of male-only elders, as soft complementarians believe? I guess this is possible. But I don't see anything in the nature of early church prophecy itself that suggests this. Perhaps it's implied from other New Testament passages like 1 Corinthians 11 and 1 Timothy 2–3. I'm excited to dig into these passages to see if this is the case.

## Chapter 7

# MARRIAGE, HEADSHIP, AND SUBMISSION (EPH. 5:21–33)

Ephesians 5:21–33 might seem off topic for this book; it's about marriage, not church leadership. But from a New Testament perspective, the lines between church and home are sometimes blurry, as we saw in chapter 4. Paul's vision for male-female relations in the home could tell us something about their roles in the church. Plus, the only other time Paul says that "man is the head of the woman" (1 Cor. 11:3 CSB) *is* in the context of a church gathering. Understanding "male headship" in Ephesians 5 will give us a running start to tackle 1 Corinthians 11 in the next chapter.

In this chapter, we'll examine three aspects of Ephesians 5:21–33: (1) the meaning of "head" (*kephalē*), (2) the sense of "submission," and (3) the significance of the unity between "head" and "body." But before we dive in, we need to situate Paul's words in the context of Greco-Roman household codes.

## Household Codes in the Greco-Roman World

Scholars use the phrase "household code" to describe a common literary trope in the ancient world. This trope is reflected in several New Testament passages—Ephesians 5:21–6:9 being the longest.[1] Paul and his audience are no doubt aware of other household codes, and Paul pens Ephesians 5 with these in mind. Understanding how the Greco-Roman world viewed household codes will shed interpretive light on what Paul is doing in Ephesians 5.

The famed Greek philosopher Aristotle is the main catalyst for the household code.[2] Here's how he launches the conversation, four hundred years before Paul:

> The primary and smallest parts of the household are master and slave, husband and wife, father and children; we ought therefore to examine the proper constitution and character of each of these three relationships, I mean that of mastership [*despotikē*], that of marriage and thirdly the progenitive relationship.[3]

---

1 See also Colossians 3:18–4:1; 1 Peter 3:1–7; cf. Titus 2:1–7 and possibly 1 Timothy 2:9–15. For surveys of household codes in the Greco-Roman world, see David Balch, *Let Wives Be Submissive: The Domestic Code in 1 Peter* (Society of Biblical Literature, 1981), 25–80; David Verner, *The Household of God: The Social World of the Pastoral Epistles* (Society of Biblical Literature, 1983), 27–81; James Hering, *The Colossian and Ephesian Haustafeln in Theological Context: An Analysis of Their Origins, Relationships, and Message* (Peter Lang, 2007), 203–62.

2 David Balch notes the scholarly consensus on seeing Aristotle's work as the most significant catalyst for this genre. "Household Codes," in *Greco-Roman Literature and the New Testament: Selected Forms and Genres*, ed. David Aune (Scholars Press, 1988), 35. Plato, Aristotle's teacher, discussed the household similarly to Aristotle. While Plato doesn't specifically pair husband and wife, father and children, and master and slave, he does emphasize that the husband is the ruler and everyone else the ruled (Laws 3.690A–D).

3 *Politics* 1.1253b. All translations of Aristotle are from *Aristotle in 23 Volumes*, vol. 21, trans. H. Rackham (Harvard University Press, 1944).

Notice the three relationship types: husband/wife, father/children, and master/slave. These are central to Aristotle's household codes and occur in Ephesians 5 as well. For Aristotle, the three pairs reflect the natural order of things—hierarchies woven into the very fabric of family life. There are, he says,

> by nature various classes of rulers and ruled. For the free rules the slave, the male the female, and the man the child in a different way. And all possess the various parts of the soul, but possess them in different ways; for the slave has not got the deliberative part at all, and the female has it, but without full authority, while the child has it, but in an undeveloped form.[4]

Aristotle's attitude toward the three pairs of relationships (husband/wife, father/children, master/slave) influenced other writers and shaped the Greco-Roman view of the family as a whole. For instance, Arius Didymus (d. 10 BC) wrote an "epitome of Aristotle's ethical, political and domestic philosophy" that became widely influential in the first century.[5] In it, he draws on Aristotle to discuss the proper way to run a household: "The man has the rule [*archē*] of this house by nature. For the deliberative faculty in a woman is inferior, in children it does not yet exist, and it is completely foreign to slaves." The father is to control the house and everything and everyone in it, since he is "the master" (*to despotikon*).[6] Didymus had a massive influence

---

4 *Politics* 1.1260a.

5 Balch, *Wives*, 40.

6 *Epitome* 2.149; cf. *Epitome* 2.148; Aristotle, *Politics* 1.1259a, 1253b.

on first-century Greco-Roman culture. He was a personal friend and mentor to Caesar Augustus, and he later became imperial procurator in Sicily. His instructions on household management became standard first-century fare.

Several other writers followed in the footsteps of Aristotle and Didymus. They saw husbands as superior rulers, and everyone else—including wives—as inferior people to be ruled.[7] Life on the ground, however, was more complicated. As we saw in chapter 4, wives often held more authority and influence than what's sometimes conveyed in the literature. But one thing is clear: The literary trope of the household code propped up the husband as the supreme ruler in the house, even if these codes were more "prescriptive and not descriptive" of real life.[8]

Paul's household code in Ephesians 5:21–6:9 bears some obvious similarities to these Greco-Roman codes. He discusses the same three pairs of relationships (husbands/wives, fathers/children, and masters/slaves) that we find in Aristotle and Didymus. Paul's language of submission and obedience also resembles aspects of the Greco-Roman codes: Wives are to submit to their husbands, children are to obey their parents, and slaves are to obey their masters. He's clearly aware of, and is interacting with, this common literary trope.

But these similarities only draw more attention to the startling differences between Paul's code and the others.

---

7 See Philo, *Hypothetica* 7.3; Josephus, *Against Apion* 2.199; Dionysius of Halicarnassus, *Rom. Ant.* 2.24.2. Some first-century Stoic writers softened this argument by encouraging mutuality and not ascribing an inferior ontology to women; see Musonius, XIIIA 11–13, 17–23. But these writers still characterized husband-wife relationships through the paradigm of ruler (husband) and ruled (wife); see Musonius, XII 40–45; Plutarch, *Advice to Bride and Groom* 33; *Moralia* 142E.

8 Carolyn Osiek and Margaret MacDonald, *A Woman's Place: House Churches in Earliest Christianity* (Fortress Press, 2006), 19.

First, Paul's treatment of the master/slave relationship is unparalleled. He doesn't tell masters to rule over their slaves. Instead, he directly addresses slaves *before* addressing masters, thus ascribing agency to slaves—something ancient authors never did. He then calls God the "master" of them both, essentially saying that even human "masters" are slaves.[9] He goes so far as to command masters to "treat your slaves *in the same way*" (literally "do the same things to them," *ta auta poieite pros autous*) as he has just instructed the slaves to treat their masters (6:9). While Paul does not dismantle the system of slavery, he challenges the social hierarchy inherent in the system itself.

Second, Paul avoids the common terms other codes used to describe husbands, such as "ruler" (*archōn*), "master" (*despotēs*), and "lord" (*kurios*).[10] Instead, he uses the metaphor of an interconnected human body, calling the husband "head" and the wife "body." While "head" might convey some sense of authority, the rest of the passage focuses on unity and interdependence, as we'll see below.

Third, while Paul tells wives to "submit" to their husbands, he doesn't tell husbands to subjugate their wives or to demand that their wives obey them.[11] It's actually quite rare for Greco-Roman codes to use the language of "submission" when referring to the wife's relationship to her husband. If they addressed the wives at all, they would tell them simply to "obey" their husbands. More often, they wouldn't

9 While some writers advocated for a more humane treatment of slaves (Philo, *Spec. Leg.* 2.137; cf. *Spec. Leg.* 2.67, 69, 83–84), Paul's treatment appears to be more radical (see Hering, *Colossian and Ephesian*, 240–45).

10 See Kelvin Mutter, "Ephesians 5:21–33 as Christian Alternative Discourse," *Trinity Journal* 39 (2018): 3–20.

11 "In general, the way *hupotassō* is employed in the New Testament within the context of a household relationship suggests a *voluntary* act, that is, yielding oneself to another." Karl Armstrong, "The Meaning of *Hupotassō* in Ephesians 5.21–33: A Linguistic Approach," *Journal of Greco-Roman Christianity and Judaism* 13 (2017): 157.

bother speaking directly to the wives; they'd just tell husbands to rule over them. It's striking that Paul talks to wives before addressing husbands and calls them to submission rather than obedience. (We'll talk more about submission later in this chapter.)

Fourth, there's no hint of ontological inferiority among women, children, or slaves in Paul's code. Even if we take wives' "submission" to be one-directional (wives submitting to husbands and not vice versa), Paul's rationale for this submission has nothing to do with women being lesser humans than men like we see in Aristotle.

Fifth, Paul's description of the husband's self-giving love for his wife is extraordinary. Some other Greco-Roman writers do talk about mutual love between husband and wife, but such love existed within a relationship where husbands ruled over their wives. I'm aware of no other writer who commands a husband to give up himself for the sake of his wife and to love her as he does his own body (5:25, 28). Paul even connects the husband's self-giving love to the work of a domestic slave: washing, bathing, and doing the laundry (5:26–27).[12] Paul flips the script: Husbands must lay down their lives for their wives, overturning the one-way hierarchy of other household codes. While Aristotle crowns the husband, Paul calls him to the cross.

In sum, Paul adopts the rhetorical husk of other household codes, but he fills it with subversive content. This dynamic should shape our interpretation of Paul's whole gospel-centered view of marriage, including his language of headship and submission.

---

12 See Cynthia Long Westfall, "'This Is a Great Metaphor!': Reciprocity in the Ephesians Household Code," in *Early Christianity in Its Hellenistic Context, vol. 1, Christian Origins and Greco-Roman Culture: Social and Literary Contexts for the New Testament*, ed. Stanley E. Porter and Andrew W. Pitts (Brill, 2013), 572; Mutter, "Ephesians 5:21–33," 17.

## "The Husband Is the Head [*Kephalē*] of the Wife" (5:23)

Paul begins his code by telling wives to submit to their husbands, since "the husband is the head [*kephalē*] of the wife":

> Submitting [*hupotassomenoi*] to one another out of reverence for Christ. Wives, [submit] to your own husbands as you do to the Lord. For the husband is the head [*kephalē*] of the wife as Christ is the head [*kephalē*] of the church, he himself [being] the Savior of the body. But, as the church submits [*hupotassetai*] to Christ, so also wives [submit] to their husbands in everything. (5:21–24, my modification of the NIV)

The Greek word *kephalē* ("head") is one of the most disputed words in the New Testament. The debate centers on whether *kephalē* conveys some sense of authority or whether it means something like "source" or "prominence" without any sense of authority. Scholars have combed through every nonliteral use of *kephalē* and reached different conclusions. Since I didn't want to just trust one scholar over another, I spent several months examining every relevant use of *kephalē* in Greek literature while interacting with scholars who debate the term. I summed up my findings in a lengthy article that I posted on my website, so if you want to verify my research, you can access it for free.[13] I concluded that *kephalē* almost always conveys some sense

13 Preston Sprinkle, "The Meaning of *Kephalē* ('Head') in Greek Literature and in Paul's Letters," available at theologyintheraw.com/womeninleadership.

of authority, especially when it refers to a person's relationship with other people.

One telling example of this pattern comes from the Septuagint version of Judges 11, where the elders of Gilead promise Jephthah that if he fights with them, they will make him "*head* [*eis kephalēn*] over all of us who live in Gilead" (v. 8). Jephthah agrees to fight, so the people make him "head and leader [*eis kephalēn eis hēgoumenon*] over them" (v. 11 ESV).[14] The entire context of Judges 10–12 highlights Jephthah becoming a military leader over the people of Gilead in their battle against the Ammonites.[15]

In Greek literature outside the Bible, we see several examples of military leaders being called the "head" while their troops are described as a body:

> Iphicrates used to resemble an army marshalled for action to the human body. The phalanx he called the breast, the light armed troops the hands, the cavalry the feet, and the general *the head*.[16]

> But after Vindex had openly declared war, he wrote to Galba inviting him to assume the imperial power, and thus to serve what was a vigorous body in need of a *head*.[17]

---

14 Codex Alexandrinus has *eis kephalēn* in Judges 11:8, while Vaticanus has *eis archonta*. In Judges 11:11, both Codex Alexandrinus and Vaticanus have *eis kephalēn*.

15 Cf. Judges 11:6: "Come and be our leader [*eis archēgon*], that we may fight against the Ammonites" (ESV).

16 Polyaenus, *Stratagems of War* 3.9.2 (second century AD), cited in Michelle Lee-Barnewall, "Turning *Kephalē* on Its Head: The Rhetoric of Reversal in Ephesians 5:21–33," in *Early Christianity in Its Hellenistic Context, vol. 1, Christian Origins and Greco-Roman Culture: Social and Literary Contexts for the New Testament*, ed. Stanley E. Porter and Andrew W. Pitts (Brill, 2013), 606.

17 Plutarch, *Galba* 4.3.

> The light-armed troops are like the hands, the Calvary like the feet, the line of men-at-arms itself like chest and breastplate, and the general is like the *head*.[18]

Paul himself uses *kephalē* to convey authority in several other places, such as Ephesians 1, where "God placed all things under" Christ's feet and "appointed him to be head (*kephalēn*) over everything" (vv. 19–23).

If *kephalē* almost always conveys some sense of "authority," then this is its most likely meaning in Ephesians 5:23, especially since *kephalē* here is surrounded by language of "submission." However, the specific nature of that authority still needs to be defined by the context. And in this context, Paul narrowly defines the kind of authority in view through the lens of self-giving love.

Before we continue, a quick word about how metaphors work. When words like *kephalē* are used metaphorically, they're typically meant to convey a specific meaning based on context. Most metaphors have more than one possible meaning, but these meanings don't all apply in every context.

For instance, the phrase "he's such a pig" can mean a lot of different things. If I see a guy shoving food down his gullet and say, "He's such a pig," I probably mean something like, "He's eating sloppily or he's eating way too much" (or possibly both). I probably don't mean that he's on all fours scarfing up rotten vegetables from a feeding trough, or anything else that might be associated with pigness. But in a different context, I might say, "That guy is such a pig! He's with

18 Plutarch, *Pelopidas* 2.1.3.

a different girl every week and treats them all like trash!" Here, the pig metaphor clearly has nothing to do with eating—just like, in the previous example, the metaphor clearly has nothing to do with how a guy treats women. Both meanings are valid interpretations of the statement "He's such a pig," but the context tells us which sense of pigness is being communicated in each case.

The same goes for all metaphors, including *kephalē*. When ancient writers use *kephalē* in a nonliteral way, it almost always conveys some sense of authority, and I think this is what Paul has in mind here. However, the context of Ephesians 5 tells exactly what kind of authority Paul has in view when he compares a husband's role as "head" to Christ's role as "Savior" and then spells out in detail what Christ as Savior looks like: self-sacrificial love and service.

Paul isn't saying that the husband has categorical authority over his wife in every way that Christ has authority over the church. He's also not saying, for example, that a husband, as "savior," does everything that Christ does as Savior—atoning for his wife's sins through his sacrificial death on a Roman cross and such.[19] "Savior" has a more particular meaning here. It refers to Christ's self-giving sacrificial love, which is spelled out in 5:25. Likewise, Paul refracts the image of the husband as "head" through *this* specific aspect of Christ's work as Savior; namely, he "gave himself up for her" (5:25).

---

19 This explains why Paul follows his statement about Christ being "the Savior" of "his body" (5:23) with the strong adversative *alla* in 5:24: "But (*alla*) as the church is subject to Christ, so also the wives *ought to be* to their husbands in everything" (NASB). As several commentators note, Paul uses *alla* in 5:24 to ensure that his audience doesn't map everything about Christ's saving work onto the husband's relationship to his wife (e.g. Lynn Cohick, *The Letter to the Ephesians*, New International Commentary on the New Testament [Eerdmans, 2020], 358).

So, *kephalē* conveys authority as it often does. But Paul tells us exactly what authority looks like in the Christian household: The husband's headship *is* his self-giving love and service to his wife.[20]

Michelle Lee-Barnewall wrote a fascinating article on Ephesians 5, which offers what I think is the most compelling treatment of *kephalē* in this passage.[21] She argues that "while *kephalē* does have definite connotations of 'authority,' the primary significance of its use is the way in which Paul reverses the cultural expectations of the 'head' according to the radical new values of the Christian community."[22] In other words, the reason Paul brings up authority is to overturn what his audience is used to hearing about authority.

When ancient writers used "head" in head-body metaphors, they were referring to a person of prominence and authority,[23] and they assumed that "a primary concern was to protect the head at all costs."[24] Paul initially seems to use the head-body metaphor in a similar way, leading his audience to "expect Paul to instruct the wife, the body, to be willing to sacrifice for the sake of the husband, the head."[25] But Paul argues the exact opposite in 5:25–33. "When Paul asks husbands, and not wives, to love and sacrifice, this reversal would be shocking in light of traditional status conventions because he tells the most honored part,

---

20 See Gregory Dawes, *The Body in Question: Metaphor and Meaning in the Interpretation of Ephesians 5:21–33* (Brill, 1998), 137.

21 See Lee-Barnewall, "Turning *Kephalē*," 599–614. For similar approaches, see Lynn H. Cohick, "Tyranny, Authority, Service: Leadership and Headship in the New Testament," *Ex Auditu* 28 (2012): 74–90; Mutter, "Ephesians 5:21–33," 3–20.

22 Lee-Barnewall, "Turning *Kephalē*," 599.

23 The emperor Nero, for instance, was called the "head" and Rome his "body" (Seneca, *Clem.* 1.4.3). Galba is also called a "head" over "a vigorous body ... meaning the Gallic provinces" over which he was invited "to assume imperial power" (Plutarch, *Galb.* 4.3, cited in Lee-Barnewall, "Turning *Kephalē*," 603).

24 Lee-Barnewall, "Turning *Kephalē*," 606.

25 Lee-Barnewall, "Turning *Kephalē*," 608.

the head, to perform the duties of the less honored member." Thus, Paul affirms that the husband is the "head," but he washes the meaning of headship with the gospel. Or as Lee-Barnewall puts it: Paul "turns *kephalē* on its head."[26]

The New Testament often promotes such kingdom reversals, as we've seen: The last will be first, the humble are exalted, and leaders serve as slaves.[27] Paul's rhetorical strategy in Ephesians 5:21–33 fits this pattern. "The passage works by seeing both how *kephalē* functions as a metaphor connoting authority and leadership as understood in the ancient Mediterranean culture and how Paul radically reorients it through his application of Christian values. It is the unexpectedness of this reversal that ultimately gives the metaphor its power in this passage."[28]

## *Kephalē* as Source?

Some scholars, however, argue that *kephalē* means "source" here in Ephesians 5:23 and that it does not convey any sense of authority.[29] Linda Belleville, for instance, believes that Paul "most certainly" uses *kephalē* to mean source.[30] This meaning "goes back to the creation of male and female," where the woman was created out of man, and Paul's allusion to this creation story (Gen. 2:21–24) in Ephesians 5:23 "is unmistakable."[31]

---

26 Lee-Barnewall, "Turning *Kephalē*," 610.

27 Matthew 19:30; 20:16; 23:12; Mark 10:31; Luke 1:51–52; 13:30; 14:11; 18:14; John 13:1–13; Philippians 2:5–11.

28 Lee-Barnewall, "Turning *Kephalē*," 613; see also David M. Park "The Structure of Authority in Marriage: An Examination of *Hupotassō* and *Kephale* in Ephesians 5:21–33," *Evangelical Quarterly* 59, no. 2 (1987): 122.

29 See e.g., Linda Belleville, "An Egalitarian Perspective," in *Two Views on Women in Ministry*, rev. ed., ed. James Beck (Zondervan, 2005), 100; Philip Payne, *The Bible vs. Biblical Womanhood: How God's Word Consistently Affirms Gender Equality* (Zondervan, 2023), 115.

30 Belleville, "An Egalitarian Perspective," 100.

31 Belleville, "An Egalitarian Perspective," 101.

Philip Payne also argues that *kephalē* means "source" in Ephesians 5:23, but he highlights the wife's social dependence upon the man in the first-century context: "The husband, in that culture, was the source of life for his wife since he provided all that was essential for her to live."[32] "Wives depended on their husbands as the source of food, clothing, shelter, the physical source of her children, and her emotional source of love."[33] Thus, "Christ is the source of life, love, and nourishment for the church as husbands should be for their wives."[34]

We should distinguish, then, between two different senses of "source." One is ontological and another social.[35] The ontological sense is derived from Eve's creation from the side of Adam, while the social sense looks to the ancient cultural context, where wives were dependent on husbands for their livelihood.

I don't find much credibility in the ontological view here. This could capture the sense of *kephalē* in 1 Corinthians 11:3 (in light of vv. 8–9), but it doesn't fit what Paul is doing in Ephesians 5. Even though Paul cites Genesis 2:24 in Ephesians 5:31, this part of the creation story speaks of the marital unity of Adam and Eve, not Eve's creation from the side of Adam. I think it's unlikely that Paul is saying something like, *Wives, submit to your husbands because, well of course, Eve was created out of Adam's side.*

Payne's understanding of source—the wife's social dependence on her husband—is more plausible, but I still don't find it as compelling as the view I've offered in the previous section.

---

32 Payne, *Bible vs. Biblical Womanhood*, 115.

33 Philip B. Payne, *Man and Woman, One in Christ: An Exegetical and Theological Study of Paul's Letters* (Zondervan, 2009), 288.

34 Payne, *Man and Woman*, 290.

35 Cynthia Long Westfall argues that both (ontological and social) senses are at work in Ephesians 5:23. *Paul and Gender: Reclaiming the Apostle's Vision for Men and Women in Christ* (Baker, 2016), 100–101.

First, *kephalē* almost always conveys a sense of authority when it's used as a metaphor in Greek literature. Payne disagrees with this, and I know I'll get an email from him (again) telling me why. But in my best reading of all the evidence, I've only found a few instances where it might mean "source" without any notion of "authority."[36]

Second, Payne argues that Paul's connection between "head" and "Savior" means that "head" does not refer to authority, since Christ's self-giving love (Eph. 5:25–29) "states nothing about Christ's authority."[37] So when "Paul calls the husbands to imitate Christ's actions in relations with his wife," this means he does "not ... assume authority over her."[38] But this is a false dichotomy and assumes a secular understanding of authority. It's certainly true that authority figures in Paul's day would *not* sacrifice themselves for the sake of another, especially one deemed inferior by the broader culture. But both Jesus and Paul turned this view of authority on its head: Service and sacrifice *is* true authority from a Christian perspective.

Third, interpreting *kephalē* as "source" would blunt the teeth of Paul's rhetorical reversal. If *kephalē* means "source" *and not* "authority," then what is Paul turning on its head? Interpreting *kephalē* as "life source" essentially has Paul *agreeing with* and *reinforcing* first-century patriarchal assumptions, where the wife was utterly dependent upon her husband for food, clothing, shelter, and so on. Saying that a wife should submit to her husband since he's her life source sounds more like Aristotle than Paul.

---

36 See my article, "The Meaning of *Kephalē* ('Head')," mentioned above.

37 Rather, Payne says, "These are his actions as savior, the source of life and nourishment of his body, the church" (*Man and Woman*, 284).

38 Payne, *Man and Woman*, 284.

In short, not only does it make more lexical sense to interpret *kephalē* as conveying authority, but it also captures the rhetorical force of what Paul's *doing* in Ephesians 5:21–33. In redefining authority to mean Christlike sacrificial love, Paul deconstructs marital hierarchy and pushes toward a view of marriage that is much more mutual and interdependent.

## Submission and Headship (5:21–24)

Paul leads into his household code with a statement about mutual submission: "submitting [*hupotassomenoi*] to one another out of reverence for Christ" (5:21 ESV). He then says, "Wives, to your own husbands as you do to the Lord" (v. 22, my translation). The word "submit" doesn't actually occur in 5:22.[39] It's implied from 5:21, where *mutual* submission is described. Does this mean that husbands and wives are to mutually submit to each other?

Some scholars say yes. Mutual submission in 5:21 shapes the rest of the passage. Wives are to submit to their husbands, and husbands submit to their wives. Philip Payne, for instance, says, "Paul does not give any command here in Ephesians 5 that *applies* only to husbands (and not to wives) or *applies* only to wives (and not to husbands)."[40] Just as husbands are told to love their wives (v. 25), all Christians are to love one another (v. 2). Just

---

39 *Hupotassō* does occur in several early manuscripts (e.g., Sinaiticus, A, I), but it's omitted in P46 (one of the earliest and most reliable attestations to Paul's letters) and in Codex Vaticanus. Most critical editions of the New Testament follow the manuscripts that omit the verb in 5:22 (NA[27], UBS[4], Nestle-Aland, Westcott-Hort), while the recent Greek New Testament published by Tyndale House (Cambridge) retains the verb. Virtually all scholars (egalitarian and complementarian alike) follow the manuscripts that omit the verb, but see Peter Gurry, "The Text of Eph 5.22 and the Start of the Ephesians Household Code," *New Testament Studies* 67, no. 4 (2021): 560–81, for an argument that the verb *hupotassō* should be retained in 5:22.

40 Payne, *Bible vs. Biblical Womanhood*, 113; cf. Payne, *Man and Woman*, 277–83 (italics in original).

as wives are told to submit to their husbands (vv. 22, 24), all Christians are commanded to submit to one another (v. 21).

Other scholars disagree: Although 5:21 refers to mutual submission for all believers, Paul commands a specific kind of submission to wives and not husbands in verses 22 and following.[41] That is, every Christian should be submissive, but not every Christian submits to every other Christian in the same way in every case.[42] All Christians "submitting to one another" includes both parents and kids, but that doesn't mean parents should submit to their kids. There can be asymmetrical relationships within "one another" statements. For instance, Revelation 6:4 says people "would slaughter one another" (CSB), but that doesn't mean everyone is slaughtering each other in the same way.[43] It simply means that "some members of the group slaughter others."[44] The phrase "one another" in Ephesians 5:21, then, might not mean every single person is submitting to every single person. In fact, whenever submission is mentioned in the context of husbands and wives, it's always the wife who is told to submit to the husband, never the other way around (Col. 3:18; Titus 2:5; 1 Pet. 3:1).[45] The Bible never says, "Husbands, submit to your wives."

I think both views make good points, and I've gone back and forth on what I think Paul is doing with submission. Here are a few things to note as we wrestle with this issue.

---

41 See Harold W. Hoehner, *Ephesians: An Exegetical Commentary* (Baker, 2002), 717; and Peter O'Brien, *The Letter to the Ephesians*, Pillar New Testament Commentary (Eerdmans, 1999), 401–4.

42 Craig Blomberg, "A Response to Linda Belleville," in *Two Views on Women in Ministry*, rev. ed., ed. James Beck, (Zondervan, 2005), 118–19.

43 See also Galatians 6:2; 1 Corinthians 11:33; cf. 2 Chronicles 20:23; James 5:16.

44 Constantine Campbell, *The Letter to the Ephesians*, Pillar New Testament Commentary (Eerdmans, 2023), 243.

45 Even though the word *submit* is absent in Ephesians 5:22, it does occur in 5:24: "Now as the church submits to Christ, so also wives should submit to their husbands in everything."

First, we must understand submission through a Christian lens, not a secular one.[46] In the Greco-Roman world, submission conveyed notions of inferiority and weakness—those with a lower social status submit to those with a higher status. But Christ radically upended this entire way of thinking. Submission is how Christ conquers dragons and is crowned King of the cosmos (Phil. 2:5–11; Rev. 5, 12–13). What was seen as a sign of weakness and inferiority has been turned into a fundamental Christian virtue. Whatever Paul means by "submission" here, we must resist reading secular notions into the term. If submission only applies to wives, this cannot mean they are called to do something degrading or demeaning, and it certainly doesn't mean wives are less valuable or important than husbands. The call to submit is a call to embody the cosmic power of King Jesus, who defeated devils and empires by submitting to the cross.

Second, even if Paul didn't say husbands should submit to their wives, his opening statement about mutual submission (Eph. 5:21) would have been startling. No ancient household code was prefaced with a statement about mutual submission. So even if we think Paul is telling only wives to submit to their husbands, we have to remember that the implied verb in 5:22 is dependent upon the mutual submission of 5:21. I like how Richard Hays puts it: "The hierarchical structure of the relations described is tempered by a comprehensive vision of the church as a people living in humility and mutual submission."[47] We can't understand

---

46 See Sydney Park, *Submission Within the Godhead and the Church in the Epistle to the Philippians: An Exegetical and Theological Examination of the Concept of Submission*, Library of New Testament Studies 361 (T&T Clark, 2007).

47 Richard Hays, *The Moral Vision of the New Testament: A Contemporary Introduction to New Testament Ethics* (HarperOne, 1996), 64.

what kind of "submission" Paul has in mind in 5:22 without appreciating the radical surprise of "submission" in 5:21.[48]

Third, while Paul doesn't explicitly tell husbands to submit to their wives, his description of the husband's love and sacrificial service toward his wife (vv. 25–28) could be understood as a kind of functional submission. Lynn Cohick, for instance, says "in terms of actual practices, Paul does in fact ask husbands to submit—in his command that they love their wives as Christ loved the church and gave himself up to death on the cross that the church might live."[49] Constantine Campbell, however, pushes back on this reading, which he believes "confuses submission with service." He argues: "Of course, all believers are to *serve* one another in a symmetrical sense, but this does not mean that all are supposed to *submit* to one another."[50]

I do wonder if we're quibbling over semantics—and, perhaps, operating out of a secular fear of submission. If the husband gives up his life for his wife—serving her in ways that the broader culture might find demeaning—how much does it matter if we call this posture "submission" or "service"? I love how Frank Thielman says it: "There may be a difference between placing oneself in the service ... of others and submitting to others (*hupotassō*), but it is not large."[51]

From my vantage point, I don't see Paul directly telling husbands to submit to their wives. And yet he clearly challenges typical hierarchical assumptions about submission and authority, pushing toward a kind of mutuality in marriage that was revolutionary in the first century.

---

48 Whatever influence 5:21 has over the rest of the household code, it ends at 5:33 and does not carry over into 6:1–9, where Paul addresses children/fathers and slaves/masters (see Payne, *Bible vs. Biblical Womanhood*, 114; Dawes, *Body in Question*, 106).

49 Cohick, *Ephesians*, 352.

50 Campbell, *Ephesians*, 244; cf. Frank Thielman, *Ephesians*, Baker Exegetical Commentary on the New Testament (Baker, 2010), 373 (italics in original).

51 Thielman, *Ephesians*, 374.

## Mutuality and Unity (5:28–32)

After redefining authority as service in Ephesians 5:25–27, Paul describes marriage in terms of profound mutuality and interdependence:

> In this same way, husbands ought to love their wives *as their own bodies. He who loves his wife loves himself.* After all, no one ever hated *their own body, but they feed and care for their body*, just as Christ does the church—for we are members of his body. "For this reason a man will leave his father and mother and be united to his wife, and the two will become one flesh." This is a profound mystery—but I am talking about Christ and the church. However, each one of you also must love his wife as he loves himself, and the wife must respect her husband. (vv. 28–33)

Gregory Dawes offers what I think is the most insightful treatment of Paul's head/body metaphor. He points out that Paul uses the body metaphor in two different ways throughout the book of Ephesians. One use is *partitive* and the other is *unitive*. The *partative* use is where the body is distinguished from the head. We see this in Ephesians 5:22–24, where Paul distinguishes Christ/husband as "head" from the church/wife as "body." But another way Paul uses the body metaphor is *unitive*: It shows how things are joined together (see 4:11–16). The head and body are different parts, but they're still part of one body.

What's striking in Ephesians 5 is that Paul begins with the partitive function (vv. 22–24) but then uses the same body metaphor in a unitive way (vv. 29–32). The head no longer stands in authority over the body; the head is at one with the body. The two are—as Paul's use of Genesis

2:24 shows—"one flesh" (Eph. 5:31). "What the author draws on here," says Dawes, "is not the distinction between the head and the body (for the term *kephalē* does not occur in these verses). Rather, what the argument relies on is the unitive use of the term *sōma* ['body'], expressing the idea that the wife and husband form 'one flesh.'"[52]

This rhetorical movement of *sōma* ("body") from partitive to unitive corresponds to Paul's redefinition of *kephalē* in terms of self-sacrificial service that we saw earlier. It's as if Paul meets his audience where they're at in 5:22–24 and then takes them on a journey toward mutuality and interdependence in verses 25–32—something he's already hinted at in verse 21. Paul's treatment of marriage here is not too far from what he says in 1 Corinthians 7:4: "The wife does not have authority over her own body but yields it to her husband. In the same way, the husband does not have authority over his own body but yields it to his wife."

## Conclusion

Ephesians 5 doesn't directly address our question about women in church leadership, but I think it still shapes how we approach the issue. For one, it provides further insight into the nature of Christian authority. As we saw in chapter 4, Christian authority and leadership are not at odds with Christian service. The two belong together like hot dogs and baseball. What Paul does with *kephalē* is an extended microcosm of this Christian redefinition of leadership.

Ephesians 5 also shows us how Paul radicalized Christian relationships while still respecting social norms.[53] As many scholars have noted,

---

52 Dawes, *Body in Question*, 201.

53 See my article, "Does Paul's Household Code Contain a Social Apologetic?" available at theologyintheraw.com/womeninleadership.

Paul had to defend the early church against outside accusations that they were a seditious movement seeking to completely overturn Roman household values.[54] For instance, Paul elsewhere directs younger women to love and submit to their husbands "*so that* no one will malign the word of God" (Titus 2:4–5). We see the same logic in 1 Timothy 5:14, where Paul instructs "younger widows [to] marry, bear children, manage their households, and *give the adversary no occasion for slander*" (ESV). Peter's household code (1 Pet. 3:1–7) shows similar concerns.[55]

Paul and Peter were deeply concerned with the church's reputation with outsiders, *specifically* how it was affected by household relationships. I think Paul had this concern in mind in Ephesians 5. He didn't completely ditch Greco-Roman expectations for household relations. Rather, he adopted a form of household management familiar to his culture—husbands are the head, and wives are called to submit—but he reconfigured what these concepts mean through the lens of the gospel.

I wonder if Paul might have been doing the same sort of thing in 1 Corinthians 11:3–12—the only other place where Paul says that man is the "head" of woman.

---

54 Craig Keener, *Paul, Women & Wives: Marriage and Women's Ministry in the Letters of Paul* (Hendrickson, 2004), 133; Alan Padgett, "The Pauline Rationale for Submission: Biblical Feminism and the *Hina* Clauses of Titus 2:1–10," *Evangelical Quarterly* 59 (1987): 39–52; P. H. Towner, "Households and Household Codes," in *Dictionary of Paul and His Letters*, ed. G. F. Hawthorne et al. (IVP, 1993), 419. Balch notes that other religions, including Judaism, also defended against similar suspicions of overturning Roman household values (*Wives*, 65–66).

55 David Balch argues extensively that Peter's domestic code (1 Pet. 3:1–7) is a social apologetic against attacks from the surrounding culture (*Wives*).

Chapter 8

# MAN IS THE HEAD OF WOMAN (1 COR. 11:3–12)

The other day, I started reciting 1 Corinthians 11 out loud in front of my wife and one of my daughters. They stared at me in shock as I quoted Paul's seemingly bizarre words: Man is God's glory, but woman is man's glory. Woman was created for man, not man for woman. Women must wear head coverings, and if they don't, they should shave their heads. Why? Well, of course—"because of the angels" (v. 10). "I'm just citing Scripture," I said at the end of my monologue, with the smug confidence of a first-year Bible college student.

I do not recommend this approach.

Hands down, 1 Corinthians 11:3–12 is *the* most difficult passage I've ever studied in my twenty years as a Pauline scholar.[1] And this isn't simply because of Paul's seemingly odd statements about women. If Paul means what he says and says what he means, then we must let Paul be Paul and not try to give him a twenty-first-century makeover.

---

1 The passage actually runs from 11:2 to 11:16, but I'll focus on verses 3–12, since this section is most pertinent for our topic.

But the difficulties in the passage aren't just about political correctness. They include the syntax, logical connections, apparent contradictions, and Greek phrases that can be translated in very different ways. We're not even sure Paul is talking about head coverings. And what's with the angels? They fly in unannounced, then flutter away before Paul can tell us why they're there.

If you meet someone who claims to have this passage all figured out, I suggest you run the other way. My goal here is not to convince you of my own (tentative) view of 1 Corinthians 11 but to act as an honest guide through this interpretive jungle.

Despite its challenges, one thing is clear: 1 Corinthians 11 says nothing about different ministry roles for men and women. The only ministries Paul mentions are public prayer and prophecy, and he is perfectly fine with women doing these things in front of men in church (v. 5). His concern has to do with what women wear *when* they pray and prophesy, not *whether* they should pray and prophesy. Thus, this passage says nothing about which church roles are available to women. But it does raise the question: Are married women under a man's (specifically, their husband's) authority when they pray and prophesy in church?

Before we dive in, I want to give a couple of preliminary thoughts. I just mentioned that there's a debate over whether Paul refers to head coverings in this passage. Some say he's talking about hair length or hairstyles, not head coverings. I've worked through this issue extensively elsewhere, so I won't get into it here.[2] While the hair length/style view

2 Preston Sprinkle, "Is Paul Talking About Hair Length/Style or Head Coverings in 1 Corinthians 11?" available at theologyintheraw.com/womeninleadership.

is commendable, I believe the head coverings view makes better sense of Paul's wording and his cultural context.

In Paul's day, married women were expected to cover their heads in public, including public worship settings. Head coverings (or veils) signaled a woman's marital status and were a sign of respectability and modesty. Women who didn't cover their heads were assumed to be single (and sexually available), prostitutes, or slaves. If a married woman went out in public without a head covering, it indicated that she was looking to have an affair. It would have been distracting, to say the least, if a woman prayed and prophesied like this in front of men. Certainly, the woman's husband would be shamed. And her behavior would be alarming to any unbeliever looking on (cf. 1 Cor. 14:23). This is why Paul concludes that a (married) woman with her head uncovered might as well shave her head (11:5–6), since this was one punishment for a wife who committed adultery.[3]

Male head coverings, however, didn't convey marital status. While some men covered their heads on various occasions, it's not always clear what this signified. But we do have extensive archaeological evidence—even from Corinth itself—depicting high-status men covering their heads while participating in pagan worship. "For those elite or high-status men taking a central role in sacrifices or worship, the Roman ethos was one in which the head was always covered."[4] I think this is the most likely rationale for Paul's prohibition of male head coverings:

---

3 In Cyprus law, "a woman guilty of adultery shall have her hair cut off and be a prostitute" (Dio Chrysostom, Or. 64.3; cf. Winter, *After Paul*, 128).

4 Mark Finney, "Honour, Head-Coverings and Headship: 1 Corinthians 11.2–16 in its Social Context," *Journal for the Study of the New Testament* 33, no. 1 (2010): 36.

He wanted to distance Christian men in Corinth from the social hierarchy and pagan practices of their day.

Thus, female head coverings said something about a married woman's horizontal relationship with men (her husband in particular), while male head coverings signaled a man's high status and vertical relationship before pagan gods.

It's also disputed whether Paul is referring to men and women generally or to husbands and wives in particular throughout this passage. Most scholars rightly say the answer is both. The Greek words for "man" and "woman" can also mean "husband" and "wife." Some verses clearly refer to men and women generally, not husbands and wives. When Paul says that "man is born of woman" (v. 12), he's not thinking of a wife giving birth to a husband. But since head coverings were worn by married women, the verses that deal directly with this attire are about wives in particular. The way I see it, Paul does appeal to men and women more generally in certain places, but he does this to serve his main argument about how married women are to present themselves in worship.

With this context in mind, let's turn to 1 Corinthians 11:3–12, paying special attention to the aspects most relevant to our question: Are married women under their husbands' authority when they pray and prophesy in church?

## Man Is the Head of Woman (11:3–6)

Paul begins this passage with a move we just saw in Ephesians 5, calling man "the head" (*kephalē*) of woman:

> But I want you to realize that the head [*hē kephalē*] of every man is Christ, and the head [*hē kephalē*] of the

> woman is man, and the head [*hē kephalē*] of Christ is God. (1 Cor. 11:3)

We have the same issue with *kephalē* here that we saw in Ephesians 5:23. It can convey "authority," "source," or "preeminence." Most scholars agree that the first two are the likely options. Unlike in Ephesians 5, though, Paul doesn't elaborate on what exactly he means by "head" in the following verses. He says that when a man prays or prophesies with a covered head, he "dishonors his *head*" (probably referring to Christ, his head, 1 Cor. 11:4). And when a woman prays or prophesies with an uncovered head, she "dishonors her *head*" (probably referring to man, her head, v. 5).[5] But this still doesn't tell us whether "head," *kephalē*, means "source" or "authority."

However, Paul might offer some clues to the meaning of *kephalē* in 11:7–10. Since he explicitly talks about man being the source of woman here, some scholars say *kephalē* must mean "source" and not "authority" in verse 3. But other scholars argue that Paul identifies man, the *kephalē*, as the "authority" over woman in verse 10. Thus *kephalē* means "authority." Both views agree that keys to unlock the meaning of *kephalē* are found in 11:7–10.

I think it's wise, therefore, to hold off defining *kephalē* in 11:3 until we've understood the rest of the passage.

---

5 It's disputed whether the phrase "dishonors his" and "her head" in 11:4–5 (CSB) refers to Christ and man respectively or to the man's and woman's literal head. I think the former is probably correct in light of 11:3; see Judith M. Gundry-Volf, "Gender and Creation in 1 Corinthians 11:2–16: A Study in Paul's Theological Method," in *Evangelium, Schriftauslegung, Kirche: Festschrift für Peter Stuhlmacher zum 65 Geburtstag*, ed. Jostein Ådna et al. (Vandenhoeck & Ruprecht, 1997), 154–55; Richard B. Hays, *First Corinthians*, Interpretation (Westminster John Knox, 1997), 184–85; contra Francis Watson, "The Authority of the Voice: A Theological Reading of 1 Cor 11.2–16," *New Testament Studies* 46, no. 4 (2000): 529–30.

## Does Man Have Authority over His Wife? (11:7–10)

After arguing that women should cover their heads while men should not (11:4–6), Paul gives his reasons for why this is the case, including an appeal to the creation of man and woman:

> A man ought not to cover his head, since he is the image and glory of God; but woman is the glory of man. For man did not come from woman, but woman from man; neither was man created for woman, but woman for man. For this reason, a woman ought [*opheilei*] to have authority [*exousian*] on/over her head [*epi tēs kephalēs*] because of the angels. (vv. 7–10, my translation)

I've come across more interpretations of this passage than I can count, but the ones relevant for our topic fit within two general approaches: (1) those that affirm a man's authority over his wife and (2) those that do not.

While many complementarians take the first approach and egalitarians the second, not everyone can be stuffed neatly into these two approaches. Some egalitarians take the first approach to verses 7–10 but say verses 11–12 give Paul's previous words a twist.[6] Some even argue that verses 7–10 represent the Corinthians' perspective, which Paul quotes and then refutes in verses 11–12.[7]

---

6 Most notably, Gundry-Volf, "Gender and Creation."

7 Lucy Peppiatt, *Women and Worship at Corinth: Paul's Rhetorical Arguments in 1 Corinthians* (Cascade Books, 2015); Alan Padgett, "Paul on Women in the Church: The Contradictions of Coiffure in 1 Corinthians 11.2–16," *Journal for the Study of the New Testament* 20 (1984): 69–86.

So if you're already committed to a complementarian or egalitarian view, you don't have to line up like sheep behind one of these two approaches to verses 7–10. Rest assured, your view of women in church leadership doesn't stand or fall on a particular interpretation of this passage. As always, we need to let Paul be Paul and understand what his words mean in his own context. Energized by curiosity, we can roll up our sleeves, dig into the text, and enjoy the exegetical journey.

There's one thing almost all scholars agree on: Paul is not denying that women are created in God's image. Paul knows Genesis 1:27, which clearly says women are created in God's image. And he elsewhere affirms that both men and women are in the image of God, or are being conformed to the image of Christ, who is the image of God.[8] Paul here simply mentions that man is the "image ... of God" and then moves on to focus on "glory," which is the key concept of 1 Corinthians 11:7–9.

Let's take a thorough look at these two interpretive approaches.

## 1. Paul Affirms a Husband's Authority over His Wife (11:7–10)

There is some variety among those who take this first approach. But in general, they say Paul appeals to the order of creation to support his claim that married women should cover their heads, which shows they are under their husbands' authority. Tom Schreiner, for instance, interprets the phrase "woman is the glory of man" (11:7) to

---

8 Romans 8:29; cf. 1 Corinthians 15:49; 2 Corinthians 3:18; 4:4; Colossians 1:15; 3:10–11; see Morna Hooker, "Authority on Her Head: An Examination of 1 Corinthians 11:10," *New Testament Studies* 10, no. 3 (1964): 411; Gordon Fee, *The First Epistle to the Corinthians*, New International Commentary on the New Testament (Eerdmans, 2014), 570. Hardly any scholar—even the most liberal ones—says Paul denies that women are in God's image, though see David Clines, "Image of God," in *Dictionary of Paul and His Letters*, ed. G. F. Hawthorne et al. (IVP, 1993), 427.

mean "she was created to honor him."[9] That is, "woman honors man by wearing a head covering, thereby showing that man is the head, i.e., the authority."[10] Paul then alludes to creation (vv. 8–9), Schreiner says, to support his point: Woman was created *from* man and *for* man—not the other way around. "If woman was created for man's sake, i.e., to help him in the tasks God gave him, then it follows that woman should honor man."[11] In this interpretation, Paul's reading of Genesis 2 draws attention to the *priority* of man in creation.[12]

Paul, then, is not simply emphasizing sex differences but role distinctions: "God created men and women with different roles in society," says Benjamin Merkle.[13] Paul is therefore dealing with issues that run deeper than mere head coverings. These are just cultural manifestations of greater theological issues at stake: "The underlying problem involves not only gender distinctions, but also role distinctions."[14] "Functionally," writes Merkle, "the wife is under the authority of her husband and therefore needs to demonstrate her submissiveness by wearing a head covering."[15]

The crux of this first approach comes in how they interpret verse 10, where Paul concludes his argument: "For this reason, a woman ought [*opheilei*] to have authority [*exousian*] on/over her head [*epi*

---

9 Thomas R. Schreiner, "Head Coverings, Prophecies and the Trinity: 1 Corinthians 11:2–16," in *Recovering Biblical Manhood and Womanhood: A Response to Evangelical Feminism*, ed. John Piper and Wayne Grudem (Crossway, 1991), 133.

10 Schreiner, "Head Coverings," 133.

11 Schreiner, "Head Coverings," 133.

12 Man's "priority" in creation could simply refer to chronology: Man was created first. "Priority" can also mean something stronger like "superiority in rank or position." Most scholars who take this first approach assume the latter.

13 Benjamin L. Merkle, "Paul's Arguments from Creation in 1 Corinthians 11:8–9 and 1 Timothy 2:13–14: An Apparent Inconsistency Answered," *Journal of the Evangelical Theological Society* 49 (2006): 537.

14 Merkle, "Paul's Arguments," 535.

15 Merkle, "Paul's Arguments," 535.

*tēs kephalēs*] because of the angels" (my translation). This approach takes the word "authority" as a metonymy for a head covering, which symbolizes the husband's authority over his wife.[16] Therefore, 1 Corinthians 11:7–10 opens up the meaning of 11:3, where "the head of the woman is man." Man, as head, is woman's authority.

## 2. Paul Does Not Affirm a Husband's Authority over His Wife (11:7–10)

A wide variety of interpretations exist within this second approach. The one thing they all have in common is that they don't think 11:7–10 affirms a husband's authority over his wife.

Some say that 11:7–9 emphasizes sex differences, not role distinctions. The phrase "woman is the glory of man" could refer to the woman's beauty or splendor; that is, she is the object of man's erotic attraction (v. 7).[17] According to Philip Payne, "Paul's appeal to woman as the glory of man affirms woman as the proper sexual partner for man."[18] Sex difference and not submission to authority is Paul's point. Some scholars go even further to say that Paul highlights a woman's power over man, not her subservience.[19] "Glory of man," writes Cynthia Westfall, refers to a woman's seductive beauty, which "is dangerous and causes men to lose control." That is, a "woman's hair is a primary part

16 A metonymy is a word associated with something that's used in place of the thing itself, like using "Hollywood" to refer to the US film industry. Iver Larson explains the logic of viewing "authority" as a metonymy for a head covering: "Since it is impossible to put an abstract idea like 'authority' on one's head, and since the context clearly talks about putting a head covering on one's head, the most reasonable solution is that the head covering in some sense is connected with or a symbol of authority." Iver Larsen, "1 Corinthians 11.10 Revisited," *Bible Translator* 48, no. 3 (1997): 348.

17 Watson, "Authority," 532.

18 Payne, *Man and Woman*, 181.

19 Cynthia Long Westfall, *Paul and Gender: Reclaiming the Apostle's Vision for Men and Women in Christ* (Baker, 2016), 66–70; see also Julie Newberry, "Paul's Allusive Reasoning in 1 Corinthians 11.7–12," *New Testament Studies* 65, no 1 (2019): 43–58.

of her beauty, which is the rationale behind veiling. If a woman prays or prophesies with an uncovered head, the glorious appearance of her hair competes with the worship of God because it displays the 'glory of man' (1 Cor. 11:15)."[20] Far from depicting man's authority over woman, "glory" here "describes the power that women have over men."[21]

Whatever "woman is the glory of man" means, this approach argues that Paul is not laying the groundwork for a husband's authority over his wife.

Scholars who take this second approach interpret Paul's reading of creation (vv. 8–9) in different ways, but they typically argue against any notion of man's superiority or authority in creation. The woman is "man's glory because she 'came from man' and was created 'for him,'" says Gordon Fee. "She is not thereby subordinate to him, but necessary for him."[22] Paul reads creation in terms of mutuality, not hierarchy. She "was created 'for the sake of man,' to fulfill man's need for an intimate sexual partner," says Philip Payne.[23] The man was the source of, and not the authority over, the woman, which is what "head" means in verse 3.

As far as verse 10 goes, this second approach interprets *exousia* ("authority") to refer to the woman's own authority, not to the man's authority over her. In the Greek, "woman" is clearly the subject of the verb "to have authority." Some say the woman's authority means she has the freedom do whatever she wants with her head.[24] Others say she's obligated to cover her head, which gives her authority to pray and prophesy.

20 Westfall, *Paul and Gender*, 68.
21 Westfall, *Paul and Gender*, 67.
22 Fee, *Corinthians*, 572.
23 Philip B. Payne, *Man and Woman, One in Christ: An Exegetical and Theological Study of Paul's Letters* (Zondervan, 2009), 181.
24 Newberry, "Paul's Allusive Reasoning," 51–52.

Still others interpret *exousia* to mean "control"; thus, a woman should have "control over her head by veiling as an affirmation of her commitment" and "faithfulness to her husband."[25] Whatever specific meaning Paul intends, it's the married woman's own authority, not her husband's, that's in view.

## Evaluating the Two Approaches to 1 Corinthians 11:7–10

I think both of these approaches have their pros and cons. I've honestly gone back and forth over the last several months. Let me give three observations to show how I'm wrestling with the passage.

First, I'm not persuaded by those who interpret "woman is the glory of man" to mean woman is man's sexual partner (Philip Payne) or has erotic power over man (Cynthia Westfall).[26] These interpretations don't seem to fit Paul's comparison between man as the "glory of God" and woman as "the glory of man" (11:7). Whatever "glory" means, it should carry the same sense in both phrases. If woman being the "glory of man" describes sexual partnership, then man being the "glory of God" would mean that man is God's sexual partner, which I find questionable. The same goes for interpreting "glory" to mean a woman's sexual power over man. The idea of a woman's hair being erotic is common in first-century

25 Jason David BeDuhn, "'Because of the Angels': Unveiling Paul's Anthropology in 1 Corinthians 11," *Journal of Biblical Literature* 118, no. 2 (1999): 303–4.

26 Westfall and others base this on a similar passage in 1 Esdras 4:18–22 (a second-century BC Jewish book), which says women "bring men glory" and cause men to lose their senses when they "see a woman lovely in appearance and beauty" (vv. 17, 18 NRSVUE; see Westfall, *Paul and Gender*, 66–70; Newberry, "Paul's Allusive Reasoning"). The parallels are certainly interesting, but Paul's argument is quite different. He's not focusing on a woman's domestic prowess, and his phrase "woman is the glory of man" is backed by his reading of creation, where he emphasizes that woman is created *from* and *for* man (1 Cor. 11:7–9). Such concerns are different from the point 1 Esdras 4 is making. I do think 1 Esdras's statements about women giving birth to men and that "men cannot exist without women" (v. 17 NRSVUE) reflect more of Paul's point in 1 Corinthians 11:11–12, but I don't think they help us interpret Paul's words in 11:7–9.

sources, and perhaps this is part of Paul's rationale for female head coverings.[27] But if "glory" refers to woman's power over man, then man being the "glory of God" refers to his power over God. This also seems unlikely, even for non-Calvinists.

I think it's best to understand "woman is the glory of man" to mean that married women are to honor their husbands—something they wouldn't be doing if they uncovered their heads in worship. The word "glory" does often mean "honor," and this fits the honor-shame context of 1 Corinthians 11.[28] A woman who prophesies with an uncovered head "dishonors" her husband (v. 5) and should receive the "disgrace," or shame, of being shorn (v. 6). Paul later contrasts "dishonor" with "glory" in verses 14–15; long hair on men is a "dishonor" (v. 14 NASB), while long hair on women is their "glory" (v. 15).

This, of course, does not mean Paul thought it was perfectly fine for husbands to dishonor their wives or that women don't need to honor God. Paul elsewhere tells all believers to "honor one another above yourselves" (Rom. 12:10), which certainly includes husbands honoring their wives! But Paul writes his words here to address a specific issue in Corinth. If married women in Corinth were praying and prophesying with uncovered heads (signaling that they were sexually available or looking to have an affair), this certainly would oblige Paul to address these women and their need to honor their husbands. Paul doesn't have to add that "married men also need to honor their wives," since that doesn't seem to be the issue he's dealing with here.

---

27 See Craig Keener, *Paul, Women & Wives: Marriage and Women's Ministry in the Letters of Paul* (Hendrickson, 2004), 28–31, who cites many sources. This, of course, is not at odds with what we said earlier about head coverings signaling marriage. Both can be true at the same time: head coverings signaling marriage and protecting married women from the male gaze.

28 See Finney, "Honour."

Second, I don't think Paul appeals to creation (1 Cor. 11:8–9) *simply* to highlight sex differences. It's true that Eve was Adam's "intimate sexual partner"[29] and was "*necessary* for him."[30] But 11:8–9 seems to emphasize man's priority in creation. Love it or hate it, Paul says "man did not come from woman, but woman from man; neither was man created for woman, but woman for man." Woman was created *from* and *for* man—not the other way around—and this serves Paul's argument that married women should wear head coverings. If sex difference and partnership were Paul's point, why stress that man was *not* created *for* woman? I appreciate the exegetical honesty of Richard Hays, an egalitarian, who says: "The man was created first and the woman 'out of' him (Gen. 2:21–23), and the woman was created for the man (Gen. 2:18), not the other way around.... Such arguments may appear unpersuasive and objectionable to modern readers, but there is no point in attempting to explain away what Paul actually wrote."[31]

Third, I used to think taking *exousia* ("authority") as a metonymy for a head covering in 11:10 was a torturous way to read the text, but I now think it has some merit. Again, if *exousia* refers to a woman's head covering, this probably signals that she's under her husband's authority. Many scholars think this is a ridiculous interpretation: "Woman" is clearly the subject of the verb "to have authority," which means the woman has authority, not her husband.[32] I thought this was the nail in the coffin of the first approach. But after taking a closer look, there's

29 Payne, *Man and Woman,* 180, 181.
30 Fee, *Corinthians*, 572.
31 Hays, *First Corinthians*, 187; see also Peppiatt, *Women and Worship*, 51–52.
32 Payne, *Man and Woman*, 182–83; Padgett, "Paul on Women," 71.

actually good evidence for taking *exousia* to refer to the woman's head covering.

For instance, the parallel between 11:7 and 11:10 makes the most sense if head coverings are in view in both verses:

> A man **ought** not [*ouk opheilei*] **to cover** [*katakaluptesthai*] **the head** [*tēn kephalēn*]. (v. 7a)
>
> A woman **ought** [*opheilei*] **to have authority** [*exousian echein*] on **the head** [*epi tēs kephalēs*]. (v. 10a, my literal rendering of the Greek in both verses)

Paul begins his argument with man's obligation *not* to cover his head (v. 7), so it makes sense that he would conclude it with woman's obligation *to* cover her head (v. 10). Notice the parallel: *Exousia* stands right where we would expect a statement about a head covering.

Also, 11:10 concludes what Paul just said in 11:7–9. It doesn't make as much sense for Paul to say that woman is the glory of man, that she was created *from* and *for* man, and then deduce ("for this reason," v. 10) that the woman has authority over her own head in verse 10.[33] Go back and re-read verses 7–9 yourself. Read them a dozen times. Does it appear that Paul is building an argument for woman's authority or

---

33 Most scholars agree that "for this reason" (*dia touto*) in 11:10a refers to 11:7–9, which is confirmed by Paul's dual use of *dia* at the end of verse 9 (*dia ton andra*) and the beginning of verse 10 (*dia touto*); see BeDuhn, "'Because of the Angels,'" 304. *Dia touto* might point both back to 11:7–9 and forward to 11:10b "because of the angels" (see Fee, *Corinthians*, 573), but it's very unlikely that it points only *forward* to the angels (contra Gundry-Volf, "Gender and Creation," 160).

man's? The latter makes much more sense of Paul's logic, even if we're bothered by his conclusion.[34]

Furthermore, the grammar of 11:10 doesn't clearly say that the woman has authority over her own head. It's true that the phrase "have authority over" (*exousian echein epi*) by itself would suggest this. But the phrase "on/over the head" (*epi tēs kephalēs*) means "on top of" a person's literal head in its other fourteen uses in the New Testament.[35] In other words, if all we had was the phrase "have authority over," then a woman's own authority would likely be in view. But the most natural meaning of *epi tēs kephalēs* ("on top of the head") complicates this reading. And since head coverings are the topic of discussion, it makes more sense that *epi tēs kephalēs* refers to a literal object on top of the woman's head, which syntactically is *exousia*.[36]

It's true that Paul earlier uses the term *exousia* to mean something like "right" or "freedom," and he even pairs *exousia* with the verb *echein* (the same terms used in 11:10) like in 1 Corinthians 9:4: "Don't *we have the right* (*echomen exousian*) to eat and drink?" (CSB).[37] But these phrases carry a meaning that cannot be what Paul means in 11:10. Throughout 1 Corinthians 7–9, Paul highlights a person's freedom

---

34 Payne pushes back on this, however. He points out that Paul begins verse 11 by addressing female independence: "Nevertheless, in the Lord woman is not independent of man...." Paul's first words in verse 11 seek to curb female independence, which show that the previous verse (v. 10) is about female authority (Payne, *Man and Woman*, 191–92). But verse 11 should be taken as a whole, since "in the Lord" occurs at the end of the verse. It literally reads: "Nevertheless, woman is not without man nor man without woman *in the Lord*." In other words, the entire verse (and not just the first bit) is a response to verse 10 (or all of 11:7–10).

35 Matthew 26:7; 27:29; John 20:7; Acts 18:6; Romans 12:20; Revelation 4:4; 9:7; 10:1; 12:1, 3; 13:1; 14:14; 18:19; 19:12. Revelation 10:1 might be the one exception, since it refers to a rainbow *over* the head (*epi tēn kephalēn*) of an angel. The rainbow is technically not on top of the head, but this sense is probably due to the nature of a rainbow, not the grammar of the phrase.

36 Roy Ciampa and Brian Rosner, *The First Letter to the Corinthians*, Pillar New Testament Commentary (Eerdmans, 2010), 523.

37 See also 1 Corinthians 9:4, 5, 6; cf. 6:12; 8:9; 9:12, 18.

to do what they want—for example, to take a wife or not take a wife (9:5). But in 11:10, Paul does not say that the married woman is free to do what she wants with her head. He says she is *obligated* (*opheilei*) to cover it (or "have authority on it"). The Greek word *opheilei* refers to a necessary (perhaps even a legal) obligation, not a person's freedom to do whatever they want.[38] In fact, if a married woman doesn't wear a head covering, Paul says her head should be shaved (11:5–6), a near death sentence for a first-century woman. The combination of "ought" with "to have authority" (11:10) means something quite different from Paul's use of "to have authority" throughout 1 Corinthians 7–9, since those uses refer to a person's *own* freedom/right and none of them are framed as necessary obligations.[39]

I don't think interpreting *exousia* as a head covering is as outlandish as some scholars think. I wouldn't bet the farm on this interpretation, but I do think it has exegetical merit.[40]

At the end of the day, both approaches to 11:7–10 have strengths and weaknesses, but the first seems most exegetically convincing: Paul appeals to man's priority in creation to argue that married women should wear culturally appropriate attire as a sign of their husbands' authority.

---

38 Loren T. Stuckenbruck, "Why Should Women Cover Their Heads Because of Angels? (1 Corinthians 11:10)," *Stone-Campbell Journal* 4 (2001): 214–15. Bruce Winter argues that the word "ought" conveys a legal obligation. *After Paul Left Corinth: The Influence of Secular Ethics and Social Change* (Eerdmans, 2000), 131.

39 We could also add that Chrysostom and other early fathers understood *exousia* as a metonymy for a head covering or veil, which shows that native Greek speakers didn't necessarily see this as an unnatural way to read the text. Chrysostom, *1 Cor. Hom.* 26.5; cf. Theophylact, "Epistulae Primae," in Migne 124:697. Irenaeus takes *exousia* to mean "veil" here (*Against Heresies* 1.8.2); see Ciampa and Rosner, *1 Corinthians*, 531.

40 One challenge to this interpretation is that *exousia* is never used as a metonymy for a head covering in ancient literature. There is a close parallel, however, in Diodorus Siculus 1.47.5 (c. 60–30 BC), where a statue is said to have "three kingdoms on the head [*treis basileias epi tēs kephalēs*]"—"kingdoms" here refers to crowns, which symbolize authority (see Ciampa and Rosner, *Corinthians*, 532).

I still think some versions of the second approach are more persuasive than others. The ones I find least credible are those that try to distance Paul from saying anything about man's priority in creation, or that Paul is making a case for woman's autonomy, freedom, or power over man. It's unlikely, for instance, that Paul is talking about a woman's freedom to do whatever she wants with her own head[41] or a married woman's authority over her husband.[42] If 11:10 does refer to a woman's own *exousia* as the second approach argues, this most likely has to do with her obligation to wear a head covering. For instance, some scholars agree that the woman has *exousia* but they interpret *exousia* in 11:10 to mean "control." That is, a woman should have "control over her head by veiling as an affirmation of her commitment" and "faithfulness to her husband."[43] Thus, Paul may not explicitly say wives are under their husbands' authority, but he still appeals to man's priority in creation to argue that the married woman is obligated to wear a head covering during worship to signal her faithfulness and commitment to her husband. This version of the second approach seems more credible, but I still think the first approach makes better sense of Paul's argument.

But we haven't hacked our way out of the exegetical jungle just yet! Paul's argument doesn't end in 11:10. It continues on through 11:12. And the next two verses throw a wrench into Paul's already complicated argument.

---

41 Padgett, "Paul on Women," 71–72.

42 Craig S. Keener, "'Let the Wife Have Authority over Her Husband' (1 Corinthians 11.10)," *Journal of Greco-Roman Christianity and Judaism* 2 (2001–2005): 146–52.

43 BeDuhn, "'Because of the Angels,'" 303–4. *Exousia* is used in a similar sense in 1 Corinthians 7:37: "The man ... is under no compulsion but *has control over* [*exousian ... echei*] his own will."

## Male-Female Relations "in the Lord" (11:11–12)

I can't overstate how crucial verses 11 and 12 are for how we understand this passage as a whole. Notice that Paul opens verse 11 with a strong contrast (*plēn*, "however")[44] and then describes male-female relations from a different perspective—one that is "in the Lord":

> In the Lord [*en kuriō*], however [*plēn*], woman is not independent of man, and man is not independent of woman. For just as woman came from man [*ek tou andros*], so man comes through woman [*dia tēs gunaikos*], and all things come from God. (vv. 11–12 CSB)

Paul's words here clash with his previous argument. While Paul highlights man's priority in creation in 11:8–9, he goes on to offer a different "in the Lord" perspective in verses 11–12. This is, I believe, the key that unlocks the entire passage. There's apparently something about verses 7–10 (or perhaps 11:3–10 as a whole) that is *not* "in the Lord," while verses 11–12 offers a perspective that *is* "in the Lord."[45]

Some scholars, however, seem to downplay the contrast. They say that Paul wrote 11:11–12 to prevent his audience from taking 11:7–10 too far; Paul wanted to remind them there's no ontological inequality

---

44 *Plēn* occurs in only four other places in Paul: Ephesians 5:33; Philippians 1:18; 3:16; 4:14. *Plēn* is a "marker of something that is contrastingly added for consideration." In all of Paul's uses, it serves as a "breaking off a discussion and emphasizing what is important." Frederick William Danker, ed., *A Greek-English Lexicon of the New Testament and Other Early Christian Literature*, 3rd ed. (University of Chicago Press, 2000), 826; see also Payne, *Man and Woman*, 189; Gundry-Volf, "Gender and Creation," 162.

45 Paul often uses the phrase "in the Lord" to describe one's existence as a member of God's redeemed community. Mary D'Angelo, "The Garden Once and Not Again: 1 Cor. 11:11–12 as an Interpretation of Gen.1:26–27 in 1 Cor. 11–12," in *Genesis 1–3 in the History of Exegesis: Intrigue in the Garden*, ed. Gregory Robbins (Edwin Mellen, 1988), 24; cf. 1 Corinthians 7:39; 16:19; Philippians 3:1; 4:1, 2, 10; 1 Thessalonians 3:8; Philemon 16, 20.

between women and men.[46] Thus, man still has authority over woman, but the two are equal in dignity and worth.

But this explanation doesn't capture the full force of Paul's words here. Paul doesn't just qualify his previous statement about man's priority in creation. Instead, he directly challenges it. Notice how Paul's wording in verse 12 interacts with the wording of his previous interpretation of Genesis 2 in 1 Corinthians 11:8–9. Even his prepositions (*ek* and *dia*) play off each other:

> For man is not **from** woman [*ek gunaikos*] but woman **from** man [*ex andros*]. (11:8)
>
> For just as the woman is **from** the man [*ek tou andros*] ... (11:12a)
>
> For also man was not created **for** [*dia*] the woman, but the woman **for** [*dia*] the man. (11:9)
>
> Thus also the man **through** [*dia*] the woman. (11:12b, my translation in these verses)

While woman was derived from man in creation, every man since then has been derived from woman. Paul's reading of creation in 11:8–9, therefore, does not represent Paul's complete perspective—indeed, his "in the Lord" perspective—without 11:11–12. In fact, his wording in

46 See e.g., Schreiner, "Head Coverings," 136–37.

11:12 is actually closer to Genesis 2:23 than his previous allusion to this passage in 11:8.[47]

I don't think this means Paul is disagreeing with himself. In 11:7–10, he makes a legitimate argument from a certain reading of creation to show that women should cover their heads while praying and prophesying in first-century Corinth. If married women were doing this with uncovered heads, this would have been a serious issue, and Paul appeals to creation to prove it. But then he adds a new-creation perspective ("in the Lord"), one that affirms man and woman's profound mutuality and interdependence.

It's interesting that Paul concludes with the phrase "all things are from God" (*ta de panta ek tou theou*, v. 12 ESV). The only other time Paul uses this exact phrase is in 2 Corinthians 5, where he refers to new-creation realities:

> Therefore, if anyone is in Christ—new creation. The old things have passed; behold—new things have come. And all things are from God [*ta de panta ek tou theou*]. (v. 17–18, my translation)

A similar logic might underlie Paul's argument in 1 Corinthians 11:7–12.[48] Verses 7–10 represent an old-creation reality, while verses 11–12 represent the inbreaking of new-creation realities. As a thoughtful missionary, Paul carefully upheld certain social codes of conduct that

47 His use of the definite article in 11:12, "from the man" (*ek tou andros*), aligns exactly with Genesis 2:23 (LXX), which also has the definite article, while 11:8, "woman is from man" (*ex andros*), lacks the definite article (see Newberry, "Paul's Allusive Reasoning," 55).

48 See D'Angelo, "Garden," 25.

were important in the first-century context, especially ones that could damage the reputation of the church. But he went on to challenge these cultural values with the new social order inaugurated by the gospel.[49]

This rhetorical movement is similar to what Paul does in Ephesians 5. He begins by affirming the social reality of a husband's authority over his wife and encourages wives to honor their husbands by donning culturally appropriate attire. But in both Ephesians 5 and 1 Corinthians 11, Paul ends up highlighting men and women's profound mutuality and interdependence in Christ.

## "Man Is the Head of Woman" (11:3)

So is man the head of woman? Well, it's complicated. One thing is for sure: No one should just quote 1 Corinthians 11:3 to prove that man is woman's authority. That would be like tuning in to the third inning of a baseball game to celebrate the winner (or the first half of a football match, for my international friends). First Corinthians 11:3 begins a long and complex argument with many twists and turns. We need to ride the wave all the way to verse 12 before we can figure out what *kephalē* means in 11:3.

When we first encounter *kephalē* in 11:3, "authority" would be the most natural meaning. But Paul continues to play with literal and metaphorical meanings of *kephalē* throughout the passage. When we get to 11:8–9 and read about woman being created "from man," this suggests that *kephalē* might mean "source." But even if *kephalē* means "source," it's unlikely that it means source *and not "authority."* From an ancient

---

49 My reading of 1 Corinthians 11:2–16 is very close to the one offered by Judith Gundry-Volf ("Gender and Creation").

perspective, to be someone's source naturally conveyed notions of authority as well.[50] We even see this dual sense in some early interpretations of 1 Corinthians 11:3.[51]

But Paul's rhetorical journey isn't over. Even if man is the source/authority of woman (11:3, 8–9), Paul goes on to say that woman is the source of man (vv. 11–12). Man's priority over woman in creation isn't the full story. Asymmetrical relationships between man and woman in the old creation become overshadowed by mutuality and interdependence through the inbreaking of the new creation.

## Pushbacks to My Interpretation

Even though I've spent several months researching this passage, I still don't think I have it completely figured out. I'm sure I'll keep coming back to it, and I want to be open to refining and revising my interpretation. For now, I'm simply offering one plausible way to read what Wayne Meeks calls "one of the most obscure passages in the Pauline letters."[52]

Every interpretation of this passage has its challenges, and mine is not immune. Here are two of the biggest ones that come to mind.

**Challenge 1:** My interpretation assumes that Paul's appeal to creation in 11:8–9 is meant to support a social custom rather than a universal theological truth. A skeptic could argue that, when Paul cites creation, he must be referring to a universal truth that transcends cultures. Jesus, for

---

50 Dale Martin, *The Corinthian Body* (Yale University Press, 1999), 232, 295n14; Gundry-Volf, "Gender and Creation," 157–58.

51 See Clement of Alexandria, *The Stromata* 4.8; Theodore of Mopsuestia, *Commentary on 1 Corinthians 11:3*; and my discussion in Preston Sprinkle, "The Meaning of *Kephalē* ('Head') in Greek Literature and in Paul's Letters," available at theologyintheraw.com/womeninleadership.

52 Wayne Meeks and John T. Fitzgerald, eds., *The Writings of St. Paul: A Norton Critical Edition*, 2nd ed. (W. W. Norton, 2007), 38.

instance, references creation to affirm the universal truth that marriage is between a man and a woman (Matt. 19:3–5; cf. Gen. 1:27; 2:24).

My response to this argument is threefold. First, anyone who doesn't think head coverings are universally binding runs up against the same issue, since Paul's exegesis in 11:8–9 ultimately supports head coverings.[53] Second, while Genesis 1–2 does often establish universal truths, this isn't always the case.[54] Jesus, in fact, builds on his statement about marriage in Matthew 19:3–5 by elevating singleness (Matt. 19:12) in a way that goes beyond what's envisioned in Genesis 1–2. Mandates to procreate, keep a six-day workweek, and maintain a vegetarian diet are all rooted in creation, yet they're not universally binding on believers under the new covenant.[55] Third, even if we believe that Paul's appeal to creation does establish a universal truth, we have to include 11:11–12 as part of that truth. We can't simply cite 1 Corinthians 11:8–9 as Paul's interpretation of creation; we have to incorporate all of 11:8–12.

**Challenge 2:** Since it's universally true that "Christ is the head of every man" and "God is the head of Christ," isn't it also universally true that "man is the head of the woman," as the same verse says (11:3 CSB)?

This excellent pushback deserves two responses. First, not every element in 11:3 plays the same role in Paul's ensuing argument.[56] Paul

---

53 Craig Blomberg, however, objects: "Head coverings are simply the situation-specific outworking in the first century of the timeless principle of male headship; we have other applications today." "A Complementarian Perspective," in *Two Views on Women in Ministry*, rev. ed., ed. James R. Beck (Zondervan, 2005), 251; see also Merkle, "Paul's Arguments," 527–48. I agree with Blomberg's logic in so far as a timeless principle can undergird a social application that is not timeless. But I think he begs the question, Where do we see Paul establishing a timeless principle of male headship in 1 Corinthians 11? Certainly, Paul's reinterpretation of Genesis in 1 Corinthians 11:11–12 would challenge this.

54 See William Webb, *Slaves, Women & Homosexuals: Exploring the Hermeneutics of Cultural Analysis* (IVP Academic, 2001), 123–52; Westfall, *Paul and Gender*, 62–63.

55 Webb, *Slaves, Women & Homosexuals*, 124–25.

56 Francis Watson probably goes too far when he says that 11:3 "plays virtually no part in the argument of the passage" ("Authority," 535). But it does appear that not every element in 11:3 is equally important for the rest of the passage.

seems to be drawing on a familiar tradition in 11:3, but he's really only focused on the middle element ("man is the head of the woman"), a statement that's unintelligible apart from what Paul says in 11:4–12 (esp. 11:7–12).[57] Even if the first and third elements of 11:3 express universal truths, this doesn't necessarily mean the second element functions the same way.

Second, it's not clear that every relationship in 11:3 (Christ/man, man/woman, God/Christ) will be the same in the new creation. God's authority over Christ refers to a temporary relationship during Christ's incarnation. But in the resurrection, Christ sits at the right hand of the Father "so that God may be all in all" (1 Cor. 15:28; cf. Phil. 2:9–11). Likewise, Christ is the head of every man, but in the resurrection, we will all be "co-heirs with Christ" who "share in his glory" (Rom. 8:17) and "participate in the divine nature" (2 Pet. 1:4). Even now, with one foot in the new creation, we are "seated ... with him in the heavenly realms" (Eph. 2:6). These are sensitive theological issues, and I don't want to read too much out of the terse statements in 1 Corinthians 11:3. But when understood through a wider theological lens, all the elements of 11:3 could describe the overlap of divine and human relationships at the intersection of old- and new-creation realities.

## Conclusion

In the end, no interpretation of 1 Corinthians 11 is without its problems, and I hold mine with open hands. In terms of our question about women

---

57 Alan Padgett suggests that 11:3 is a Corinthian slogan, which "Paul affirms" before he "goes on to correct the excesses derived from the slogan's misinterpretation" ("Paul on Women," 80). While I don't think there's enough evidence to say that 11:3 is a direct quote of a Corinthian slogan, it does seem to represent a familiar tradition that Paul uses to find common ground, while building off it to expand upon (and perhaps even correct) the Corinthians' undeveloped understanding of what it means.

in church leadership, this passage does not support a complementarian view. Not even "soft complementarian" versions (where women teachers must speak under the authority of male elders), since elders are nowhere to be found in this chapter or 1 Corinthians as a whole. At the very least, complementarians should not look to this passage as clear support for their view, and egalitarians have little reason to be troubled by it.

But we're not out of the Corinthian weeds just yet. Just a few chapters later, Paul says that women should not even speak in church. Or so it seems.

Chapter 9

# WOMEN BE SILENT IN ALL THE CHURCHES (1 COR. 14:34–35)

So far in my journey, I'm seeing more and more biblical evidence for women leaders in the early church. But I'm cautious about forming firm conclusions just yet, because Paul seems to restrict women from leading or teaching in two key texts: 1 Corinthians 14 and 1 Timothy 2–3. I've always known these passages would require deep study. If they truly prohibit women from teaching or leading men, I'll have to revisit my earlier conclusions, since I don't believe Paul contradicts himself. Some people refer to apparently contradictory passages like these as "problem passages"—but if there's a problem, it's with me, not Paul. My task is to let Paul be Paul, interpreting his words with curiosity and heeding them with delight.

First Corinthians 14:34–35 is particularly jarring, because Paul flat out says women should be silent and aren't permitted to speak in church. Toward the end of his discussion about tongues and prophecy, Paul writes:

> The women *should be silent* [*sigatōsan*] in the churches, for they are not permitted *to speak* [*lalein*], but *are to submit themselves* [*hupotassesthōsan*], as *the law* [*ho nomos*] also says. If they want *to learn* [*mathein*] something, *let them ask* [*eperōtatōsan*] their own husbands at home, since it is disgraceful for a woman *to speak* [*lalein*] in the church. Or did the word of God originate from you, or did it come to you only? (vv. 34–36 CSB)

But didn't Paul just say women were praying and prophesying in church (1 Cor. 11:5)? Surely he can't mean that women shouldn't utter a peep in the gathering. This would make him not just a complementarian on steroids but a terrible writer who contradicts himself. There's got to be something else going on here.

Scholars have offered several different interpretations of this passage, not all of which can be neatly placed into egalitarian or complementarian camps. What I'm going to do is simply sum up and evaluate four of the most common interpretations and then show why I think one of them is the most credible. Keep in mind that the issues we'll discuss can get technical, especially with this first interpretation.

## 1. Paul Didn't Write 14:34–35

Several scholars claim that Paul never wrote these words; rather, they were added later by a scribe.[1] Arguments for this view are both *external* and *internal*. *External* evidence has to do with which ancient manuscripts include this section and which ones don't. *Internal* evidence has to do with the content and context of the passage itself. Does it fit with what Paul is saying? Does it contradict other passages in Paul? Are there other clues in the text suggesting that Paul didn't pen these words?

As far as external evidence goes, every single Greek manuscript we have includes this passage, although there's some discrepancy over *where* the passage is placed. A few manuscripts, for instance, place verses 34–35 after verse 40.[2] One important manuscript (Codex Vaticanus) includes verses 34–35 right where they're at in our modern Bibles (after v. 33), but there are scribal notations in the margins that some scholars interpret to mean that the scribe didn't think this section was original. These notations are two tiny dots that look like a German umlaut (the dots over the *u* in *über*), called "distigmai" by textual critics. Scholarly debates have erupted over the meaning of these two dots. Standing in one corner is Philip Payne, who has argued extensively that these notations indicate that the scribe who copied Vaticanus didn't think verses 34–35 were

---

1 Gordon Fee, *The First Epistle to the Corinthians*, New International Commentary on the New Testament (Eerdmans, 2014), 780–92; Richard B. Hays, *First Corinthians*, Interpretation (Westminster John Knox, 1997), 245–49.

2 Manuscripts that include verses 34–35 after verse 40 include D, E, F, G, 93, Old Latin manuscripts ar, b, d, f, g, eighth-century Vulgate manuscript R, along with Ambrosiaster (AD 366–384) and Sedulius Scottus (ninth century); see Anthony Thiselton, *The First Epistle to the Corinthians: A Commentary on the Greek Text*, New International Greek Testament Commentary (Eerdmans, 2000), 1150.

original.[3] In the other corner are several other textual critics who have rebutted Payne's argument, suggesting that the scribal notations should be dated to the ninth to sixteenth centuries.[4] They also point out that it's not at all clear what these notations even mean.

Payne's research is meticulous and thorough, no doubt. So are many of his critics' responses. Their back-and-forth has become so technical that it's difficult to weigh in unless you're skilled in ancient textual criticism and love to geek out over dots and stuff. Such expertise is above my pay grade.

Whatever the distigmai in the margins of Codex Vaticanus mean, I think the external evidence we have makes it much more likely that Paul penned these verses. Here are two reasons why.

First, we can't forget that *every single* manuscript we have contains this passage. If Paul never wrote these words, we would expect at least some manuscripts to leave them out. Some (mostly later and almost exclusively Western) manuscripts place verses 34–35 after verse 40, which is a discrepancy worth mentioning. But this is weak evidence for Paul not writing these words at all.

---

3 Payne's view is summed up in his popular-level book *The Bible vs. Biblical Womanhood: How God's Word Consistently Affirms Gender Equality* (Zondervan, 2023), 79–101, and more thoroughly explored in his scholarly book *Man and Woman, One in Christ: An Exegetical and Theological Study of Paul's Letters* (Zondervan, 2009), 217–67.

4 For instance, Peter Head argues that these scribal notations are from a much later, perhaps ninth-century, scribe. "The Marginalia of Codex Vaticanus: Putting the Distigmai (Formerly Known as 'Umlauts') in Their Place," paper presented at the Society of Biblical Literature's annual conference, 2009. Curt Niccum argues they're from the sixteenth century ("The Voice of the Manuscripts on the Silence of Women: The External Evidence for 1 Cor. 14.34-5," *New Testament Studies* 43 [1997]: 244–45). Jan Krans-Plaisier argues that the "date and the identification of variant readings" indicated by the scribal notes (the distigmai) are "clouded in uncertainty." "Paragraphos, Not Obelos, in Codex Vaticanus," *New Testament Studies* 65 (2019): 252–57. See also J. Edward Miller, "Some Observations on the Text-Critical Function of the Umlauts in Vaticanus, with Special Attention to 1 Corinthians 14.34–35," *Journal for the Study of the New Testament* 26, no. 2 (2003): 217–36.

Second, some of the earliest and most reliable ancient manuscripts include verses 34–35 right where they are. This includes the great fourth-century Codex Sinaiticus, the late second-century P46, the fifth-century Codex Alexandrinus, and even the Codex Vaticanus (if the distigmai don't indicate what Payne thinks they do).[5] The scholars who compiled the United Bible Society's fourth edition of the Greek New Testament said it "is almost certain" that Paul wrote verses 34–35.[6]

What about internal evidence? Some scholars argue that verses 34–35 interrupt the flow of Paul's argument, and there is some truth to this. Verses 34–35 feel like they come out of nowhere, and I don't think anyone except Doug Wilson would miss them if they were gone.

But I don't think the abruptness of verses 34–35 suggests Paul didn't write them. Why? Well, "because of the angels" (11:10). As we saw in 1 Corinthians 11, it's not at all odd for Paul to say things that seem unexpected from our modern perspective. What may seem unclear to us was probably much clearer to the original readers.

Plus, there are several words in verses 34–35 that Paul uses throughout this chapter. I disagree with Gordon Fee, who says that some words in this passage "seem altogether foreign to the Paul we know from both this letter and the rest of the Pauline corpus."[7] The only word that strikes me as uncharacteristic of Paul is his use of "law."[8] Otherwise, almost every word in this short passage is used elsewhere in Paul, and several words (like "silent," "speak," "submission," and "church") are used throughout 1 Corinthians 14.

---

5 E.g., 33, 88 mg, Vulgate, Old Syriac, and most other manuscripts.

6 See the marginal notes under 1 Corinthians 14:34–36; Thiselton, *Corinthians*, 1148.

7 Fee, *Corinthians*, 786.

8 Richard Hays says "the Law" is "uncharacteristic of Paul's way of appealing to Scripture as a source of behavioral norms" (*First Corinthians*, 247).

Other scholars note that Paul's statement about "churches" (plural) in verse 34a is an odd way to address a single congregation at Corinth. Richard Hays takes the plural "churches" as evidence that "the passage was added at a later time when the letter was being circulated for the guidance of a wider circle of communities."[9]

I admit that it's a little strange for Paul to say "women ... in the churches" if he's only thinking of women in the Corinthian church (v. 34). But Paul uses the plural "churches" right before this verse: "as in all the churches of the saints" (v. 33 CSB). Perhaps he's letting his first plural carry over into his command to the women at Corinth. Or maybe he's including the Corinthian women in a broader rule that he established in other churches. While the second plural does feel odd, I don't think this is strong evidence that Paul didn't write this passage. At the very least, we should consider other interpretive options to see if there are better ways to understand the passage.

A final internal argument says that 14:34–35 contradicts what Paul says in 11:2–16, where he assumes women are prophesying and therefore speaking.[10] But it's only a contradiction if Paul literally means that women aren't permitted to pray, prophesy, or even open their mouths. As we'll see, there's good reasons to believe that Paul is prohibiting certain *kinds* of speech, not *all* speech.

## 2. Paul Is Quoting a Corinthian Slogan

Some scholars argue that verses 34a–35 are a Corinthian slogan that Paul quotes and then refutes in verse 36: "*Or* [*ē*] did the word of God

9 Hays, *First Corinthians*, 246; Fee, *Corinthians*, 790.

10 Fee, *Corinthians*, 702; cf. Hays, *First Corinthians*, 246.

originate with you? Or are you the only people it has reached?" According to this view, the Greek particle *ē* (which normally means "or") should be interpreted as a strong objection—something like "What!" or, as Gilbert Bilezikian creatively renders it, "Nonsense!"[11] Some scholars also point out that the phrase "only people" ("alone" in some translations) is masculine in Greek (*monous*), indicating that Paul is *now* addressing the men in his audience. The sense would then be: "What! Did the word of God originate with you *men*, or are you *men* the *only ones* [*monous*] it has reached?"[12]

It's true that Paul mentions Corinthian slogans in order to refute them in this letter (e.g., 6:12; 7:1; 8:1; 10:23). So it's not crazy to suggest that Paul is doing the same thing here. But I think it's unlikely, for four reasons.

First, this passage isn't structured like Paul's other interactions with Corinthian sayings. When Paul quotes other Corinthian phrases, he partially affirms them or seriously qualifies them. He doesn't just denounce them altogether.[13]

Second, the particle *ē* is best rendered "or," not as an adversative "What!" I looked at several other passages where Paul uses *ē* when interacting with an idea he disagrees with, and in every case, he affirms, not disagrees with, what he just said.[14] I agree with D. A. Carson that "in every instance in the New Testament where the disjunctive particle

---

11 Gilbert Bilezikian, *Beyond Sex Roles: What the Bible Says About a Woman's Place in Church and Family*, 3rd ed. (Baker, 2006), 233–34 n27.

12 "It may be," writes Lucy Peppiatt, "that 1 Cor 14:34–35 is an indication, not of Paul's anti-feminism, but of his opposition to a male-dominated group in Corinth." *Women and Worship at Corinth: Paul's Rhetorical Arguments in 1 Corinthians* (Cascade Books, 2015), 111.

13 See Craig Keener, *Paul, Women & Wives: Marriage and Women's Ministry in the Letters of Paul* (Hendrickson, 2004), 76.

14 For example, Romans 3:29; 4:9; 6:3; 1 Corinthians 6:2, 9, 15–16, 18–19; 9:4–5; 10:21–22.

in question [*ē*] is used in a construction analogous to the passage at hand, its effect is to reinforce the truth of the clause or verse that precedes it."[15]

Third, when Paul uses the masculine form of "only people" in verse 36, this probably doesn't mean he's singling out men. Masculine plural forms are used all the time in Greek to include both men and women. When Paul uses a masculine plural word, we should assume by default that he's speaking to everyone in the community he's writing to, not addressing only the men.[16]

Lastly, as I said before, Paul has already used many of the words in verses 34–35 in previous verses. Verses 34–35 seem more likely to be an extension of Paul's own argument than a quotation of someone else's.

While the slogan-quoting view is possible, I think it's speculative and rests on sketchy evidence. At the very least, we should explore other views to see if they can better explain what's going on here.

## 3. Paul Is Prohibiting Women from Judging Prophecies

This view is held by several complementarian scholars who argue that Paul is not silencing *all* kinds of speech among women but only one kind of speech: judging prophecies.[17] Just a few verses earlier, Paul tells the church to weigh prophecies and see if they are true: "Two or three prophets should speak, and the others should *evaluate*" (*diakrinetōsan*,

---

15 D. A. Carson, "'Silent in the Churches': On the Role of Women in 1 Corinthians 14:33b–34," in *Recovering Biblical Manhood and Womanhood: A Response to Evangelical Feminism*, ed. John Piper and Wayne Grudem (Crossway, 1991), 151. I removed the emphasis in Carson's original quote.

16 Keener, *Paul*, 75; Carson, "'Silent in the Churches,'" 149.

17 Wayne Grudem, *Evangelical Feminism & Biblical Truth: An Analysis of More Than 100 Disputed Questions* (Crossway, 2012), 232–35; Carson, "'Silent in the Churches,'" 140–53.

14:29 CSB; cf. 12:10). According to this view, Paul then explains how the Corinthian *men* should judge prophecies in 14:30–34a and prohibits women from judging prophecies altogether in 14:34b–35. Wayne Grudem says that "only men can give spoken corrections to prophecies,"[18] so this passage enforces female submission to male prophets "in matters of doctrinal or ethical instruction."[19] (Ironically, we also saw Grudem argue in chapter 6 that prophecy *isn't* a matter of doctrinal or ethical instruction, just "the speaking of merely human words to report something God brings to mind."[20]) Carson agrees with Grudem's analysis: "Paul refused to permit any woman to enjoy a church-recognized teaching authority over men (1 Timothy 2:11ff), and the careful weighing of prophecies falls under that magisterial function."[21]

To be clear, Grudem and Carson argue that Paul prohibits women from judging prophecy *altogether*, not simply from doing so in the wrong *manner*. In Grudem and Carson's view, manner has nothing to do with it. Women are prohibited from judging prophecies, even if they do so in a perfectly orderly fashion. The passage commands female submission to male authority in church, and when women evaluate prophecy, they are violating "the law" (v. 34).

I believe this view suffers from several exegetical problems.

First, there's no indication that Paul refers only to men in 14:30–34a when he talks about judging prophecies. Paul addresses the whole congregation, giving instructions about "when *you* [plural] come together"

18 Grudem, *Evangelical Feminism*, 235.
19 Grudem, *Evangelical Feminism*, 233.
20 Wayne Grudem, *The Gift of Prophecy in the New Testament and Today*, rev. ed. (Crossway, 2000), 141.
21 Carson, "'Silent in the Churches,'" 152.

(v. 26). When prophets speak, "the *others* [plural] should weigh carefully what is said" (v. 29). And so on. Thus, Paul makes no gender distinctions when he directly addresses the judging of prophecies.

Second, there's no linguistic evidence that 14:34–35 is about "judging prophecy." Paul has a word for "judging prophecy" (*diakrinō*). He just used it in 14:29, and he uses the noun form in 12:10 (*diakrisis*). But these words don't occur in 14:34–35. If he wants to forbid women from judging prophecy, why doesn't he use the same word he's already used for "judging prophecy"?

Third, there's no indication in the text that "judging prophecy" is more authoritative than prophecy itself or that this gift is distributed only to men.[22] Interpreters have to assume this from another passage (there is none), or it could reflect a previously held theological position. But 1 Corinthians 14 doesn't say this. In fact, Paul lists the gift of prophecy—which is distributed to men and women alike—right before "judging prophecy" in 12:10. There's no evidence that the latter is more authoritative than the former.

Paul doesn't seem to be dealing with *who* can judge prophecy but *how* they do so. Nowhere does Paul say that only "men should give such a correction"[23] to prophecies, while women are not to give one.

Fourth, when Paul says that women "must be in submission" (14:34), he is not talking about women submitting to their husbands or male authorities. Paul uses the same verb in 14:32 to say that prophets must submit to other prophets while they are prophesying. This is most likely

22 Keener, *Paul*, 79.
23 Grudem, *Evangelical Feminism*, 234.

what Paul means by "submission" in 14:34—women (like men) are to submit to other prophets when they are prophesying.

While this view has some strengths, I think the next view makes much better sense of the passage.

## 4. Paul Prohibits Women from Speaking in a Disruptive Manner

According to this view, Paul isn't prohibiting women from speaking altogether or even from judging prophecies. Instead, he's prohibiting them from speaking in a disorderly manner during the gathering: specifically, from speaking while another prophet is speaking.

This view does the best job interpreting our passage in light of its immediate context. In fact, Paul uses several words in verses 34–35 that he has already used throughout this chapter. It makes good sense to interpret them in light of his previous uses. Let's look at four of these words: "speak" (*laleō*), "be silent" (*sigaō*), "submit" (*hupotassō*), and "learn" (*manthanō*).

Paul uses the verb "speak" (*laleō*) twice in 14:34–35. This same word occurs twenty-one times in 1 Corinthians 14 alone, and in twenty of those instances, it refers to specific kinds of speech: speaking in tongues, prophesying, and speaking with understanding so others may be instructed (v. 19). Just before verses 34–35, Paul addresses disruptive and disorderly speech (vv. 26–33). He commands the community to stop speaking in tongues with no interpreter present (vv. 27–28) and to stop prophesying in a disorderly manner and interrupting each other (vv. 29–32). When Paul talks again about "speaking" (*laleō*) in verses 34–35, we should interpret him in light of how he's been using this same verb all along. Thus, Paul is not prohibiting women from speaking altogether but speaking in a disorderly manner—interrupting prophets and such.

Context also informs what Paul means by "be silent" (*sigaō*) in 14:34. Paul uses this word only three times in his letters, and all three are clustered right here in 1 Corinthians 14 (vv. 28, 30, 34). In 14:28, *sigaō* refers to being silent (that is, not speaking in tongues) when no interpreter is present. In 14:30, Paul says a prophet should "be silent" (*sigaō*) when another prophet receives a revelation. Prophets shouldn't interrupt each other; they should submit to the one speaking (v. 32).[24] Therefore, when Paul tells women to "be silent" (*sigaō*) in verse 34, he doesn't mean that women should never talk out loud in church. The context is clear: Women should be silent when another prophet is speaking.

"Submit" (*hupotassō*, v. 34) is another word informed by its context. Paul uses this word only one other time in 1 Corinthians—two verses earlier, in 14:32, where he commands prophets to submit to another prophet who is prophesying. If context is king, as the adage goes, Paul almost certainly has something similar in mind when he tells women to "be in submission" in 14:34. He's not telling women to submit to their husbands, as he does elsewhere (e.g., Eph. 5:22–24). And it's very unlikely that he's talking about submission to male authority in the church—that idea appears nowhere in this passage. Context shows that Paul is commanding women to submit to the prophet who is already speaking.[25]

24 See Thiselton, *Corinthians*, 1144; Fee, *Corinthians*, 771.

25 As noted, it's not clear what Paul is referring to when he writes "as the law says" (1 Cor. 14:34). He could mean the Torah, the Old Testament as a whole, some kind of Greco-Roman legislation, his own ruling or principle, Genesis 3:16 in particular, or the creation order as a whole (Gen. 1–2). I think the latter view has the fewest problems (see Keener, *Paul*, 87; and Thiselton, *Corinthians*, 1153–54, who has the most thorough and convincing explanation).

Last but not least, "learn" (*manthanō*) is also shaped by Paul's earlier use. In 14:35, Paul advises women who "want *to learn* [*mathein*] something" to "ask their own husbands at home" (CSB).[26] Paul uses this same word for "learn" in 14:31, where he corrects disorderly speaking: "But if something has been revealed to another person sitting there, the first prophet should be silent. For you can all prophesy one by one, so that everyone may *learn* [*manthanōsin*]" (vv. 30–31 CSB). When people prophesy in a disorderly manner, they prevent learning. Paul probably has this same point in mind when he talks about women "learning" just a few verses later in 14:35. By interjecting or asking questions while the prophet was speaking, the women were disrupting the prophecy and preventing learning from happening. Paul's next statement, that "it is disgraceful for a woman to speak in the church" (v. 35), suggests that the women were being belligerent or disrespectful in how they were interrupting the prophet.

Studying Paul's words "speak," "be silent," "submit," and "learn" in their larger context helps us clarify their meaning in 14:34–35. Paul is commanding women to not interrupt another prophet while he or she is speaking but to submit to the one speaking. It may be that some of these women had gotten into the habit of interrogating the prophet, asking questions, or evaluating his or her prophecy as it was happening. Whatever the case, they had been speaking in a disorderly manner, which is precisely Paul's concern throughout this passage (vv. 33, 40).

In short, Paul was *not* making a categorical statement that it's disgraceful any time any woman opens her mouth in church. It pains me

---

26 Since men were typically more educated than women at that time, it was common for husbands to educate their wives at home. Plutarch, *Mor.* 138a–146a; cf. Lynn Cohick, *Women in the World of the Earliest Christians: Illuminating Ancient Ways of Life* (Baker, 2009), 245.

to think of how many women throughout the ages have felt this way. Not only is this interpretation sexist and dehumanizing, but it's also bad exegesis. Context informs the meaning of Paul's words, and the context rather clearly suggests that Paul had something more specific in mind.

This interpretation also makes sense considering Paul's historical context. The Greco-Roman world held certain codes of conduct when a person was giving a public speech or lecture. The first-century writer Plutarch says this about lecture-listening etiquette: "Those who instantly interrupt with contradictions, neither hearing nor being heard, but talking while others talk, behave in an unseemly manner; whereas the man who has the habit of listening with restraint and respect, takes in and masters a useful discourse." Plutarch considered it rude for one listener to even whisper to another during a lecture.[27] If he had seen the kind of interruptions and interrogations apparently happening in the Corinthian church, he would have been horrified.

It would have been doubly disrespectful in Greco-Roman culture for a woman to interrupt a male speaker. Plutarch didn't think it was appropriate for married women to speak in public at all: "A wife should speak only to her husband or through her husband, and should not feel aggrieved if, like a piper, she makes nobler music through another's tongue."[28] The satirist Juvenal didn't agree with Plutarch that women ought to *never* talk publicly, but he grumbled about women who dominated dinner party discussions: "I loathe the woman who is forever referring to Palaemon's *Grammar* and thumbing through it, observing all the laws and rules of speech ... she rattles on at such a rate that you'd

---

27 Plutarch, *Mor.* 45d.

28 Plutarch, *Conj. praec.* 32.

think all the pots and pans in the kitchen were crashing to the floor or that every bell in town was clanging.... She should learn the philosophers' lesson: 'moderation is necessary even for intellectuals.'"[29]

Paul didn't share the same low view of women that we find among Greco-Roman writers like Plutarch and Juvenal. He had no problem with women prophesying to men in church. But he was also sensitive to the social conventions of his day. He had already expressed concern over an outsider coming to a church gathering and witnessing what appeared to be a madhouse (v. 23). The reputation of the church would be threatened if outsiders saw a bunch of women appearing to "upstage their male peers"[30] by questioning or interrupting them while they were speaking. By commanding women not to be disruptive, Paul was protecting these women's ability to continue praying and speaking prophetically in their church without offending their Greco-Roman neighbors more than necessary.

## But What About...?

As I did with my view of 1 Corinthians 11 in the last chapter, let's address some of the best pushbacks to my interpretation of 1 Corinthians 14:34–35. This way, you can decide for yourself if the pros outweigh the cons.

The most obvious challenge to my view is that Paul's words in 14:34–35 appear to be unqualified. He says that women are to be silent, submit, and not speak in church—period. When Paul uses these terms earlier, he makes it clear that he is thinking of a specific kind of silence

29 Juvenal, *Sat.* 6.34–56.
30 Susan Hylen, *Women in the New Testament World* (Oxford University Press, 2018), 136.

and submission. For instance, when he says a person "is to keep silent in the church," it's obvious he's referring to speaking in tongues "if there is no interpreter" (v. 28 CSB). And when he says "the first prophet should be silent," he's undoubtedly talking about being silent when another prophet has just received a revelation (v. 30 CSB). In both cases, we know what "silence" means, since Paul tells us. He doesn't give these same qualifications in 14:34–35.

Then again, I don't think he needs to. He's just used all these same terms and qualified them in the preceding context. When Paul uses the word "speak" (*laleō*) no less than twenty times in 1 Corinthians 14 to refer to a specific kind of speech, I don't think it's a stretch to assume that his audience would read "speak" through the same lens in verses 34–35. When "be silent" (*sigaō*) occurs three times within a span of a few verses (vv. 28–34), the first two uses almost certainly inform the third. This is a standard principle in writing: Once you've already qualified what you mean, you don't need to keep giving the same qualifications over and over again.

In fact, it's not uncommon for Paul to use unqualified words or phrases as shorthand for something he has already explained earlier. He does this, for instance, with the term "the day" in 1 Corinthians 3:12–13: "If anyone builds on the foundation with gold, silver, costly stones, wood, hay, or straw, each one's work will become obvious. For *the day* will disclose it, because it will be revealed by fire" (CSB). Paul doesn't tell us what "day" he's thinking of. But he doesn't need to, since he earlier told the Corinthians that they would "be blameless on *the day of our Lord Jesus Christ*" (1:8). "The day" in 3:13 is shorthand for "the day of our Lord Jesus Christ" (that is, Christ's second coming). Likewise, when Paul says we are "justified by faith" in Romans 3:28, he's not referring to just *any* kind of faith, but "faith in Jesus Christ" (Rom. 3:22, 26) and "faith in His blood" (v. 25 HCSB). The unqualified use of "faith" derives its meaning from previous qualified uses.[31]

Here's another critique of the interpretation I'm proposing: If Paul is concerned with *disruptive* women, why does he seem to direct his prohibition to *all* women in Corinth? Surely they weren't all being disruptive. And why doesn't he also forbid disruptive *men* from interrupting the prophet?[32]

Let me respond to this critique with four brief observations. First, Paul is likely referring to married women in this passage, since he tells them to "ask their own husbands at home" (1 Cor. 14:35)—even though we know there were single women in the Corinthian church (1 Cor. 7). Paul probably doesn't mean that single women are therefore allowed to interrupt prophecies. But married women in the first century typically had a higher social status than unmarried women, especially younger virgins. If any woman in Corinth had the chutzpah to interrupt a prophet, it most likely would have been a married woman.

Second, Paul refers to women in this passage with the definite article, "*the* women" (*hai gunaikes*). Definite articles sometimes indicate that a writer has a particular subgroup of people in mind, not an entire group. We should be careful not to read too much into this phrasing; Paul could have had all married women in mind when he wrote this. But if he wanted to single out a certain group of married women, using the definite article would be one way to do so.

---

31 Scholars have identified dozens of places in Galatians where Paul uses a word or short phrase as a "theological formula" to convey "key theological concepts in abbreviated form." B. C. Lategan, "Formulas in the Language of Paul: A Study of Prepositional Phrases in Galatians," *Neotestamentica* 25, no. 1 (1991): 75–87. Clearly, Paul was comfortable using words that appear as absolutes but are intended as shorthand for a more specific idea.

32 Carson, "'Silent in the Churches,'" 147.

Third, we should keep in mind the size of the Corinthian church. As we saw in chapter 4, the average first-century house church had around twenty to thirty people, or fifty at most.[33] This number includes men, children, and unmarried women, as well as the married women Paul is addressing here. There might have been no more than a dozen married women in the church. If some of them were being disruptive by interrupting the prophet, we can imagine that the Corinthians would know exactly who "*the* women" were that Paul was referring to. It may not be that every married woman was being disruptive but that Paul had in mind "the women" who were.

Fourth, why didn't Paul expand his prohibition to include disruptive men? Well, he actually does: Paul gives a general ruling in verses 29–33 against *anyone* who speaks while another prophet is speaking. He's not giving men a free pass to interrupt when they want. Both men and women are to prophesy in an orderly manner. It might just be that a specific group of married women in the Corinthian church was being particularly disruptive.

## Conclusion

This passage is difficult, but I don't think it's as tough as 1 Corinthians 11. I was honestly a bit shocked when I found out that all the key terms in 14:34–35 are used throughout the chapter. It makes good sense to interpret these words in light of their immediate context, which is all

33 This number may be higher if Paul was thinking of the entire body of Christians in Corinth gathering in one home (cf. 1 Cor. 14:23; Rom. 16:23), rather than one of the individual house churches. Vincent Branick suggests that "the whole church of Corinth" had "no less than thirty people." *The House Church in the Writings of Paul* (Wipf and Stock, 1989), 64. Roger Gehring proposes that the number might have been a bit higher: "not less than thirty and probably from fifty to ninety members." *House Church and Mission: The Importance of Household Structures in Early Christianity* (Hendrickson, 2004), 139.

about disorderly speech and conduct. All the other interpretations seem to create more problems than they solve.

First Corinthians 14, then, does not present a problem for my conclusions thus far about women leading and teaching in first-century house churches.

Of course, I know plenty of complementarians (especially "soft complementarians") who aren't looking to any part of 1 Corinthians to build their understanding of male-only eldership. For them, the key passage is 1 Timothy 2–3. So, last but not least, let's take a deep dive into this passage, which has played such a massive role in the egalitarian-complementarian debate.

Chapter 10

# WOMEN, TEACHING, AND AUTHORITY (1 TIM. 2–3)

A few years ago, I invited New Testament scholar Bill Mounce onto my *Theology in the Raw* podcast to talk through 1 Timothy 2:8–15. Most seminary students know Mounce's name, since he wrote a widely used New Testament Greek textbook. He also wrote one of the most in-depth commentaries on the Pastoral Epistles—a commentary that took him fourteen years to write.[1] I'll never forget what Mounce said in our podcast conversation when we came to 1 Timothy 2:13 (where Adam is created first, not Eve): "If verse 13 weren't there, I'd be egalitarian."[2]

I think Mounce was being a bit provocative, and he gave several other reasons why he's a "soft complementarian." But his comment attests to the importance of this verse for our topic. For many years, I felt the same

1 William Mounce, *Pastoral Epistles*, Word Biblical Commentary 46 (Thomas Nelson, 2000).
2 Preston Sprinkle, host, *Theology in the Raw*, podcast, episode 1058, "A Complementarian Interpretation of 1 Tim 2:8–15," March 13, 2023, https://theologyintheraw.com/podcast/a-complimentarian-interpretation-of-1-tim-28-15-dr-bill-mounce.

way Mounce does about 1 Timothy 2:13.[3] I used to wonder, *How in the world do egalitarians get around this verse?* After all, Paul seems to say that women can't teach or have authority over men (v. 12) *because* Adam was created first, not Eve (v. 13). Creation, not culture, appears to be Paul's rationale.

As you might have guessed, this passage—like the last two we've looked at—is complex. Some Greek words in 2:8–15 are difficult to interpret, Paul's logical connections could be understood in different ways, and the passage ends with one of the oddest statements in the entire New Testament: Women "will be saved through childbearing." Dozens of books and hundreds of articles have been written on these eight verses alone,[4] to say nothing of the rest of 1 Timothy 2–3.

I'm sure this chapter will end up being my longest one. But this passage is so important for our debate that it's worth treating it more like a marathon than a wee stroll in the woods.

## Wealthy Women (2:9–10)

We're going to spend most of our time in 2:11–14, but it's worth noting that Paul begins his exhortation by addressing women in Ephesus who lavishly displayed their wealth:

3 Other thoughtful studies arguing for a complementarian view of 1 Timothy 2:8–15 include Andreas J. Köstenberger and Thomas R. Schreiner, eds., *Women in the Church: An Interpretation & Application of 1 Timothy 2:9–15*, 3rd ed. (Crossway, 2016); Douglas Moo, "What Does It Mean Not to Teach or Have Authority Over Men?: 1 Timothy 2:11–15," in *Rediscovering Biblical Manhood and Womanhood: A Response to Evangelical Feminism*, ed. John Piper and Wayne Grudem (Crossway, 1991), 179–93; and Wayne Grudem, *Evangelical Feminism & Biblical Truth: An Analysis of More Than 100 Disputed Questions* (Crossway, 2012), 65–74.

4 See the massive bibliography compiled in Mounce, *Pastoral Epistles*, 94–102.

> I also want the women to dress modestly, with decency and *propriety* [*sophrosunēs*], adorning themselves, not with elaborate hairstyles or gold or pearls or expensive clothes, but with good deeds, appropriate for women who profess to worship God. (vv. 9–10)

Paul's concern about female attire might seem odd (or legalistic) to modern readers. Are elaborate hairstyles, gold, and pearls sinful? Would Paul lose his mind if he saw what women wear at American megachurches?

Such attire probably signaled something in the cultural context of Ephesus that it might not mean today. I don't think Paul was placing a universal ban on perms and pearls. We'll explore this cultural context later. For now, we should simply note that Paul's concerns over female attire—and the wealthy women who could afford such stuff—can't be separated from the rest of the passage. In fact, Paul repeats verse 9's word *sophrosunē* ("propriety") in verse 15, bookending the passage to show that it fits together as a whole.[5] He also shifts from addressing Ephesian women (vv. 9–12) to talking about Eve in the garden (vv. 13–14), then returns to the Ephesian women (v. 15), which shows that 1 Timothy 2:9–15 is a single unit addressing issues related to the women at Ephesus.[6]

---

5 See Osvaldo Padilla, *The Pastoral Epistles: An Introduction and Commentary*, Tyndale New Testament Commentary 14 (IVP Academic, 2022), 84.

6 Philip H. Towner, *The Letters to Timothy and Titus*, New International Commentary on the New Testament (Eerdmans, 2006), 200; Padilla, *Pastoral Epistles,* 83–97.

The fact that 2:9–15 all fits together and speaks to what's going on in Ephesus doesn't necessarily tell us how to interpret Paul's words in 2:11–12. But however we interpret 2:11–12, we have to take seriously the overarching context of the passage.

## To Teach and *Authentein* a Man (2:11–12)

We now come to the only place in the New Testament where Paul explicitly prohibits a woman's teaching.[7] He writes:

> A woman should learn in quietness and full submission. I do not permit a woman to teach or *authentein* a man; she must be quiet. (1 Tim. 2:11–12)

By the way, I'm leaving the Greek word *authentein* untranslated, since its meaning is widely disputed, as we'll see. In any case, Paul goes on to connect his prohibition to Adam being created first (v. 13) as we noted earlier.

These verses play an important role in my personal journey in this topic, since they offer the strongest support for complementarian views. It's certainly not the only passage, but it is the main one. Whenever I entertained the possibility of an egalitarian view, I just couldn't get around what seems to be the plain meaning of 1 Timothy 2. But as we've seen throughout our study, the meaning of Paul's words isn't always as plain as it seems—because of the angels. If you're a biblicist like me, you'll agree that we need to dig deep into the text and scrutinize familiar interpretations *for the sake of*, and not *in spite of*, being biblical.

---

7 Craig Keener, *Paul, Women & Wives: Marriage and Women's Ministry in the Letters of Paul* (Hendrickson, 2009), 101.

And that's what I want to do with this passage. I'll summarize the best complementarian arguments and then analyze these arguments in light of the text.

Wayne Grudem sums up the view held by many complementarians:

> When Paul bases his argument on the order of creation of Adam and Eve, it indicates that his command about women not teaching or having authority in the assembled congregation transcends cultures and societies. It applies to men and women as they were created by God at the beginning, and it is not due to any distortion brought on by sin or the Fall. It applies, then, to all churches for all time, and it is a means by which the beauty of manhood and womanhood as God created them to be can be manifested in the church.[8]

Grudem's interpretation represents what may be called a "strong complementarian" view: Women can never teach in church gatherings where men are present. Scholars who defend this interpretation of 1 Timothy 2:11–13 most often do so with three main arguments.

First, the Greek word *authentein* (v. 12) refers to Christian authority in general, not to a negative kind of authority (e.g., "domineering authority"). Thus, men are allowed to *authentein* both men and women, and women are allowed to *authentein* other women, but women are not allowed to *authentein* men.

---

8 Grudem, *Evangelical Feminism*, 69.

Second, *authentein* is joined with the positive word "to teach" (*didaskein*) in 2:12: neither *teach* nor *authentein* a man. The grammatical construction "neither … nor," they argue, always joins two positive words or two negative words.[9] Since *didaskein* is positive, *authentein* must also be positive. Paul therefore doesn't just prohibit women from some kind of bad teaching or domineering authority; he prohibits women from exercising any kind of teaching or authority, including good Christian teaching and authority, over men.

Third, Paul defends this prohibition by saying, "*For* [*gar*] Adam was formed first, then Eve" (v. 13). The Greek word *gar* ("for," "because") is causal; it gives the reason for the prohibition. This makes Paul's command universal. It's not simply limited to some women in Ephesus, since Paul roots his command in the pre-fall creation order.

This "strong complementarian" reading should be distinguished from a "soft complementarian" perspective. According to this view, Paul doesn't prohibit women from *all* kinds of teaching over men; he only prohibits a specific kind of authoritative teaching that's reserved for male overseers.[10] Scholars who hold this view interpret the phrase "to teach and *authentein*" together to mean "authoritative teaching," which is reserved for the highest level of leadership in church (i.e., elders, overseers). They support their reading by pointing out that Paul's qualifications for overseers in 1 Timothy 3 include both being able to teach and being a husband of one wife (v. 2). Thus, they conclude, women can teach in the church assembly as long as they do so under the authority of male-only overseers.

---

9 See Andreas J. Köstenberger, "A Complex Sentence: The Syntax of 1 Timothy 2:12," in *Women in the Church: An Interpretation & Application of 1 Timothy 2:9–15*, 3rd ed., ed. Andreas J. Köstenberger and Thomas R. Schreiner (Crossway, 2016), 117–61.

10 See e.g., Craig Blomberg, "A Complementarian Perspective," in *Two Views on Women in Ministry*, rev. ed., ed. James R. Beck (Zondervan, 2005), 168–70.

So let's follow the posture of the noble Bereans in Acts 17:11 and search the Scriptures to discern the truth. We'll start with the meaning of *authentein*.

## The Meaning of the Verb *Authentein*

I can't overstate how important *authentein* is for our understanding of this passage, and for the whole debate over women's church leadership. A word of warning: The following discussion will get very technical. But in this case, I think the technical details are worth the hassle. We need to let the depth of our study determine the strength of our conclusion.

The word *authentein* has been scrutinized in dozens of studies, making it one of *the* most examined words in the Bible (second, perhaps, to *kephalē*).[11] The debate centers on whether the word refers to positive authority (which godly men can exercise but godly women cannot) or to some kind of negative authority (domineering authority, unauthorized authority, etc.) that neither men nor women should exercise in the church. The "strong complementarian" view—and, to some extent, the "soft complementarian" view—largely depends on a positive rendering of *authentein*.

---

11 There are too many studies to list, but some important ones include George Knight III, "*Authenteō* in Reference to Women in 1 Timothy 2:12," *New Testament Studies* 30 (1984): 143–57; Cynthia Long Westfall, "The Meaning of *Authenteō* in 1 Timothy 2.12," *Journal of Greco-Roman Christianity and Judaism* 10 (2014): 138–73; Philip Payne, *Man and Woman, One in Christ: An Exegetical and Theological Study of Paul's Letters* (Zondervan, 2009), 361–97; Jamin Hübner, "Revisiting *Authenteō* in 1 Timothy 2:12: What Do the Extant Data Really Show?," *Journal for the Study of Paul and His Letters* 5, no. 1 (2015): 41–70; and several by Albert Wolters, "A Semantic Study of *Authentēs* and Its Derivatives," *Journal of Greco-Roman Christianity and Judaism* 1 (2000): 145–75; "*Authentēs* and Its Cognates in Biblical Greek," *Journal of the Evangelical Theological Society* 52, no. 4 (2009): 719–29; "The Meaning of *Authenteō*," in *Women in the Church: An Interpretation & Application of 1 Timothy 2:9–15*, 3rd ed., ed. Andreas J. Köstenberger and Thomas R. Schreiner (Crossway, 2016), 65–115; "An Early Parallel of *Authentein* in 1 Tim 2:12," *Journal of the Evangelical Theological Society* 54, no. 4 (2011): 673–84.

Unfortunately, figuring out the meaning of *authentein* is quite challenging. The verb occurs only once in the New Testament (here in 1 Tim. 2:12), it's not in the Septuagint, and it rarely occurs in extrabiblical Greek literature around the time of Paul.[12] The noun form *authentēs* occurs more frequently, but there's debate over how relevant the meaning of the noun is to the meaning of the verb.

I hope you don't mind tedious word studies, because I want to look closely at every occurrence of the verb *authentein* in Greek literature prior to AD 312. I want you to see for yourself how the word is used elsewhere so you can fact-check how I'm interpreting it. I'll then survey the meaning of the noun *authentēs* and explore its relationship to the verb *authentein*.

The first extrabiblical use of *authentein* we'll look at is considered by both egalitarian and complementarian scholars as the most significant for understanding Paul's use in 1 Timothy 2:12.[13] It comes from a papyrus dated less than a century before Paul:

> Since I had authority [*authentēkotos*] with respect to him, he immediately granted Kalatytis the ferryman a concession to make a profit at the same rent.[14]

The larger context of this passage features four characters: an unnamed slave, his master Asklepiades, a ferryman named Kalatytis, and

---

12 We do have several uses of the verb after AD 312, but these later uses are less valuable for understanding Paul's use in 1 Timothy.

13 See Payne, *Man and Woman*, 365; and Knight, "*Authenteō*," 154. See also the thorough discussion in Wolters, "Meaning of *Authenteō*," 73–76.

14 Papyrus *BGU* 1208.38 (27/26 BC).

the narrator, a man named Tryphon.[15] Tryphon is with Asklepiades's slave, and he's looking for a ride from Kalatytis, the ferryman. The unnamed slave refuses to pay the ferryman for the ride, so Tryphon exercises *authentēkotos* (a perfect participle of *authentein*) over the slave, and the slave pays the ferryman. Tryphon later writes to Asklepiades and apologizes for *authentein*-ing his slave.

Is Tryphon's use of *authentēkotos* over another man's slave positive, neutral, or negative?

Some scholars say the word is neutral or positive, since slave owners in the ancient world had authority over slaves. Tryphon might have overstepped his bounds by ordering around another man's slave, hence his apology to Asklepiades. But the verb itself does not carry a negative connotation in this context.[16]

But notice the glaring context: *Authentein* here describes a kind of authority that a master has over a slave. Of course from a secular perspective, this kind of authority would not be considered negative. But does it resonate with the authority described by Jesus: "Whoever wants to become great among you must be your servant, and whoever wants to be first must be slave of all" (Mark 10:43–44)? Even if Tryphon isn't using *authentein* negatively in his mind, he's still wielding a kind of authority wholly unfit for Christian leaders, who should never exercise master-like authority over the ones they're called to lead.[17]

---

15 See Payne, *Man and Woman*, 365, for a reconstruction for this scenario.

16 Knight, "*Authenteō*," 145.

17 Payne argues that *authentein* is negative because Tryphon assumed an authority that was not his (*Man and Woman*, 367–68). This may be true, but I think the negativity of the term runs deeper than that; that is, *authentein* captures a master-slave kind of authority. Even if Tryphon had wielded authorized authority over the slave, that authority still wouldn't be a kind of authority fit for Christian leaders.

Another passage dated from roughly the same era implies a similar meaning of *authentein*:

> Hermes in the post-ascension of the place of access signifies an artisan, a handicraftsman … but when benefics [that is, planets bearing good omens] are squaring, *one who has full command* [*authentounta*] of everything in an art but gains nothing.[18]

The final phrase where *authentein* occurs can also be translated, "the one who *is superior to* the foregoing [*ton toutōn authentounta*] in his occupation, yet earns nothing."[19]

This astrological text conveys a familiar trope where "planetary positions in the heavens correspond to social positions on earth."[20] Hermes (the planet Mercury) "is the planet which determines occupations."[21] The larger passage lists seven different occupations in order from highest to lowest: (1) "a leader and ruler," (2) "a royal man," (3) "a great man," (4) "an artisan, a handicraftsman," (5) "one who works with fire or iron," (6) "a fence or one who takes care of seaside business," and (7) "one who has full command of everything [or "is superior to the foregoing," *authentounta*] in an art but gains nothing."

The first three occupations "are high in the social hierarchy of the ancient world," while the next three "are much lower in that hierarchy,"

---

18 *Methodus Mystica* (ca. 100 BC–AD 50); the translation is from Robert Schmidt, *Astrological Record of the Early Sages in Greek* (Golden Hind Press, 1995), 11. See Wolters, "Early Parallel," 673–84, for a discussion of the date of this work.

19 F. Cumont, ed., *Catalogues codiucum astrologorum graecorum*, vol. 8.1 (Lamertin, 1929), 177, cited in Wolters, "Meaning of *Authenteō*," 76n46.

20 Wolters, "Early Parallel," 677–78.

21 Tamsyn Barton, *Ancient Astrology* (Routledge, 1994), 119, cited in Wolters, "Early Parallel," 677.

and the last one "designates the lowest of them all."[22] Thus, *authentein* here refers to a person who should be, according to the social hierarchy of the day, superior to even leaders and rulers, royal men, and great men but who will unfortunately live at the bottom rung of the social ladder (probably as a slave) thanks to Mercury.[23]

Albert Wolters (a complementarian) argues that *authentein* is not negative in this text: "It simply refers to the way a person is superior … to others in the same business."[24] In one sense, Wolters is right. *Authentein* does not refer to abuse or to one person dominating another (necessarily). But as in the previous text, *authentein* conveys a kind of superiority that resonates perfectly with the secular social hierarchy of the day—a kind of hierarchy that Paul does *not* endorse for church leaders.

When considering whether *authentein* refers to good authority or bad authority, we have to again ask, Good or bad according to whom? According to secular notions of authority or Christian ones?

Three more astrological texts use *authentein* in similar ways. Here's one:

> If Saturn alone is ruler [*tēn oikodespoteian*] of the soul
> and dominates [*authentēsas*] Mercury and the moon …
> he makes his subjects lovers of the body.[25]

---

22 Wolters, "Early Parallel," 678.

23 Wolters, "Meaning of *Authenteō*," 76.

24 Wolters, "Early Parallel," 680.

25 A second-century AD text; Ptolemy, *Tetrabiblos* 3.14.10, in *Claudii Ptolemaei opera quae exstant omnia*, vol. 3.1, *Apotelesmatika*, ed. Wolfgang Hübner (Teubner, 1998), cited in Wolters, "Early Parallel," 680.

This text dates near the time of Paul, and *authentein* occurs in a grammatical position similar to 1 Timothy 2:12.[26] Here, Saturn is "the ruler [*tēn oikodespoteian*] of the soul" and "dominates [*authentēsas*] Mercury and the moon."[27]

Wolters translates *authentein* as "dominates" and argues that the word is not negative in this passage.[28] But I think Wolters's own translation, along with Paul's view of leadership, suggests otherwise. Once again, *authentein* is tethered to a secular understanding of hierarchical relationships, where those at the top dominate those at the bottom.[29]

Here's another astrological text:

> If Mars appears in triangular relation to the latter [Jupiter] and to Saturn, this causes great happiness, and he will make acquisitions and *rule* [*authentēsei*] ... an occupation.[30]

Wolters interprets *authentēsei* here as referring to "a person's future good fortune, which has to do with authority or dominance of some kind related to his occupation."[31] He also cites an expert on ancient astrology,

---

26 The verb *authenteō* is followed by a genitive, as in 1 Timothy.

27 Wolters, "Early Parallel," 681. According to LSJ, *katakrateō* can mean "prevail, gain the mastery, gain the victory ... gain mastery over, become master of one's purpose," and when used of "planetary influence," it means "predominate" (H. G. Liddell et al., *A Greek-English Lexicon* [Clarendon Press, 1996], 896).

28 Wolters, "Early Parallel," 684.

29 Payne is probably closer to the mark when he notes, "The verbs that parallel *authenteō*, 'dominate' and 'overcome,' reinforce that *authenteō* conveys a negative sense in this passage" (*Man and Woman*, 381; cf. Hübner, "Revisiting," 57).

30 *P. Tebt.* 276 (second/third century AD), in *The Tebtunis Papyri: Part II*, ed. Bernard P. Grenfell and Arthur S. Hunt (Henry Frowde, 1907), 31. The text is damaged but has been reconstructed by the editors of these papyri.

31 Wolters, "Early Parallels," 681–82.

Simonetta Feraboli, who translates *authentēsei* to mean that a person has "absolute powers."[32]

Again, this smells a lot like the stuff Jesus denounced in Mark 10. In a world where masters rule their slaves, "absolute power" would be seen as a virtue, not a vice. But in the church, leaders are servants, not masters possessing "absolute power" over their subjects.

Let's look at one more astrological text:

> But if Saturn shares its place, or is in aspect with it according to the manner indicated, it makes people reprehensible, and in their honorary offices makes them not *masters* [*authentas*], but subordinates [*praxantas*] of others, or else people who entrust their own affairs to others.[33]

As in the previous texts, the arrangement of the planets determines a person's social status. Here, *authentas* refers to a "master" as opposed to a "subordinate," yet again conflicting with a Christian understanding of authority.

Finally, let's look at a text that uses *authentein* to discuss rhetoric, the art of speaking:

---

32 Wolters, "Early Parallels," 681n54.

33 CCAG 8.4 (ca. second/first century BC), cited in Wolters, "Early Parallels," 682. The word *authentas* sure looks like a noun to me, not a verb. But Wolters says that *authentas* here is "a denominative verb based on [the noun] *authentēs* in the sense of 'master'" ("Early Parallels," 682). He might be gathering this from the parallel with the participle *praxantas*. Greek nerds can fact-check me, but the *-ntas* ending of *praxantas* means it's a participle, while the *-ntas* ending of *authentas* does not, since *-nt* is part of the stem, not an indicator of the participle. In any case, Al Wolters knows Greek far better than I know English, so I'm going to default to his expertise and treat *authentas* here as a verb. At the end of the day, it's doesn't matter a whole lot for our study.

> But if one is to speak the truth the rhetoricians do greatly harm many [and] great men [*megalous*], and concerning those things (ambitions) which are aimed at with strong desires against distinguished personages [*epiphan*...]—on each occasion they contend earnestly and with *dominating masters* [*authent*...]—to similar ends.[34]

The original Greek text is fragmentary, so this translation is based on a reconstruction. It's not even clear that the verb *authentein* is being used. All we have in the original manuscript is *authent-*, which could be a noun or a verb.

In any case, scholars translate *authent-* in various ways: "dominating masters," "authorized rulers," "rule," "powerful lords," or "have authority over."[35] *Authent-* seems to be correlated with the previous "great men" and "distinguished personages," which might be persons of high status. If this is correct, then *authent-* is being used in a way similar to how it's used in the previous texts we looked at.[36]

In sum, in every occurrence of the verb *authentein* prior to AD 312, few though they may be, the word conveys an authority characteristic of rulers and masters at the top of the secular social hierarchy—the kind of authority both Jesus and Paul directly and consistently denounce.

---

34 Philodemus, *De rhetorica* 2.1333 (= *P.Herc.* 220, frag. 4) (ca. 110–40/35 BC). This translation is from Payne, *Man and Woman*, 371, based on the reconstruction of the Greek text by S. Sudhaus, ed., *Philodemi: Volumina rhetorica*, vol. 3 (Teubner, 1896), 133. Payne points out that the phrase "aimed at with strong desires" seems to be quoting Euripides, and since eight out of nine uses of the noun *authentēs* in Euripides mean "murderer," Payne suggests that *authent-* should be interpreted along similar lines (*Man and Woman*, 372).

35 See the discussions in Payne, *Man and Woman*, 370–73, and Wolters, "Semantic Study," 48.

36 See Westfall, "Meaning of *Authenteō*," 158n45.

*Authentein* captures the social position of "rulers" and "those in high positions" who "act as tyrants" and "lord it over" their subjects, rather than describing the servants who Jesus authorizes to lead his church (Mark 10:42–45).

## The Meaning and Relevance of the Noun *Authentēs*

The verb *authentein* is quite rare. Thankfully, we have many more examples of its noun form *authentēs*. As we'll see, the noun often conveys a negative meaning similar to what we have seen with the verb.

In classical Greek (fifth to fourth century BC), the noun *authentēs* most often means "murderer" (twenty-four times). Around Paul's time, in addition to "murderer," it could also mean "master/owner."[37] The latter sense occurs in the early Christian work *The Shepherd of Hermas*:

> "Let us go to the tower; for the owner [*authentēs*] of the tower cometh to inspect it." And we came to the tower, and there was no one at all by it, save the virgins alone. And the shepherd asked the virgins whether the master [*despotēs*] of the tower had arrived.[38]

Notice how the "*authentēs* of the tower" is also called the "*despotēs* of the tower."[39] *Despotēs*, where we get our English word "despot," refers to

37 It means "murderer" in several first- and second-century AD texts: Wisdom of Solomon 12:6; Josephus, *Jewish War* 1.582, 2.240; Philo, *Det.* 78; Clement of Alexandria, *The Stromata* 3.18.106, 4.4.16.3; Appian, *Bell. Civ.* 2.13, sec. 115.17; 3.2, sec. 16.13; 4.17, sec. 134.40; and *Hist. Rom.* 12.4, sec. 23. Wolters lists five instances where *authentēs* means "master" and not "murder" prior to AD 100 (see "Semantic Study," 45). Wolters overstates his case when he says, "By the first century AD ... the meaning 'murderer' was largely forgotten" ("Semantic Study," 47).

38 *Shepherd of Hermas* 9.5.6 (first to second century AD).

39 See too *Shepherd* 9.5.7, 9.7.6.

"one who has legal control and authority over persons," such as a master over a slave, a ruler over a city, or an owner over an object they own.[40] Elsewhere in *The Shepherd*, the "master of the tower" is called the "lord [*kurios*] of the tower."[41] These terms aren't negative in the sense that the owner is murdering or beating up his tower, but they still convey a secular kind of authority similar to what we saw in the verb *authentein*. Christian leaders aren't like masters over slaves, nor do they resemble lords who own towers. Service—not ownership or mastery—is the mark of *Christian* authority.

Another interesting use of *authentēs* occurs in the first-century BC text 3 Maccabees. Notice how the context is all about the hierarchical status of citizens and slaves:

> He proposed to inflict public disgrace on the Jewish community, and he set up a stone on the tower in the courtyard with this inscription: "None of those who do not sacrifice shall enter their sanctuaries, and all Jews shall be subjected to a registration involving poll tax and to the *status of slaves*. Those who object to this are to be taken by force and put to death; those who are registered are also to be branded on their bodies by fire with the ivy-leaf symbol of Dionysus, and they shall also be reduced to their former limited *status* [*authentian*]." ... "But if any of them prefer to join those who have been initiated into the mysteries, they shall have

40 See William F. Arndt and F. Wilbur Gingrich, ed., *A Greek-English Lexicon of the New Testament and Other Early Christian Literature*, 2nd ed. (University of Chicago Press, 1979), 220.

41 *Shepherd* 9.5.2, 9.7.1. Wolters, "*Authentēs* and Its Cognates," 729.

> *equal citizenship* with the Alexandrians." (2:27–30 NRSV)

The NRSV translates *authentian* as "status," which is technically correct. But the context shows that the status in question is "the status of slaves," in contrast to "equal citizenship with the Alexandrians."[42] Again, the noun points to the kinds of social hierarchies that have no place in Christian leadership.

Another occurrence of *authentēs* comes in a first-century astrological text, where it clearly conveys a master-slave relationship:

> If the Moon is waning it does not make them *masters* [*authentas*], but *servants* [*hupēretoumenous*] of such persons.[43]

In the following century, the adjective *authentikōs* occurs in a similar context with the same meaning:

> For if the Moon waxes, they will be *high-ranking* [*authentikoi*] officers; if it wanes, they will be servants of the leaders [*hupēretai ... tōn hegemonōn*].[44]

---

42 Philip Payne translates *authentian* as "domination," which makes sense in light of the context (*Man and Woman*, 380). Linda Belleville, however, translates it as "origin." "Teaching and Usurping Authority: 1 Timothy 2:11–15," in *Discovering Biblical Authority: Complementarity Without Hierarchy*, ed. Ronald W. Pierce and Rebecca Merrill Groothuis (InterVarsity, 2004), 211. Wolters states that the "abstract noun *authentia* ... almost always refers to authority or sovereignty, and is thus also clearly based on *authentēs* 'master'" ("Semantic Study," 50).

43 *Carmen astrologicum* 346 (first century AD), cited in Wolters, "Early Parallel," 683.

44 *Vettii valentis anthologiae* 381.21 (second century AD), cited in Wolters, "Early Parallel," 683. Wolters goes on to note that the adjective *authentikos* occurs five times in Ptolemy's *Tetrabiblos* "to indicate authority or dominance of some kind" ("Early Parallel," 683, citing Ptolemy, *Tetrabiblos* 4.3.6, 4.4.11, 4.7.5, 4.7.10, 4.10.9).

Wolters notes that these latter two texts are consistent with how "the verb [*authentein*] and its cognates are generally used in astrological texts before about 200 AD."[45] In fact, the "*authentēs* word family seems to be used throughout to refer to authority or dominance of some kind ... which is particularly relevant for understanding *authentein* in 1 Tim 2:12."[46] I agree. I would only suggest that Christian authority is not about "dominance."

In sum, the noun *authentēs* often means "murderer" in its earliest uses. Closer to Paul's time, it can still mean "murderer," but it also conveys the same kind of master-slave hierarchical relationship we saw in the few uses of the verb.[47]

Some scholars argue that the meaning of the noun *authentēs* is irrelevant for determining the meaning of the verb *authentein*.[48] But both complementarian and egalitarian scholars have critiqued this assumption and rightly so.[49] Linguistically, many verbs are derived from nouns, and *authentein* is one of these verbs.[50] Certainly, a noun's cognates can take on meanings different from the original noun. Just because the noun *authentēs* can mean "murderer" doesn't mean Paul uses the verb *authentein* to prohibit women from slaughtering men

45 Wolters, "Early Parallel," 683.

46 Wolters, "Early Parallel," 683–84.

47 From the second century onward, we begin to see other more neutral uses of *authentēs*. For instance, the word is used throughout the second-century papyrus *P.Fam.Tebt.* to refer to the "*keeper* of the archives" (15.31, 32, 48, 141–42; 24.21, 69, 78, 87, 102); see B. A. van Groningen, *A Family-Archive from Tebtunis* (E. J. Brill, 1950), 60n48. Wolters notes that after AD 312, the noun can also mean "doer" (a meaning he says is only attested three times prior to AD 312; "Semantic Study," 45).

48 Knight, "*Authenteō*," 153.

49 Westfall, "Meaning of *Authenteō*," 143.

50 Verbs derived from nouns are called "denominal" verbs. Such verbs are common in ancient Greek, and the forms of *authentein* and *authentēs* suggest that *authentein* is a denominal verb derived from *authentēs*. For more on the morphological relationship between denominal verbs and the agent nouns from which they're derived, see Laura Grestenberger, "To *V* or Not to *V*? Theme Vowels, Verbalizers, and the Structure of the Ancient Greek Verb," *Glossa: A Journal of General Linguistics* 47, no. 1 (2022): 1–42.

in the church, though I'm pretty sure he would oppose this. In any case, as Wolters points out, the verb *authentein* and other cognates "are all based on *authentēs* in the meaning 'master.'"[51] Our survey above agrees with Wolters—even though he doesn't think the term is negative.

From my best reading of the sources, then, *authentēs* (often) and *authentein* (always) denote a type of authority grounded in secular social structures, such as the power masters have over slaves. Paul's Greco-Roman world saw nothing wrong with this kind of authority. But Paul himself considered this kind of authority wholly unfit for Christian leaders, regardless of their sex.

When writers use rare words, they often do so for a specific purpose. If Paul's use of the rare verb *authentein* was deliberate, it may be that he chose it to convey a specific point—namely, that he did not permit wealthy women to exercise the kind of domineering authority over men that masters exercised over slaves within the first-century secular hierarchy.[52]

But I want to hold this conclusion with an open hand, since we still have a lot more to work through. Our understanding of *authentein* must make sense not only of the word's meaning but also how Paul uses it in his argument.

## *Didaskein* and the "Neither ... Nor" Construction (2:12)

Let's return to the context of 1 Timothy 2:12. How is *authentein* connected with the previous verb "to teach" (*didaskein*)?

---

51 Wolters, "Semantic Study," 47.

52 See Hübner, "Revisiting," 44–56.

As noted earlier, some scholars argue that *authentein* must be a positive word, since it's joined to *didaskein* with "neither ... nor" (*ouk ... oude*). Since *didaskein* is positive, *authentein* must be positive. Therefore, they argue, Paul doesn't forbid women only from teaching false doctrine or exercising ungodly authority; rather, he prohibits all forms of teaching and authority over men, or at least all authoritative teaching (as "soft complementarians" argue).

I think the meaning of *authentein* challenges this logic. Why not let *authentein* shape our understanding of *didaskein* rather than the other way around? But before we make a decision, let's consider the meaning of *didaskein* on its own terms.

Paul uses *didaskein* fifteen times in his letters, and in almost every case he uses the term positively.[53] It would be misleading, though, to say that *didaskein* is an intrinsically positive word. The term is actually neutral; it simply means "to teach." Whether it's used positively or negatively depends on what's being taught, how it's being taught, or who's doing the teaching.

In most New Testament uses, *didaskein* is positive—but that's because the context makes it positive. When Paul tells Timothy to "command and teach these things" (1 Tim. 4:11), we know this is positive, not because *didaskein* is intrinsically positive but because it's obvious from the context that Paul is using it positively.

In Titus 1:10–11, however, Paul clearly uses *didaskein* negatively. "For there are many rebellious people," Paul says, "... disrupting whole households by *teaching* things they ought not *to teach*—and that for the

53 Romans 2:21; 12:7; 1 Corinthians 4:17; 11:14; Galatians 1:12; Ephesians 4:21; Colossians 1:28; 2:7; 3:16; 2 Thessalonians 2:15; 1 Timothy 2:12; 4:11; 6:2; 2 Timothy 2:2; Titus 1:11.

sake of dishonest gain." In this context, *didaskein* is negative because of the content of the teaching and the motivation of the teacher.

Other passages are more complicated. In Galatians 1:12, Paul writes, "I did not receive [the gospel] from any man, nor was I *taught it* [*edidachthēn*]; rather, I received it by revelation from Jesus Christ." Paul contrasts the *teaching* of human beings with direct revelation from Christ. Humans teaching the gospel is certainly a positive thing. But in Paul's specific argument, *didaskein* conveys a negative point: It refers to *mere* human teaching as opposed to direct revelation from Christ.

We see a similar use in Romans 2:21: "*You ... who teach* [*ho ... didaskōn*] others, do *you* not *teach* [*didaskeis*] yourself?" Paul here addresses hypocrites who teach others but don't teach themselves. The content of their teaching might be good: They're telling others the truth (v. 20). But since they're doing so in a hypocritical manner, Paul criticizes their teaching. "Do you not teach yourself?" is a jab at hypocrisy, not a wholly positive use of *didaskein*. Paul views their "teaching" negatively not because of its content but because of the manner in which it's done.[54]

*Didaskein* is not an innocent word until proven guilty, positive unless it's shown to be negative. It's a neutral word that's rendered positive or negative based on the context. And there's nothing in the context of 1 Timothy 2:12 that shows *didaskein* is a positive kind of teaching (which men can do but women cannot). In fact, if *authentein* refers to a negative kind of authority, which is probably the case, then *didaskein* more likely refers to a negative kind of teaching.

This brings us to the "neither ... nor" (*ouk ... oude*) construction that joins *didaskein* to *authentein*. Paul frequently employs this construction

54 See also Matthew 5:19; Revelation 2:14, 20.

to join two words into a single idea: what linguists call a hendiadys. For instance, Paul says in Romans 2:28, "A person is *not* [*ou*] a Jew who is one only outwardly, *nor* [*oude*] is circumcision merely outward and physical." Being a Jew "outwardly" overlaps with "circumcision" to form a single idea (cf. 2 Thess. 3:7–8).[55]

Throughout 1 Timothy 2, Paul also uses word pairs that overlap in meaning, like "peaceful and quiet" (v. 2), "godliness and holiness" (v. 2), and "I am telling the truth, I am not lying" (v. 7).[56] It wouldn't be unusual for Paul to join *didaskein* to *authentein* with the *ouk ... oude* construction to convey a single idea—namely, that women are not permitted to teach (*didaskein*) in a domineering manner (*authentein*) over man.

This interpretation also fits Paul's concern with the *manner* of Christian behavior throughout 1 Timothy 2: *how* to pray (vv. 2, 8), *how* to dress (vv. 9–10), and *how* to learn (vv. 11–12). In fact, Paul begins his prohibition of *didaskein* and *authentein* by highlighting the manner in which women should learn—"in quietness and full submission" (v. 11) and with a "quiet" demeanor (v. 12).[57] Paul's emphasis on this humble posture, in contrast to the secular social hierarchy implied by *authentein*, suggests that he's concerned with *how* women teach, not *whether* they teach.[58]

In short, from my best reading of the linguistic evidence, *authentein* refers to a secular kind of domineering authority, not a godly kind of

---

55 See also Romans 2:28; 3:10; 9:6–7, 16; 11:21; 1 Corinthians 15:50; Galatians 1:1, 11–12; 4:4; Philippians 2:16; 1 Thessalonians 5:5; see Payne, *Man and Woman*, 33.

56 See Blomberg, "Complementarian Perspective," 169.

57 The phrase "in full submission" (*en pasē hupotagē*) does not refer to a wife's submission to her husband, nor a woman's submission to man, but to a woman's posture while learning. The syntax of the verse "indicates that the silence was to be exercised during instruction." Bruce Winter, *Roman Wives, Roman Widows: The Appearance of New Women and the Pauline Communities* (Eerdmans, 2003), 114.

58 See Hübner, "Revisiting," 67. Schreiner and Moo both agree that when it comes to women learning, Paul's focus is on the manner in which they are to learn. Schreiner, "Interpretation," 97; Moo, "What Does It Mean," 183.

authority fit for Christian leaders. While Paul often uses *didaskein* positively, the context always makes this clear, and such clarity is lacking in 1 Timothy 2:12. Because Paul joins *didaskein* with *authentein*—a word that most likely conveys a negative kind of authority—Paul is therefore prohibiting women from teaching men in a domineering manner.

This is, at the very least, an exegetically plausible way to interpret Paul's words. But please don't just believe everything I'm saying without scrutinizing my argument. These are complicated issues that require patient study and critical thinking, and I'm sure brilliant scholars will disagree with some of my conclusions thus far. I'm only offering my most thorough and honest evaluation of the text with the hopes that readers will do as the Bereans did and see if these things are so.

Let's move on to the verse that's keeping Bill Mounce from being egalitarian.

## Adam's Priority and Eve's Deception (2:13–14)

Paul follows the prohibition in 1 Timothy 2:12 by appealing to Adam and Eve's creation:

> For [*gar*] Adam was formed first, then Eve. And Adam was not the one deceived; it was the woman who was deceived and became a sinner. (vv. 13–14)

Complementarians say Paul's appeal to creation means the prohibition of verse 12 is a universal principle applying to all churches in all times. The word *gar* ("for," "because") gives Paul's reason for prohibiting women from teaching and exercising authority over man—namely, Adam was formed first, not Eve.

I used to think this was a slam-dunk argument for the complementarian view. And I still think it has some merit. But after looking at the text more closely, I've found it faces some challenges.

The first challenge should now be obvious. Even if 2:13 establishes a universal principle, then Paul is universally prohibiting women from teaching men in a domineering manner. No egalitarian would (or should!) disagree with this. Complementarians assume that "teach and *authentein*" is a positive description of godly teaching and authority, something appropriate for men but not for women. But if *authentein* does not refer to godly, Christlike authority, then Paul's reference to creation offers no support for a complimentarian view.

But before we declare the case closed, let's just assume that everything I've said about *authentein* and *didaskein* is wrong. Let's say Paul is prohibiting women from teaching and exercising a kind of godly authority that's reserved only for men. Does Paul's appeal to creation in verse 13 establish this prohibition as a universal principle?

Our answer depends largely on the meaning of the Greek word *gar* ("for," "because"). Many complementarians say this word is causal ("because"); it gives Paul's reason for his prohibition in verse 12. But while Paul often uses *gar* as a causal word, this isn't the only way he uses it. Sometimes he includes *gar* to introduce an illustration. Thus *gar* could be translated as "for example."[59] Paul even employs *gar* to continue his train of thought in ways that make it almost unnecessary

---

59 BAGD lists thirty-nine instances in the New Testament where *gar* is a "marker of clarification" ("for, you see") and fourteen instances in Paul where *gar* is not used to describe cause or reason (Rom. 1:18; 2:25; 4:3; 9:5, 7; 12:3; 14:5; 1 Cor. 10:1; 2 Cor. 1:12; 10:12; 11:5; Gal. 1:11; 5:13; 1 Tim. 2:5). Bauer, Arndt and Gingrich, *A Greek-English Lexicon*, 152. Mounce argues that seven of the New Testament's thirty-nine instances of "clarification" listed in BAGD are debated (*Pastoral Epistles*, 132). Payne identifies even more instances where Paul uses *gar* in noncausal ways (*Man and Woman*, 399–401).

to translate the word at all, like in 1 Timothy 3:13 (see also 2 Tim. 3:6; Titus 3:3).[60]

But we can't determine the meaning of *gar* by simply citing how Paul uses it elsewhere. Context must determine the meaning of *gar*.[61] We have to consider the point Paul is making about Adam and Eve in 2:13–14 and determine whether his logic makes the most sense as a *reason* or an *illustration* in relation to 2:12.

Most who interpret *gar* causally (to give a *reason*) say that Paul alludes to the principle of primogeniture (the right of inheritance ascribed to the firstborn) that comes with Adam's firstborn status.[62] Women shouldn't teach or *authentein* man (v. 12) *because* Adam was created first, not Eve (v. 13). This may seem like the "plain" reading of the text. But if you remember our discussion of Genesis back in chapter 1, the primogeniture reading is anything but plain. Adam was *created* first, not *born* first; Eve is his wife, not his sibling; Adam doesn't have a father who died and passed on his inheritance; and so on.

But perhaps Paul is referring to some general priority of being born (or created) first and not specifically to ancient primogeniture principles. This still faces the problem that God frequently overturns the priority of the firstborn throughout Scripture. Paul himself appeals to Adam's priority over Eve in 1 Corinthians 11:8–9 only to turn around and refute it (or at least significantly qualify it) in 11:11–12.[63] It's theologically ques-

---

60 The NIV rightly doesn't translate *gar* in 1 Timothy 3:13. See Payne, *Man and Woman*, 399, who cites Romans 8:18 as another example of this use.

61 Cf. A. T. Robertson: "The precise relation between clauses or sentences is not set forth by *gar*. That must be gathered from the context if possible." *A Grammar of the Greek New Testament in the Light of Historical Research* (Broadman Press, 1934), 1191, cited in Payne, *Man and Woman*, 402.

62 See e.g., Andreas J. Köstenberger, *1–2 Timothy & Titus*, Evangelical Biblical Theology Commentary (Lexham Press, 2021), 116.

63 Timothy Harris, "Why Did Paul Mention Eve's Deception? A Critique of P. W. Barnett's Interpretation of 1 Timothy 2," *Evangelical Quarterly* 62 (1990): 344.

tionable, then, that Paul is alluding to a universalized primogeniture (or priority of the firstborn) principle that conflicts with his own view in 1 Corinthians 11 and is at odds with the biblical theme of overturning the priority of the firstborn.

Interpreting *gar* causally to establish a universal principle faces a second challenge—one that deserves an extended reflection. Paul's reference to creation doesn't stop at Adam being created first; it extends to Eve's deception: "And Adam was not the one deceived; it was the woman who was deceived and became a sinner" (1 Tim. 2:14). If Paul's appeal to creation has universal relevance, then we shouldn't stop at Eve being created second. We should keep going to include her deception. If Eve's second-born (or -created) status applies universally to *all* women (i.e., it's why all women can't teach or *authentein* men), then her deception also applies universally to *all* women. Does this mean all women are more easily deceived than men?

Through much of church history, the answer was yes. Women were excluded from teaching and leading men because they were believed to be by nature more easily deceived and intellectually inferior to men. First Timothy 2:14 was often cited as proof of this belief.[64]

But many complementarians today don't argue for this. Most now agree with Wayne Grudem that "Paul is not saying anything about the natural abilities of men and women."[65] Instead, they argue, Paul is talking about generalities, not absolutes. "*Generally speaking*," writes Tom Schreiner, "women are more relational and nurturing and men are more given to rational analysis and objectivity."[66] Grudem agrees: "God gave

---

64 See William Webb, *Slaves, Women & Homosexuals: Exploring the Hermeneutics of Cultural Analysis* (IVP Academic, 2001), 226–27, 263–68; William Witt, *Icons of Christ: A Biblical and Systematic Theology for Women's Ordination* (Baylor University Press, 2021), 21–29.

65 Grudem, *Evangelical Feminism*, 70.

66 Schreiner, "Interpretation," 145 (italics in original).

men, *in general*, a disposition that is better suited to teaching and governing in the church, a disposition that inclines more to rational, logical analysis of doctrine ... and God gave women, *in general*, a disposition that inclines more toward a relational, nurturing emphasis that places a higher value on unity and community in the church (v. 14)."[67]

Grudem and Schreiner don't think Paul is saying *all* women are more prone to deception or are less rational than *all* men. And I agree. But I don't think their exegesis of 2:14 is compelling or consistent. If 2:13 establishes an absolute principle with no exceptions, then why isn't 2:14 also an absolute principle with no exceptions? There's no indication in Paul's words that he's shifting from an absolute principle (v. 13) to a general one (v. 14). He simply continues his thought: "*And* Adam was not deceived, but the woman was deceived." Paul's wording in 2:14 even parallels 2:13:

> For Adam was formed first, then Eve; (v. 13)
> and Adam was not deceived, but the woman was deceived. (v. 14 ESV)

It seems odd to interpret 2:13 universally but 2:14 more generally. Plus, if Grudem and Schreiner are right and Paul really is describing women's general disposition, then what about the exceptions to this general rule? If a minority of women are just as rational and deception-proof as men, shouldn't *these* women be allowed to teach?[68]

---

67 Grudem, *Evangelical Feminism*, 72 (emphasis mine).

68 Grudem addresses this pushback but offers a circular counterargument. He says that exceptions to 2:14 (i.e., the few women who aren't easily deceived) are still excluded from teaching and authoritative positions in the church, since 2:13 is universal and absolute (*Evangelical Feminism*, 73). But he never shows exegetically how Paul moves from an absolute statement (2:13) to a more general one (2:14).

And besides, if women really are more relational, nurturing, and unity-focused as Grudem argues, should these things be disqualifications for leadership? Paul himself describes his apostolic ministry as one that is nurturing (1 Thess. 2:7), and few things impassioned him more than the unity of the church. I can't imagine Paul advocating for male-only teachers and authority figures in the church since he believed that men are more rational, less relational and nurturing, and don't place a high "value on unity and community in the church." I've been in churches run by such pastors. I don't recommend it.

Other complementarians say 2:14 "makes no ontological statement about women" at all, not even in generalities.[69] Rather, 2:14 is "making a statement about what happens when roles are interchanged and women take leadership."[70] In other words, 2:13 gives a *reason* while 2:14 provides an *illustration*. Thus, Eve's deception is hers alone, not an indictment of all (or most) women.

This view seems more credible, but it doesn't seem very consistent. It interprets Adam's firstborn status as the universal *reason* for male leadership in the church, but it believes Eve's deception is an *illustration* that says nothing universal about women. Why take Adam out of the garden but leave Eve there? It's more exegetically compelling to take 2:13–14 together as either giving a universal *reason* or providing an *illustration*.[71] As we'll see, it's likely that Paul is doing the latter in both verses.

---

69 Mounce, *Pastoral Epistles*, 137.

70 Mounce, *Pastoral Epistles*, 137.

71 Craig Blomberg takes a different route. Instead of connecting 2:14 to 2:13, he takes 2:14 and 2:15 together: "Verse 14 then functions to set up verse 15 by recalling that things got worse before they got better" ("Complementarian Perspective," 172). But there's no indication that 2:14 should be logically disconnected from 2:13, especially since, as noted, the two verses have a parallel structure connected by "and" (as Mounce rightly observes, *Pastoral Epistles*, 142).

It's worth noting that Paul talks about deception elsewhere without linking it to gender. Paul frequently warns entire churches—males and females—about the dangers of deception, often in the context of false teachers.[72] In fact, the only other place where Paul mentions Eve's deception is in 2 Corinthians 11:3, where Eve's deception is an illustration applied to both men and women in the Corinthian church. Paul doesn't seem to treat Eve's deception as proof of a universal principle about all (or most) women. Rather, he appeals to it in an ad hoc way that suits his particular point in different contexts.[73]

Perhaps, then, 2:13–14 as a whole is an illustration and not a universal reason for Paul's prohibition in 2:12. As noted, the Greek word *gar* can set up an illustration ("for example"). Paul's appeal to creation in 2:13–14 would then illustrate the point of 2:12. That is, he cites creation to draw a parallel between Adam and Eve and the situation at Ephesus.

I think this interpretation makes good sense of Paul's reference to Eve's deception (v. 14). He doesn't bring up Eve to make a universal or general point about women. Rather, he mentions Eve's deception to illustrate something about the local situation in Ephesus (as he did with the situation in Corinth in 2 Cor. 11:3). We know that women in Ephesus were being deceived by false teachers, so it makes sense for Paul to appeal to Eve as an illustration of a woman being deceived like the Ephesian women were.[74]

---

72 General warnings: Romans 7:11; 16:18; 1 Corinthians 3:18; 6:9; 15:33; Galatians 6:3, 7; 2 Thessalonians 2:3; 2 Timothy 3:13; Titus 3:3. False teachers in particular: 2 Corinthians 11:3–4; 2 Timothy 2:17–18; 3:6–8. See Cynthia Westfall, *Paul and Gender: Reclaiming the Apostle's Vision for Men and Women in Christ* (Baker, 2016), 109–10.

73 Westfall, *Paul and Gender*, 111.

74 Padilla, *Pastoral Epistles*, 95.

In fact, Paul's language subtly correlates Eve with the women at Ephesus. He moves from "Eve" (v. 13) to "the woman" (v. 14) to "she" (v. 15 CSB) and then to "they" (v. 15 CSB)—that is, the women at Ephesus who must "continue in faith, love and holiness with propriety [*sophrosunēs*]" (v. 15)—the key word that bookends our passage (vv. 9, 15). Paul brings us back to the wealthy women of Ephesus who have been his focus all along (vv. 9–10).[75]

While the illustration view of *gar* makes sense of 2:14, I think it has a tougher time with 2:13. How would Adam being created first and Eve second illustrate Paul's prohibition in 2:12? One plausible suggestion is that Paul is refuting some kind of genealogical myth believed by the Ephesians, in which woman preceded man. After all, "myths and endless genealogies" were part of the false teaching alive in Ephesus (1 Tim. 1:4).

I'll come back to this possibility later, since it'll take some time to unpack. For now, I want to simply note that both the causal and illustrative interpretations of 2:13 face some challenges. But the illustrative interpretation makes much better sense of 2:14 than the causal interpretation does. Paul appeals to Eve's deception not to support a universal principle applied to all women but to offer an illustration tailored to the local situation at Ephesus. Either way, it makes more exegetical sense to take all of 2:13–14 as either causal or illustrative. For me, the scales are tipped in favor of the latter.

In sum, I don't think complementarian interpretations of 1 Timothy 2:13–14 are as "plain" as I used to think. It's certainly possible to interpret 2:13 as a universal principle based on creation and

---

75 David Pao, *1–2 Timothy, Titus*, Brill Exegetical Commentary Series (Brill, 2023), 186–87.

2:14 as an illustration but not a universal principle. But this isn't the only, or even the best, way to interpret these verses.

This brings us to Paul's final, and most jarring, statement in the passage: "Yet *she* will be saved through childbearing—if *they* continue in faith and love and holiness, with self-control" (2:15 ESV).

This verse has elicited all sorts of interpretations. Are women saved (in the theological sense) by bearing children? Are they saved (theologically) by living out their God-given duties as wives and mothers? Are they saved (theologically) through the birth of Christ? Are they physically saved (that is, delivered from death) while giving birth?[76]

I think the last interpretation is the most probable, but it's not essential to how we interpret this passage as a whole.[77] However we understand this enigmatic verse, one thing seems clear: Paul isn't making a universal statement about women, childbirth, and salvation.[78] Rather, he's probably addressing a local belief about women and childbirth that's prevalent in Ephesus.

But what is this belief? And how does 2:15 shape our reading of 2:8–15 as a whole? To answer these questions, we need to take a visit to the bustling town of first-century Ephesus.

---

76 See Westfall for a survey of interpretive options (*Paul and Gender*, 130–40). Sandra Glahn has recently argued convincingly for this view. *Nobody's Mother: Artemis of the Ephesians in Antiquity and the New Testament* (IVP Academic, 2023).

77 One of the greatest challenges to this view is that it's a false promise: Certainly some women still died in childbirth. But this is also a problem for other statements in the New Testament, where a promise of healing appears to be absolute. James says that the "prayer of faith will save [*sosei*] the sick" (James 5:15 CSB), but certainly not every sick person is always healed when they're prayed for. Paul says that "the Lord will rescue me from every evil attack" (2 Tim. 4:18), and yet he was executed a few years later (see Westfall, *Paul and Gender*, 138). I think it's best to take such statements as general promises even though they are stated in language that appears absolute.

78 One could say that the "birth of Christ" view of 2:15 universally applies to all women. I think this interpretation is the least credible. But even if we go with this, it's almost certain that Paul writes what he does in 2:15 to address some local belief in Ephesus.

## The Cultural Context of Ephesus

We should be cautious in reconstructing ancient contexts we've never lived in. We'll never know with certainty what ancient cities were like. Fortunately, we do have an abundance of knowledge about first-century Ephesus. And the parallels between the cultural situation at Ephesus and Paul's argument in 1 Timothy, especially 2:8–15, are striking.

Paul's focus on rich women (vv. 9–10) makes perfect sense considering the historical situation in Ephesus and its surrounding regions. Archaeological and literary evidence shows us that a surprisingly high number of women occupied positions of authority in civic, political, and especially religious spheres.[79] Many of these prominent women belonged to the upper class, since wealth was required for acquiring such prominent offices.[80] In fact, "female benefactors are honored in inscriptions for providing substantial support for others 'as frequently as in those for men.'"[81] Paul Trebilco notes that "a significant group of wealthy and prominent women" in first-century Asia Minor "had the freedom to use their wealth as they saw fit."[82] This picture is magnified when we look at the religious, social, and economic heartbeat of the city: its patron deity Artemis and the religious cult dedicated to her supremacy.

Artemis was worshipped as the supreme deity in Ephesus and the city's benefactor, protector, and savior. She was ascribed various titles,

79 See Paul Trebilco, *Jewish Communities in Asia Minor*, Society for New Testament Studies Monograph Series 69 (Cambridge University Press, 2006), 104–26. Steve Baugh reminds us that, even though a number of women held prominent positions in Ephesus, it was still "an ancient patrichal" city ("A Foreign World: Ephesus in the First Century," in Andreas J. Köstenberger and Thomas R. Schreiner, eds., *Women in the Church: An Interpretation & Application of 1 Timothy 2:9–15*, 3rd ed. [Crossway, 2016], 50).

80 Trebilco, *Jewish Communities*, 125.

81 Pao, *1–2 Timothy, Titus*, 177, citing Riet van Bremen, "Women and Wealth," in *Images of Women in Antiquity*, ed. Averil Cameron and Amélie Kuhrt (Routledge, 2017), 224–42.

82 Trebilco, *Jewish Communities*, 125.

such as "Artemis of the First Throne," "Most Holy," "Most High," "Lord," "Savior," and "Queen of the Cosmos," who wielded power and authority over creation.[83] It was believed that devotion to Artemis secured the economic prosperity of the city. The massive temple dedicated to Artemis was not just a religious center; it also functioned as a bank which controlled the city's wealth.[84] Artemis's influence over Ephesus cannot be overstated. Mythologies about her permeated the social, political, religious, and economic fabric of the city. [85] Paul, of course, experienced this firsthand when he clashed with devotees to Artemis in Ephesus, which nearly started a riot (Acts 19).

Artemis mythology was especially important to Ephesian women. According to Greek legend, Artemis had protected the Amazons—female warriors independent of men—who founded the city of Ephesus, and they reflected the powerful and ferocious character of their god.[86] The Artemis cult in Ephesus was primarily led by female virgin priestesses, typically high-status and wealthy women who were able to finance their own duties in the cult and served as generous benefactors

---

83 Richard Oster, "The Ephesian Artemis as an Opponent of Early Christianity," *Jahrbuch für Antike und Christentum* 19 (1976): 40.

84 See Dio Chrysostom, *Or.* 31.54; Oster, "Artemis," 32–34. Artemis's temple was four times larger than the Parthenon in Athens and was hailed as one of the seven wonders of the ancient world (see Pliny, *Nat.* 36.95–97).

85 See Oster, "Artemis," 27; Morna Hooker, "Artemis of Ephesus," *Journal of Theological Studies* 64, no. 1 (2013): 41.

86 Pausanias, *Description of Greece* 4.31.8, 7.2.7. Homer, the first to mention the Amazons, describes them as *antianeirai* (translated as "antagonistic to men" or "the equal of men"); *Iliad* 3.189, 6.186. Herodotus describes the Amazons as "killers of men" (*Histories* 4.110); an Amazon woman, he says, doesn't get married until "she has killed a man of the enemy," and in some cases they "grow old and die unmarried" (*Histories* 4.118). Aeschylus says the Amazons "loathe all men" (*Prometheus Bound*, 724); cf. C. L. Brinks, "'Great Is Artemis of the Ephesians': Acts 19:23–41 in Light of Goddess Worship in Ephesus," *Catholic Biblical Quarterly* 71, no. 4 (2009): 779. Sandra Glahn notes that while "many scholars have downplayed any Amazon connections" to the city of Ephesus, "open-air stone carvings in a temple in Ephesus ... feature Amazon women as integral to the city's origins" (*Nobody's Mother*, 41).

of others.[87] Priestesses had many religious responsibilities, including performing cultic duties during festivals, adorning statues of Artemis with lavish decorations, and financially underwriting the cult.[88] They also wielded power beyond the religious sphere, which "is evident by the relatively high number of women occupying the leadership position[s]" in the city. [89]

There are several interesting parallels between the Artemis cult and the issues Paul addresses in 1 Timothy. These parallels could be a clue that Paul has this cult in mind in his letter, especially in 2:8–15.[90]

One of the most common titles ascribed to Artemis is "Savior" and "the Savior of Ephesus." It's interesting that Paul almost never calls God or Christ "Savior" outside the Pastoral Epistles (Phil. 3:20 is the only place), but in the Pastorals, he refers to God/Christ as "Savior" ten times, four of which are in 1 Timothy. "In the same way that kryptonite evokes thoughts of Superman without uttering his name," suggests Sandra Glahn, "Paul could refer to Jesus as *the/our Savior* in Ephesus and listeners would know he was exalting Christ over their local deity."[91]

The Artemis cult was led by women with wealth and social power, and Artemis herself was viewed as the financial benefactor of the city. Throughout 1 Timothy, Paul addresses issues of wealth and wealthy

---

87 Glahn, *Nobody's Mother*, 85. Pao notes that there were a "disproportionate number of women" who "serve[d] as high priestesses even for male deities ... and for related imperial cults ... found throughout Ephesus ... and the surrounding area (*1–2 Timothy, Titus*, 176); cf. the extensive documentation in R. A. Kearsley, "Asiarchs, *Archiereis*, and the *Archiereiai* of Asia," *Greek, Roman, and Byzantine Studies* 27 (1986): 183–92.

88 Glahn, *Nobody's Mother*, 86. There were two main yearly festivals associated with the Artemis cult; one of them (the Artemision) lasted for an entire month (Brinks, "'Great Is Artemis,'" 782).

89 Pao, 1–2 *Timothy, Titus*, 176.

90 Paul never names Artemis in 1 Timothy, but Paul never mentions foreign deities in any of his letters. (Luke does throughout Acts, however.) Certainly, Paul dealt with the influence of pagan deities throughout his letters, but he always avoids mentioning the names of pagan gods (see Glahn, *Nobody's Mother*, 122).

91 Glahn, *Nobody's Mother*, 121.

women in particular (2:9–10; 3:3; 6:2–10, 17–19). It would be difficult to detach the city's wealth, and the Christians who were misusing it, from the Artemis cult and its influence over the city's economic success.

Paul's emphasis on marriage in 1 Timothy (4:3; 5:11–15) makes sense if the Artemis cult—with all its emphasis on female autonomy and virginity—nurtured a more negative view of marriage in Ephesus.[92] Artemis was a virgin hailed as the "wife of Ephesus."[93] Her power and authority over Ephesus were completely disconnected from a male figure.[94] Her independent status may have influenced a sense of female autonomy among some women in the city.[95]

There are also several noteworthy linguistic connections between 1 Timothy and a first-century book about Ephesus called *Ephesiaca*.[96] *Ephesiaca* uses the term "braided hair" to "refer to a hairstyle ... worn by those who served and desired to imitate Artemis."[97] Paul uses the same root term when he forbids women from wearing "braided hair" (*plegmasin*) in 1 Timothy 2:9 (ESV). In fact, this is the only time this word occurs in the New Testament.

The adjective "adorned" (*kosmios*) occurs only twice in the New Testament—both times by Paul in 1 Timothy (2:9; 3:2). And Paul uses the verb form of this term only in Titus 2:10 and here in 1 Timothy

---

92 "Her [Artemis's] perpetual virginity was indicative of her freedom from men rather than of any kind of morality, and in fact she is still embraced today as a symbol of female independence" (Brinks, "'Great Is Artemis,'" 778).

93 Lynn R. LiDonnici, "The Images of Artemis Ephesia and Greco-Roman Worship: A Reconsideration," *Harvard Theological Review* 85, no. 4 (1992): 409.

94 Glahn, *Nobody's Mother*, 59–60.

95 Glahn raises the question, "If Artemis *and* her Amazonian devotees were single, did the women in Ephesus seek to emulate their city's founders and the goddess they worshiped by remaining unmarried?" (*Nobody's Mother*, 43).

96 Gary Hoag, *Wealth in Ancient Ephesus and the First Letter to Timothy: Fresh Insights from Ephesiaca by Xenophon of Ephesus*, Bulletin for Biblical Research Supplement 11 (Eisenbrauns, 2015).

97 Hoag, *Wealth*, 75.

2:10. *Ephesiaca* uses several forms of this same word to describe young women leading an annual procession to celebrate Artemis's birth. The girls were "adorned [*ekekosmēto*] as for a lover,"[98] and the leader of the group, Anthia, donned "*the adornment* [*kosmos*] of her dress."[99] Anthia, who also has her hair *braided* (*peplegmenē*),[100] is even portrayed as imitating Artemis: "Often when seeing her at the shrine, the Ephesians worshiped her as Artemis."[101] In fact, "the practice of imitating Artemis is portrayed in *Ephesiaca* as a cultural expectation for all young women, and prominent ones led the way in exhibiting piety to Artemis in this fashion."[102]

Paul forbids women in 1 Timothy 2:9 from dressing in "costly" (*polutelei*, ESV) clothing, and this is the only time Paul uses this word in his letters. *Ephesiaca* uses the same word four times to refer to a woman's "costly" attire.[103] Paul's only use of the term "gold" (*chrusion*) is also in 1 Timothy 2:9, and this word occurs fifteen times in *Ephesiaca*. The word "self-control" (*sophrosunē*, ESV), a key word that bookends our passage (1 Tim. 2:9, 15), occurs twenty-one times in different forms throughout *Ephesiaca*.[104]

If 1 Timothy and *Ephesiaca* had only one or two words in common, we probably shouldn't think much of it. But cumulatively, these parallels are suggestive. Paul uses these terms only here in 1 Timothy 2, and they all occur in a book written around the same time and in the same place as 1 Timothy to describe women associated with the Artemis cult.

---

98 *Ephesiaca* 1.2.4–5; cf. 1.2.2.
99 *Ephesiaca* 1.2.4–5.
100 *Ephesiaca* 1.2.6.
101 *Ephesiaca* 1.2.4–5.
102 Hoag, *Wealth*, 79.
103 Hoag, *Wealth*, 77.
104 Hoag, *Wealth*, 76.

Another potential connection between Paul's letter and the Artemis cult comes from the myths of Artemis's origin. Artemis was believed to be the firstborn of Zeus and Leto, hailed as preeminent over her twin brother Apollos.[105] Glahn sees evidence that some of her followers believed "she was superior because she was born first."[106] A second-century (AD) writer, Pausanias, even notes that in Artemis's temple, "there is a stone wall above the altar of Artemis," where she is called "Goddess of the *First Throne* [*Artemis prōtothroniē*]."[107] It seems that "firstness" was part of Artemis's identity—both in terms of her birth and her superiority. Many devotees to Artemis, in fact—including the women in *Ephesiaca*—believed she was the same deity as the Egyptian goddess Isis. In Isis's origin story, she usurps the authority of the sun god Ra and forms a serpent to bite him. In this creation account, as Gary Hoag points out, the male deity Ra "was the one who was deceived."[108] Artemis's and Isis's origin stories might easily have shaped the imagination of their religious devotees: The female is the firstborn, and the male is the one who falls into deception.[109]

These origin stories are perfectly contradicted by Paul's appeal to Adam's priority in creation and Eve's deception (2:13–14). We can't be sure this is what Paul is doing by bringing up Genesis; I wouldn't base my interpretation on it. But the parallels are too striking to dismiss out of hand. If I had to guess what "myths and endless genealogies" Timothy was dealing with in Ephesus (1:4), I think something related to the Artemis cult would be a good candidate.

---

105 Hooker, "Artemis of Ephesus," 43, citing Homer, *Iliad* 21.470.

106 Sandra Glahn, "The First-Century Ephesian Artemis: Ramifications of Her Identity," *Bibliotheca Sacra* 172, no. 668 (2015): 463.

107 Pausanias, *Description of Greece*, 10.38.6.

108 Hoag, *Wealth*, 91.

109 See Glahn, *Nobody's Mother*, 97.

Here's one more parallel I find especially striking: Artemis was believed to deliver people from their afflictions, especially women during childbirth.[110] As a kind of cosmic midwife, Artemis supposedly relieved women from their birth pains, saved them from death, or allowed them to die without experiencing pain. As Hoag explains, "Women who chose to serve God rather than the goddess of childbearing would put their lives at risk because of the possibility of the wrath of the goddess."[111]

This context might explain Paul's cryptic statement that "*she* will be saved through childbearing—if *they* continue in faith and love and holiness, with self-control" (2:15 ESV). It's certainly plausible that Paul, writing to a city whose famed deity was celebrated as a divine midwife who saved mothers in childbirth, had this in mind when he penned 2:15. He wanted to redirect people's hope from Artemis to God—our true "Savior" who saves women from dying in childbirth. Since 2:15 wraps up and bookends Paul's argument in verses 8–15, this makes it even more likely that the Artemis cult might linger behind Paul's whole passage.

Lastly, it's worth noting that Paul stationed Timothy in Ephesus to "command certain people not to teach false doctrines" (1:3). Such false teaching includes "myths and endless genealogies" (1:4; cf. 4:7), negative views of marriage and procreation (4:3; cf. 5:14), a misuse of wealth (6:3–10, 17–19), and a mishandling of the Mosaic law to justify their teaching (1:7–11), and the false teachers targeted women in particular (especially widows) with their doctrine (5:15; cf. 2 Tim. 3:6).

---

110 See Glahn, *Nobody's Mother*, esp. 45–80, 128–46.
111 Hoag, *Wealth*, 91–92.

All these same concerns are present in 1 Timothy 2:9–15. There is a genealogy (v. 13), concern over wealth (vv. 9–10), an appeal to the Mosaic law (vv. 13–14), and a weird statement about procreation (v. 15), and the whole passage is directed toward women, whom the false teachers were particularly targeting. I don't think it's a stretch to think Paul might be addressing local issues related to false teaching in Ephesus in 1 Timothy 2:9–15, rather than giving universal commands for every church throughout all time.

## Summarizing 2:8–15

To sum it all up, I think it's plausible that Paul prohibits wealthy women from teaching men in a domineering way (1 Tim. 2:12), then appeals to the Genesis creation account (vv. 13–14) to combat a local genealogical myth (Artemis's firstborn status and Ra's deception) that empowered female religious leaders to think they were superior to men. Paul then concludes by confronting another Artemis myth, declaring that God—not Artemis—is the one who saves women through childbirth (v. 15). "What we see in Paul's appeal to Genesis," writes Nijay Gupta, "is not a generic appeal to gender roles based on creation principles but a 'clash' of origins and how they shape social identity. Genesis was brought into the discussion not to prevent women from teaching anywhere and everywhere but to refute any justifications for women trying to overpower men."[112]

In the end, it's impossible to know exactly why Paul wrote what he did. Reconstructions of an ancient context always contain a degree of

---

112 Nijay Gupta, *Tell Her Story: How Women Led, Taught, and Ministered in the Early Church* (IVP Academic, 2023), 179n45.

speculation. To be clear, my exegesis of 1 Timothy 2:8–15 rests primarily on the text itself, not on the cultural context surrounding Artemis. While this context might help color in Paul's argument, the text itself must direct our interpretation.

I believe "strong complementarian" interpretations of 1 Timothy 2:8–15 have some merit, but they also face several challenges. I'm most confident that they misinterpret *authentein* as referring to a kind of Christlike authority that's valid for men but not for women. All the available evidence about the meaning of *authentein* works against this interpretation. I think complementarian interpretations of Paul's use of Adam and Eve in verses 13–14 are possible but also face several exegetical difficulties. They're certainly not the only way—or even the best way—to read this passage.

"Soft complementarian" interpretations of 1 Timothy 2 strike me as problematic for similar reasons. If Paul prohibits women from teaching and exercising domineering authority (v. 12), then he's not excluding them from simply being overseers—even male overseers shouldn't emulate this kind of secular leadership. And even if one takes 2:12 as a prohibition of women from exercising godly teaching and authority, it's not altogether clear that Paul's appeal to creation (vv. 13–14) establishes this as a universal principle.

If we're going to make a compelling case for male-only overseers, I think we'd have to do so from 1 Timothy 3.

## 1 Timothy 3:1–7 and Male-Only Overseers

In 1 Timothy 3:1–7, Paul lists qualifications for an overseer (*episkopon*) of a church. His list is not a job description but a character description. That is, he doesn't highlight what overseers are to do but the kinds of virtues they are to emulate and vices they are to avoid.[113] Most English translations contain male-specific language throughout the passage, but the Greek is not male-specific. For instance, the NIV translates 3:4 as "*He* must manage *his* own family well," but the Greek does not contain a male pronoun. It simply says "managing one's own family well."[114]

There is one character trait in this list that might exclude women: Paul says an overseer must be a "husband of one wife," or literally "one-woman man" (*mias gunaikos andra*, 3:2 CSB).[115] This verse is, in my view, the strongest argument for the male-only overseer view. It might even be the only argument. The phrase is clearly gender-specific. After all, Paul knows how to say "wife of one husband," as he does in 5:9 (CSB). But he doesn't in 3:2. He uses a phrase that seems to assume overseers are male: "one-woman man."

Some interpreters, therefore, say this passage excludes women from occupying the role of overseer.[116] Others, however, say Paul's words are more descriptive than prescriptive—he doesn't explicitly prohibit women from being overseers, but presumes a historical situation where male heads of households were the norm.

One way to scrutinize these two options is to ask, Who is Paul trying to keep out of being an overseer with the phrase "one woman-man"?[117] Is he intentionally excluding people who practice polygamy? Or does he

---

113 Paul gives five vices for them to avoid and six virtues to pursue in addition to fidelity within marriage. The qualification that an overseer must be an "able teacher" (*didaktikon*, 3:2 HCSB) is the closest thing to a job description; but Paul doesn't say they must teach, merely that they are capable of doing so. First Timothy 5:17 also implies that only some elders had a regular teaching role in the church.

114 The words are masculine in the Greek (as opposed to feminine or neuter), but this does not mean they're limited to males, since masculine verbs and nouns are often inclusive of women.

115 Paul gives the same requirement for deacons (1 Tim. 3:12) and elders (Titus 1:6).

116 See chapter 4 for the meaning of "overseer."

117 See Sydney Page, "Marital Expectations of Church Leaders in the Pastoral Epistles," *Journal for the Study of the New Testament* 15, no. 50 (1993): 105–20.

not want overseers who are remarried (after divorce or the death of a spouse)? Or does Paul believe single men are unqualified to be overseers? Or is "one-woman man" just a generic phrase for being faithful to your spouse if you're married?

Paul probably isn't focused on polygamy, since monogamy was the norm in the Greco-Roman world.[118] Of course, the phrase *does* logically rule out polygamy, but it's unlikely that this is why Paul used it. It's also unlikely that he's prohibiting remarriage after the death of a spouse, since he allows for this elsewhere (Rom. 7:1–3; 1 Cor. 7:8–9, 39–40) and even prefers it in Ephesus (1 Tim. 5:14).[119] Prohibiting remarriage after divorce is possible, but there are no clues in the context that Paul specifically has divorce in mind.

Most scholars believe that Paul is making a general statement about marital faithfulness.[120] In a society where it was common for married men to have sex with unmarried women (especially prostitutes and slaves), it makes sense that Paul would require overseers to be faithful to their wives.

What about singleness? Is Paul saying that single men cannot be overseers?[121] If we interpret Paul's words in the most literal way, the answer is yes: Overseers have to be married. If we take this very literal reading, though, we should also interpret 3:4 the same way, where Paul says an overseer must "see that his *children* obey him." An overseer, then,

---

118 Philip Towner, *The Letters to Timothy and Titus*, New International Commentary on the New Testament (Eerdmans, 2006), 250n42.

119 Though C. H. Dodd notes that this was "the dominant view in early times." "New Testament Translation Problems II," *Bible Translator* 28, no. 1 (1977): 114.

120 E.g., I. Howard Marshall, *The Pastoral Epistles*, International Critical Commentary (T&T Clark, 2000), 478; George W. Knight III, *The Pastoral Epistles*, New International Greek Testament Commentary (Eerdmans, 1999), 158–59.

121 Sydney Page says, "I am not aware of any contemporary scholar who supports this position" ("Marital Expectations," 106).

must not only be male but a male who is currently married and has at least two children.

My friend and theologian Gerry Breshears interprets the passage this way: He believes overseers must be married men (or widowers whose wives have passed away) with at least two children.[122] I commend Breshears for his attempt at consistency, but there are at least three challenges to this view.

First, Paul elsewhere commends singleness and says singles are freer to be "concerned about the Lord's affairs" (1 Cor. 7:32), living "in undivided devotion to the Lord" (v. 35). Certainly, overseers would do well to have such dedication to the Lord. When Paul enthusiastically invites believers to remain single, it seems odd to think that following Paul's advice would disqualify them from serving the church as overseers.

Second, Jesus was single and never married, and he's called an overseer (*episkopon*) in 1 Peter 2:25. It's unlikely that Peter would use this title for Jesus if the early church believed this role was off-limits to unmarried men like Jesus. Plus, Jesus isn't just any overseer; he's the ultimate "*Overseer* [*episkopon*] of your souls" (1 Pet. 2:25). If Jesus is the overseer of *the church*, I can't imagine Paul would forbid him to be an overseer of *a church*.

Third, Breshears argues that a widowed man who is no longer married is still qualified to be an overseer, as long as he was faithful to his former spouse. But if our goal is to interpret the phrase "one-woman man" as literally as possible, then overseers would need to be *currently* married,

122 Gerry has expressed his views to me through many personal conversations, and through his extensive comments on earlier drafts of this book.

not just *formerly* married. Paul says an overseer must *be* a "one-woman man," not that they *used to be* one. In other words, even Breshears tacitly admits that Paul's requirement that an overseer must be a "one-woman man" shouldn't be taken in its most literal sense.

In first-century Greco-Roman culture, most people qualified to be church overseers would have been currently married men with multiple children. But it's unlikely that Paul's words in 1 Timothy 3:2 and 3:4 are *requiring* all overseers to be currently married men with at least two children. Breshears comes the closest to making this argument of any scholar I've seen, and even he makes allowances for not-currently-married men.

So if you're with me and don't think all overseers of all time must be currently married and have at least two children, then what grounds do we have—if we're being consistent—to say they all must be male? Robert Yarbrough, for instance, argues, "The Greek is explicit that the overseer is a male who, *if married*, has a female wife to whom he is fully and exclusively dedicated."[123] But why say "*if* married" and not "if male"? It seems more consistent either to take Paul's phrase even more literally and absolutely than Breshears does (all overseers must be male, be *currently* married, and have at least two children) or else to take this phrase more conditionally: Those who are male and married must be faithful to their wives, and those with children must manage them well.

It's worth noting that almost everything in Paul's list of overseer qualifications is applied to women elsewhere in 1 Timothy.[124]

---

123 Robert Yarbrough, *The Letters to Timothy and Titus*, Pillar New Testament Commentary (Eerdmans, 2018), 195 (emphasis mine).

124 The following list was compiled by Payne, *Man and Woman*, 449–52. The requirement that overseers must be "able teacher[s]" (*didaktikon*, 3:2 HSCB) is not applied to women in 1 Timothy, though Paul does say older women should "teach what is good" in Titus 2:3. In any case, most complementarians don't say that women aren't able teachers, only that they should not teach men, regardless of how able they might be at it.

- "good work" (3:1 KJV)—of women: "good works" (5:10 CSB)
- "irreproachable" (3:2 NABRE)—of women: "irreproachable" (5:7 NABRE)
- "one-woman man" (marital faithfulness; see 3:2)—of women: "one-man woman" (marital faithfulness; 5:9)
- "temperate" (3:2)—of women: "temperate" (3:11)
- "sober" (3:2 CEB)—of women: "sobriety" (2:9, 15 KJV)
- "gravity" (or "respect," 3:4 KJV)—of women: "be grave" (3:11 KJV)
- "fall under ... judgment" (3:6)—of women: "fall under judgment" (5:12, my translation here and below)
- "must have a good witness [*marturian*]" (3:7)—of women: "witnessed [*marturoumenē*] by good works" (5:10)
- "manage their own household" (3:4 CEB)—of women: "to manage their homes" (5:14)

Paul's requirement that overseers and women manage their households is particularly interesting. Paul uses the term *proistemi* ("to manage, care for") to describe overseers (3:4) but a different word (*oikodespoteō*) to describe women (5:14). Wayne Grudem takes this as proof for male-only overseers: "The NT never uses *proistemi* to speak of women 'managing' or governing a household, but only of men."[125] But I think Grudem overstates his case in three ways. First, female heads of

125 Grudem, *Evangelical Feminism*, 263n107.

households most certainly did manage and govern their households, as we saw in chapter 4. Second, Paul uses *proistemi* elsewhere in gender-inclusive contexts (Rom. 12:8; 1 Thess. 5:12), where there's no exegetical reason why women are excluded. Third, *oikodespoteō*, the word Paul uses when he talks of women managing their homes in 1 Timothy 5:14, is an even stronger term than *proistemi* in 3:4.[126] *Oikodespoteō* is used in other places to describe a household's "ruler," even God's rulership.[127] Based on these three pieces of evidence, it's unlikely that Paul uses *proistemi* in 1 Timothy 3:4 to exclude women.

This sends us back to our original question: Does Paul's list of qualifications in 3:1–7 (1) require overseers to be men or (2) assume qualified overseers would be married men with children who were household heads?

I think the second option makes the most sense of Paul's words and the historical situation. As we saw in chapter 4, first-century Christians gathered in homes of wealthier believers who were household heads—most of whom were men, but some of whom were women. Paul presumes these social norms when he lists qualifications for overseers. He's not mandating that overseers must be currently married men who have at least two children. As Andrew Clarke says, "A common error in reconstructing Paul's views about leadership is the failure to distinguish between what Paul prescribes and what he describes."[128]

---

126 While Paul is addressing widows, he tells them "to marry, to have children," and then "to manage their homes," suggesting that the latter is a postmarital duty (1 Tim. 5:14).

127 Matthew 13:27, 52; 20:1; cf. Josephus, *Against Apion* 2.128; Epictetus, *Discourses* 3.22.4; Philo, *On Dreams* 1.149. See Luke Timothy Johnson, *The First and Second Letters to Timothy: A New Translation*, Anchor Bible Commentary 35A (Yale University Press, 2008), 267–68.

128 Andrew Clarke, *A Pauline Theology of Church Leadership*, Library of New Testament Studies 362 (T&T Clark, 2008), 6.

Andrew Clarke has been researching New Testament leadership and church structures for over three decades, and he's one of the leading authorities on this subject. As I was putting the finishing touches on this book, I had the opportunity to sit down with him at a coffee shop in Cambridge, England. I didn't know where Andrew stood on the question of women in church leadership, but I couldn't resist asking, "Do you think 1 Timothy 3 rules out women from being overseers?" Here's what he said:

> We miss Paul's point when we read our modern church structures into the first-century context. Christians gathered in homes, and Paul was addressing Christian leadership according to social norms of first-century households. Paul does not *prescribe* that women can't be overseers. He's simply *describing* a situation where men typically were.[129]

Andrew went on to illustrate his point like this:

> Imagine if I were to ask you seventy-five years ago, 'Do you like your doctor? Is he a good man? Is he faithful to his wife?' My questions wouldn't imply that all doctors had to be men. They just presume a situation where almost every doctor was.

129 Towner makes the same point: Paul was "spelling things out in terms of the broad norms of society," but "we cannot be certain that he would have ruled out the possibility of women householders serving as overseers" (*Timothy and Titus*, 254n67; see also Witt, *Icons*, 327).

Of all the ways we could interpret Paul's words in 1 Timothy 3, Andrew's explanation makes the most sense to me. And it reflects what many other experts have said about the first-century church. Within Paul's ancient context, most qualified overseers would have been married men with children. But Paul is not trying to rule out the possibility of women overseers.

## Conclusion

Paul's words in 1 Timothy 2:8–3:7 provide the strongest support for complementarian views, and I still believe their interpretations have some merit. I'm not on the side of those who consider complementarians outlandish for thinking that Paul requires teachers and overseers to be men. However, there are other exegetically credible ways to interpret this passage. And from my vantage point, I think complementarian interpretations of this passage face more challenges than the interpretation I've offered in this chapter.

While I hold my interpretation cautiously and I'm open to changing my view upon further study, I don't believe 1 Timothy universally excludes all women from positions of teaching and leadership over men in the church.

# LANDING THE PLANE

I finished my first draft of this book in January 2025, but I wasn't satisfied with it. I kept going back through it to refine my thoughts, triple-check my exegesis, and revisit some of my conclusions. The first draft turned into a second ... and a third, and a fourth. Finally, with the ink still fresh on the sixth draft, I sent the manuscript to several scholars on all sides of the debate, inviting them to shred my argument to pieces. And indeed, they did.

A seventh draft, an eighth draft—*Will I ever actually arrive at a final draft?*

I knew I had to submit the manuscript eventually, so I flew to Cambridge for one last push. I spent twelve days in the Tyndale House Library, combing through my book once more. Those were probably the most mentally exhausting twelve days of my life. For fourteen hours a day, I tweaked my argument, refined my language, and scurried around the library searching for books and articles that challenged every nitty-gritty detail of what I'd written. Once my brain was fried and my eyes were bleeding, I finally called it a day.

As I write these words, I've just boarded my plane from Heathrow to Idaho. When I land, I'm going to send the manuscript off to my editor. And I'll finish writing this conclusion as I fly back across the pond to return home.

It should be clear by now where I've landed in this debate. I believe the Bible says that women can teach and exercise leadership at every level in the church. I don't hold this view with the same level of confidence as I hold doctrines like the Trinity or the deity of Christ. I still think some complementarian arguments have exegetical credibility. But after a long and sometimes tedious journey, I believe the egalitarian view is more biblically persuasive. Here are my primary reasons why.

Genesis 1–3 doesn't appear to establish a universal principle that man should exercise authority or leadership over woman. The text doesn't demand this, and some elements of the passage work against male-only leadership. The only explicit "ruling" language applies to both male and female (1:26–28) or negatively to a fallen kind of rule that man wields over his wife (3:16). Some interpreters see Paul's allusions to this Genesis passage (1 Cor. 11:8–9; 1 Tim. 2:13–14) as confirmation of male authority over women (or wives), but their interpretation is uncertain at best and problematic at worst.

The rest of the Old Testament—the early church's Bible—reveals a variegated picture of male-female relations. In key parts of the story, the writers highlight the faithfulness and agency of women in contrast to the faithlessness and passivity of men. Some characters, like Abigail, model godly leadership traits in contexts where men exhibit the exact opposite. Most formal leaders in the Old Testament are men, but some are women (like Deborah and Huldah) who exercise authority over men, and the writers of Scripture don't censor their behavior. And Israel's all-male priesthood does not appear to reflect a universal principle that only men should be teachers in God's covenant community.

The Gospels don't give us a list of leadership qualifications for the church. But the Gospel writers do portray women as emulating the traits of radical discipleship, often in contrast to men—especially the twelve apostles. Most significantly, in the one place where Jesus addresses the category of leadership, he highlights "service" as the true mark of authority. And throughout the Gospels, women are the ones who most clearly embody this key leadership trait.

Paul identifies leaders in a variety of ways. Sometimes he uses words like *overseer*, *elder*, or *pastor-teacher*, while he also describes leaders with other terms like *servant*, *coworker*, *working hard*, and *managing*—terms used of both men and women. Paul's descriptions of Phoebe, Priscilla, and Junia in particular suggest these women were leaders in the early church.

The leadership of women may also be implied, once we understand the social context of the first century. Paul singles out Apphia alongside other male leaders in his letter to Philemon, suggesting that she too was a leader. Female hosts of house churches would have been presumed leaders in those gatherings. Priscilla and Aquila hosted churches in more than one city, and they are always described together as doing the same kinds of ministry.

New Testament prophets played leadership roles in the early church, and prophecy has a functional overlap with teaching. Some women were undoubtedly prophets and prophesied. The New Testament doesn't distinguish between male prophets who led and taught and female prophets who did not. If female prophets were excluded from teaching and authority roles, this must be derived from other passages, not from the nature of New Testament prophecy itself.

The household code in Ephesians 5 doesn't directly address our question of church leadership, but it does inform our understanding of male-female relations in the home, which was the social location of early church gatherings. Paul says that the husband is the "head" of his wife, but he purges "headship" of its secular connotations and redefines it in terms of self-giving sacrifice and love. Paul's household code contains the husk of hierarchical language used in other Greco-Roman codes, but Paul challenges these notions with the gospel-shaped language of mutuality.

Three New Testament passages might exclude women from teaching or exercising authority over men: 1 Corinthians 11:2–16; 1 Corinthians 14:34–36; and 1 Timothy 2–3. In all three cases, other interpretations are more plausible. First Corinthians 14, to my mind, offers the weakest evidence of the three for male-only teachers. First Corinthians 11:3–10 seems to say that a woman can only prophesy while recognizing the authority of her husband, but Paul's words in 11:11–12 disrupt this argument. The passage as a whole is very complex, and every interpretation must be held tentatively. Either way, 1 Corinthians 11 presumes that both men and women were engaging in the same kinds of ministry.

First Timothy 2–3 offers what I believe is the strongest case for complementarian perspectives (both "strong complementarian" and "soft complementarian"). But these interpretations face several challenges, and there are other more plausible ways to understand this passage. *Authentein* most likely conveys the kind of secular authority that a master has over his slave; therefore, Paul isn't prohibiting women from teaching or exercising *godly* authority over men. While Paul certainly roots his prohibition in the creation order of men and women, it seems most likely that he appeals to this Genesis account as an illustration to address a local situation in Ephesus.

The "soft complementarian" (or "male-elder") view largely rests on interpreting the phrase "one-woman man" (see 1 Tim. 3:2) to exclude women (as well as single men and married men with fewer than two children) from the role of overseer. But this interpretation is suspect. Not only is it inconsistent, but it also reads more into the verse than Paul intends. It's more likely that Paul is speaking to the social context of the first century, where most qualified overseers would have been married men with children. Paul presumes a situation where most qualified overseers will be married men with children, but this doesn't mean he's forbidding everyone who doesn't fit this norm from serving in the role.

I also think the "soft complementarian" view wrongly presumes a monolithic church structure and leadership, where the "overseer/elder" occupies the highest level of leadership in the church, while "pastors" and "teachers" and "prophets" are under their authority. Modern churches may operate this way, but the New Testament does not affirm this kind of leadership structure. Paul's view of leadership was more diverse and contextual. "Overseer" and "elder" are two terms that describe leaders in the church, but other churches have leaders performing similar functions who are not described with these terms. Quite frankly, I think the "soft complementarian" view has less biblical evidence than "strong complementarian" or egalitarian views.

In the end, I think the best interpretation of all the Bible's evidence shows us that both women and men can be equally qualified and gifted for all forms of church leadership.

I guess this makes me egalitarian.

But I actually don't love the label "egalitarian." This modern term can get entangled with secular perspectives about equality, some of which try to erase male-female differences. I still believe passionately that men and women are different by design; I just don't think our differences determine who can teach or lead our churches.

Apart from the word *egalitarian* in particular, I don't like labels in general. They can give the impression that everyone who shares a label holds the same views on the same passages, arguing with the same manner and tone. Labels can also foster an "us versus them" mentality, which is toxic for the church. I'd prefer to describe my view from the text of Scripture and have people see me living it out consistently, rather than just slapping on a label that ends the conversation.

Some complementarians have argued that churches becoming egalitarian will lead to them affirming same-sex marriage for Christians. This claim deserves a lengthy evaluation, which we don't have space for here. But since I've written extensively defending sex difference (male and female) as an essential part of marriage, let me say a few words.

First, it's hermeneutically inaccurate to compare the biblical debate over women in church leadership with the debate over same-sex marriage, as William Webb thoroughly pointed out more than twenty-five years ago.[1] The Bible consistently says that sex difference is an intrinsic part of what marriage *is*, and it prohibits same-sex sexual relationships each time they are addressed. Scripture shows no diversity on these points. The same is not true of women in church leadership. Many passages suggest that women were leading. And there are better ways to interpret the few passages that seem to say otherwise.

Second, the claim that affirming same-sex marriage and women in leadership derives from recent cultural trends is not accurate. Throughout

1 William Webb, *Slaves, Women & Homosexuals: Exploring the Hermeneutics of Cultural Analysis* (IVP Academic, 2001).

church history, women were considered intellectually inferior and more easily deceived than men, and this is why they were prohibited from teaching and leading men. *This* was the traditional view. But all egalitarians and even most complementarians disagree with this historical position. It's not that egalitarians have drunk the punch of modern society and revised the Bible in light of it, while complementarians have the Bible and church history on their side. Both have revised traditional views of women. And both have appealed to Scripture to do so.

Third, plenty of evangelical egalitarians believe the Bible is clear about male-female marriage and male-female sex differences. If some egalitarians also end up affirming same-sex marriage, such change is not intrinsic to the hermeneutic that leads to supporting women in leadership. In case some are wondering about me in particular, all I can say is the more I've studied the question of marriage, the more I am convinced—using the same exegetical method employed in this book—that the Bible clearly teaches the traditional view. And I don't see this as some negotiable issue that Christians should waver on. I see it as a matter of Christian orthodoxy. Using the same hermeneutic, I now see more biblical evidence for women in leadership.

Does this mean I also think that affirming women in all areas of leadership is a matter of orthodoxy? No, I don't think it is. While women in leadership is a very important topic, I think the Bible is less clear on this topic than, say, the doctrines affirmed in the Nicene Creed—or what it says about marriage. I do believe the Bible advocates for women serving in all positions of leadership, but I'm happy to admit that it's an exegetically complex issue.

So I wouldn't say complementarians are in sin simply for being complementarian, nor should complementarians accuse egalitarians of the same. Accusations like these reflect exegetical naivete and theological hubris more than a humble appreciation of the complexity of the biblical text. I still have great admiration for complementarian scholars and pastors who have a high view of women and are constrained by their honest reading of Scripture. I don't agree with egalitarians who say that all complementarians are dehumanizing women or that the abuse of women is intrinsic to the complementarian view. Abuse and dehumanization can exist in churches across the spectrum of views, and the temptation for men to dominate women is a perennial one. Simply being egalitarian on paper does not automatically free women from oppression.

In any case, my focus in this book has been exegetical, not pastoral. I've been primarily focused on exploring what the Bible says, not sorting out all the implications of my study for the modern church. I certainly hope that this book will serve Christians, and leaders in particular, as they seek to align their lives and ministries with the ancient text of Scripture.

Let me be clear: This book represents where I'm currently at on this topic. I've only spent three years and about a thousand hours researching it. Some of my friends have applauded me for investing so much time and energy, and I'm grateful for their encouragement. But three years isn't a lot of time compared to what some scholars have invested. Philip Payne, an egalitarian scholar, has spent more than forty years researching the topic and has published thousands of pages on the issue. So has Wayne Grudem, who arrives at a complementarian view. Several scholars used to hold one view but have changed their minds upon further study. I would either be naive or arrogant (probably both) to think that my conclusions are etched in cement, never again to be revisited. This book is simply my entry into the conversation, and I look forward to refining my view in the coming years—especially from the barrage of critiques that's about to come my way.

My plane is about to land, but before the flight attendant asks me to stow my laptop, I want to offer two last theological observations that are more reflective than strictly exegetical.

First, I think the egalitarian view—or whatever we call it—provides a better theological rationale than the complementarian view. Most thoughtful complementarian scholars today agree with egalitarians that women are not (on the whole) intellectually inferior to men or less gifted than men in teaching and leading. The rationale by which many of these complementarians arrive at their view comes down to a questionable interpretation of a few New Testament passages and Genesis 1–2, leading them to conclude that women are excluded from certain kinds of teaching and leadership over men, since Adam was created first. If this truly is what the Bible says, then I agree with my grandma: "God said it; I believe it; that settles it." I don't think the Bible says this, but either way, the rationale certainly seems arbitrary.

The rationale that underlies the egalitarian view is more theologically compelling. It says that men and women are beautifully different, but neither is intellectually or spiritually inferior to the other. Both are empowered by the same Spirit, who distributes a diversity of gifts to both men and women. The mere fact that Adam was created first and called his partner "woman" in no way limits the opportunity for a mature, godly woman who's skilled in biblical exegesis and demonstrates gifts in teaching and leading to shepherd God's people.

Second, since the church is a family, it makes sense that we should have both mothers and fathers. Churches with only male or only female leaders may face challenges similar to the challenges faced by single parents. And I don't think it's enough for women to teach and provide spiritual leadership only to other women, while male leaders do the same for both men and women. I think men miss out when we don't sit under the teaching of godly and gifted women whose maturity and wisdom is shaped by their unique experiences *as* women.

Imagine Junia stepping into her first household gathering, her body branded by the scars of a Roman prison. Her experience as a woman compounded her suffering—dealing with menstruation in a filthy cell packed with depraved men, under constant threat and perhaps even a victim of rape and sexual assault, beaten and broken, harassed and humiliated. Through it all, she clung to the blazing hope that Jesus is King. No dungeon or empire could deter her from announcing his reign to the nations.

When she stood again among the faithful, her very presence hushed the room. The church saw not just a sister returned but the gospel incarnate. Her body proclaimed Christ's triumph—every scar a sermon, every breath a testimony. For the sake of the gospel, she defied the empire as a woman in a male-dominated world, and she won.

These are the fires in which true leaders are forged. To forbid men from sitting at Junia's feet—from her wisdom and witness and instruction, authenticated by her resilience as a woman—would strip us of the breadth and depth of Christian discipleship.

And I would be robbed if I never let myself be led by Junia today.

# ACKNOWLEDGMENTS

An earlier draft of this book was over a hundred pages longer—and was much more scholarly in tone and content—than the one you're holding in your hands. But I didn't want the final product to be a lengthy academic tome accessible only to people with PhDs. So I spent several months whittling the book down to make it more readable, without losing key points in my argument. Some words that I cut were extensive footnotes dissecting every minutia of my claims and listing endless sources to show that I am aware of all the exegetical issues that aren't crucial to my argument. This was painful. But I took the advice of the prolific English novelist Sir Arthur Quiller-Couch, who once said, "Murder your darlings"—that is, cut the parts of your prose that you love dearly but are unnecessary for your reader. My darlings are two-hundred-word footnotes that cite ten sources to support every jot and tittle of every sentence I write. Most of these darlings have now deceased. But I did keep a few alive as extended articles on my website which you can access for free (theologyintheraw.com/womeninleadership).

During the final stages of writing, I sent off earlier drafts (or portions of them) to many scholars who are on all sides of the debate—complementarians, egalitarians, and others who are undecided on the issue. These include: Lynn Cohick, Gerry Breshears, Sandy Richter, Tom Schreiner, Nijay Gupta, Wayne Baxter, Michelle Lee-Barnewall, Dru Johnson, Osvaldo Padilla, and Carmen Imes. Their criticism and comments proved to be invaluable. Several others gave me feedback on specific points along the way: Peter Williams, Cynthia Westfall, Kevin Grasso, Andrew Bartlett, Sam Choi, David Warren, and others whose names escape me. I'm especially grateful for my indelible editor, Greg Coles, who combed through the final manuscripts several times with painstaking precision. Whatever mistakes that remain are, of course—Greg's.

Most of all, I thank my wife and kids, who encouraged me along the way and who put up with me saying, "I'm about to finish my book," every other week for the last year before I actually finished my book. This time it's real. I finally finished my book. Thank you for your grace and love, and for keeping me grounded in real life.